THE LATIN LANGUAGE

A Handbook for Students

PREPARED BY
The Scottish Classics Group

Oliver & Boyd

This Handbook was prepared by the following members of the Scottish Classics Group:

Mary S. R. Burns	Assistant Deputy Principal and formerly Principal Teacher of Classics in The Mary Erskine School, Edinburgh
Andrew Kilgour	formerly Principal Lecturer in Classics, Jordanhill College of Education, Glasgow
Iain R. Macaskill	Principal Teacher of Classics, Knox Academy, Haddington
M. Barclay Miller	formerly Depute Rector and Principal Teacher of Classics, Perth Academy
Richard M. Orr	Adviser in Classics, Glasgow Division, Strathclyde Region
Henry L. Philip	formerly HM Inspector of Schools and Headmaster, Liberton High School, Edinburgh
William F. Ritchie	formerly Depute Rector and Principal Teacher of Classics, Arbroath High School
Kenneth G. Silver	formerly Rector, Jedburgh Grammar School, and Principal Teacher of Classics, Falkirk High School
Geoffrey Suggitt	formerly Headmaster, Stratton School, Biggleswade, and Principal Teacher of Classics, George Watson's College, Edinburgh

Since publication of this book in 1989, run or changes have been made to the following pages: 7, 11, 26, 29, 35, 52, 57, 103, 107, 109, 161, 191 and 192.

Cover photograph
The photograph on the cover shows the Arch of Titus in the Forum, Rome.

Acknowledgements
We are grateful to the following for giving permission to include extracts from copyright works: Oxford University Press, from *The Chronicle of Jocelin of Brakelond* (Oxford Medieval Texts); The University of Chicago Press, from "The Exempla of Jacques de Vitry" in K. P. Harrington, *Medieval Latin* (No. 20).

Oliver & Boyd
Pearson Education Limited
Edinburgh Gate, Harlow,
Essex CM20 2JE, England
and Associated Companies throughout the world.

An Imprint of Pearson Education Ltd

© The Scottish Classics Group 1989

All rights reserved. No part of this publication may be reproduced, stored in a retrieval system, or transmitted in any form or by any means, electronic, mechanical, photocopying, recording or otherwise, without either the prior written permission of the publishers or a licence permitting restricted copying in the United Kingdom issued by the Copyright Licensing Agency Ltd, 90 Tottenham Court Road, London W1P 9HE.

First published 1989
Sixteenth impression 2005

ISBN-10: 0-05-004287-4
ISBN-13: 978-0-05-004287-8

The publisher's policy is to use paper manufactured from sustainable forests.

Set in Linotron 10/12 Garamond and Optima Regular
Printed in China.   EPC/16

Designed by Cauldron Design Studio

Contents

Introduction		4	

Part I: Syntax

	Page		
Nominative Case	5	Accusative and Infinitive	34
Vocative Case	5	Direct Questions	36
Accusative Case	5	Indirect Question	39
Genitive Case	7	Indirect Command	41
Dative Case	10	Purpose	44
Predicative Dative	13	Result	47
Ablative Case	15	Fearing	49
Time Phrases	18	Time Clauses	51
Place	20	Conditional Sentences	54
Prepositions	22	Impersonal Verbs	57
Relative Clauses	26	Gerunds and Gerundives	60
Participles	28	Correlatives	63
Ablative Absolute	30	Days, Months and Years	66
Infinitives	32	Roman Names	69

Part II: Translation

Preamble	70	**quam**	100
Case Recognition	71	**qui** + Subjunctive	103
Agreement of Adjectives	74	**quin**	105
Dative or Ablative?	76	The Subjunctive in Main	
Word Building	78	Clauses	107
Latin Word Families	84	The Subjunctive in	
cum	88	Subordinate Clauses	109
dum	91	Reported Speech (Oratio	
ut	93	Obliqua)	110
ne	96	**se** and **suus**	114
quod	98	Translation	117

Part III: Medieval Latin	132
Part IV: Tables	140
A Simplified Guide to Pronunciation	166
Vocabulary	168
Index	191

Introduction

Traditional Latin grammar books were designed mainly to help students produce correct Latin when translating passages of English into Latin. Those grammar books were usually very comprehensive, describing in detail not only the regular linguistic forms and rules but also the many exceptions and peculiarities of usage which are to be found in Latin.

For the reading and translation of Latin, however, such an exhaustive description of accidence and syntax is not only unnecessary but can even confuse rather than assist students, since the mass of detail often results in their not being able to "see the wood for the trees". Indeed, it is possible that a student may never encounter many of the "exceptions" in the course of quite an extensive reading programme.

This Handbook has been designed to meet the needs of modern approaches to the study of Latin. It should be particularly useful to students who have progressed beyond their introductory course books and are now reading Latin authors either in the original or in an edited form. It is by no means an exhaustive or definitive account of Latin grammar. It ignores those Latin usages which are sufficiently close to the English idiom to be unlikely to cause difficulty in translation, and concentrates on the normal usages rather than on the exceptions. Throughout, the notes have been written in such a way as to help students understand the Latin they are reading.

Although it is intended mainly as a handy reference book, the Handbook tries to train students to use clues as they meet them in the sentence so that they are in a better position to predict intelligently (rather than guess) how the sentence is likely to develop. In particular, it is important that students learn to suspend judgment on those words whose use is not confined to one construction. The notes and exercises which are to be found on pages 117–131 have been specifically written to give students practice in handling such problems.

After the description of each construction, there are graded exercises to give students practice in recognising and translating that construction. Since the A exercises concentrate almost exclusively on the grammatical input of the section, they are suitable for additional practice immediately after students have studied the construction(s). The B exercises are more difficult in that they usually contain more than one grammatical construction. They will therefore be more useful as revision at a later stage in learning.

Since the vocabulary contains all the words used in the exercises, this Handbook should prove a useful extension to any Latin course.

Part I: Syntax

Nominative Case

The nominative is the case of the subject of the sentence, e.g.

servus laborat. *The slave is working.*

and of the complement, e.g.

Marcus est **puer Romanus**.
Marcus is a Roman boy.

Vocative Case

The vocative is used when addressing a person or thing. It is identical in form to the nominative case, except in the singular of Group 2 nouns ending in **-us**, e.g.

veni celeriter, **domine**!   salve, **mi fili**!
Come quickly, master!   Greetings, my son!

Masculine Group 1/2 adjectives ending in **-us** also show the vocative ending, e.g.

ave, **optime** Caesar! *Hail, most excellent Caesar!*

In poetry, this usage is extended to participles, e.g.

quo, **moriture**, ruis?
Where are you rushing to, you who are about to die?

Accusative Case

The most common uses of the accusative are:

(*a*) as DIRECT OBJECT of a transitive verb, e.g.

puella **pupam** habet.
The girl has a doll.

Two accusatives may be found with certain verbs such as **docere**, **rogare** and **creare**, e.g.

magister **pueros multa** rogabat.
The teacher asked the boys many questions.

Cincinnatum dictatorem creaverunt.
They appointed Cincinnatus dictator.

(b) WITH CERTAIN PREPOSITIONS. (See pages 22–23.)

(c) to denote MOTION TO A PLACE. Usually it is preceded by a preposition, but with the names of towns, small islands and a few other words, notably **domus** and **rus**, the preposition is omitted (see page 20), e.g.

Neapolim cras iter faciemus.
We shall travel to Naples tomorrow.

rus aestate semper redimus.
We always return to the country in the summer.

(d) to denote DURATION OF TIME, e.g.

ibi **paucos dies** manebant.
They remained there for a few days.

urbs Troia **decem annos** obsidebatur.
The city of Troy was besieged for ten years.

(e) to denote EXTENT OF SPACE, e.g.

murus erat **tres pedes** altus.
The wall was three feet high.

multa milia passuum progressi erant.
They had advanced many miles.

(f) in EXCLAMATIONS, e.g.

o praeclarum custodem ovium, ut aiunt, lupum!
What an excellent protector of sheep, so they say, the wolf is!

o tempora! o mores! *What times! What customs!* (implying "What is the world coming to?")

(g) as the subject of the infinitive in ACCUSATIVE AND INFINITIVE CLAUSES (see page 34), e.g.

audio **Caesarem** in Britanniam **transiisse**.
I hear that Caesar has crossed into Britain.

audio **Britannos** a Caesare **victos esse**.
I hear that the Britons have been defeated by Caesar.

EXERCISE

Translate:
1. Capuam cras proficisci in animo habemus.
2. consul senatores sententiam rogavit.
3. eruditissimus erat ille magister qui me linguam Latinam docuit.
4. cives te aedilem creaverunt quod magnas divitias habes.
5. urbem Athenas magnopere amamus quia ibi sunt aedificia pulcherrima.
6. quoniam in oppidum nocte ambulare timebamus, in villa manere constituimus.
7. paedagogus multa et mira pueris cotidie demonstrabat.
8. duos iam menses invitus in urbe habito; rus igitur redire valde cupio.
9. me caecum! quot annos contra me coniuratis?
10. Caesar milia passuum tria ab eorum castris castra posuit.

Genitive Case

1 The genitive case is most often found along with another noun, the two nouns together forming a phrase. In such a phrase, the genitive case DEFINES, DESCRIBES or CLASSIFIES the other noun, e.g.

filia **senatoris**	the daughter of the senator / the senator's daughter
turba **servorum**	a crowd of slaves
arbores **horti**	the trees in the garden
viae **urbis**	the streets of the city / the city streets
custos **portae**	the guard at the gate / the gate-keeper
dux **belli**	the leader in war / the war-leader
praemium **virtutis**	the reward of valour / the reward for valour
timor **coniuratorum**	the fear of the conspirators, i.e. either the fear that they feel (Subjective Genitive) or the fear that they inspire (Objective Genitive)

7

2 The genitive case is used also

(*a*) WITH CERTAIN ADJECTIVES, e.g.

memor **patriae**	*mindful of (his) country*
plenus **hominum**	*full of people*
cupidus **rerum novarum**	*eager for (political) change*
rei militaris peritus	*skilled in warfare*
similis **patris**	*like his father*

(*b*) WITH CERTAIN VERBS, e.g.

eum **furti** accusaverunt.	*They accused him of theft.*
tui semper meminero.	*I shall always remember you.*
patriae numquam obliviscemur.	*We shall never forget our country.*
eum **sceleris** pudet.	*He is ashamed of his crime.*
laboris me taedet.	*I am tired of work.*
capitis damnatus est.	*He was condemned to death.*

(*c*) to express PRICE OR VALUE, e.g.

quanti hanc domum emisti?	*How much did you pay for this house?*
magni amicitiam tuam aestimo.	*I value your friendship greatly.*

(*d*) with the ablative case of the nouns **causa** and **gratia**, meaning *for the sake of* or *for the purpose of*. These nouns always follow the genitive, e.g.

natandi causa	*for the purpose of swimming* / *to swim*
exempli gratia	*for the sake of an example* / *for example*
honoris causa	*as an honour*

(*e*) to describe a PERSONAL QUALITY, e.g.

vir **summae virtutis**   *a man of outstanding bravery*

(*f*) with the verb **esse** to describe a DUTY OR CHARACTERISTIC, e.g.

civis Romani est pro patria pugnare.
It is the duty of a Roman citizen to fight for his country.

prudentis est pecuniam conservare.
It is characteristic of a sensible man to save his money.

(g) to denote the whole, of which some group, person or thing is a part (PARTITIVE GENITIVE), e.g.

plerique **civium**	*most of the citizens*
nonnulli **vestrum**	*some of you*
nihil **periculi**	*no danger*
satis **pecuniae**	*enough money*
quid **novi**?	*What news?*
plus **vini**	*more wine*

(h) to indicate PLACE AT WHICH, most frequently with the names of towns. There existed in early times a *locative* case which performed this function; but, by classical times, the locative of singular nouns of Groups 1 and 2 had the same ending as the genitive singular, e.g.

Romae	*at Rome*
Brundisii	*at Brundisium*
Corinthi	*in Corinth*
humi	*on the ground*

EXERCISE

Translate:
1 viae urbis erant plenae viatorum, mercatorum, servorum.
2 filii senatoris, quod feriati sunt, ad patrui villam laeti abeunt.
3 quod te sceleris paenitet, capitis te non damnabunt iudices.
4 numquam vestri amicorumque vestrorum obliviscar.
5 Romani iter quinque dierum per fines Helvetiorum fecerunt.
6 quanti tu vendidisti illos servos? ego eos magni aestimabam.
7 multi vestrum cupidi rerum novarum esse videntur.
8 iuvenis, quamquam nec belli nec imperii peritus erat, omnium consensu dux factus est.
9 immemores suorum patriaeque suae milites in hostium castra transfugerunt.
10 praedae causa milites universi in oppidum desertum decurrerunt.
11 nonne ille senator, vir summi ingenii ac maximae probitatis, consul creabitur?
12 est sapientis virtutem pluris quam divitias aestimare.

Dative Case

1 The most frequent use of the dative case is to indicate the person(s) *to* whom something is "transferred" or *for* whom something is done, e.g.

viator pecuniam **praedonibus** tradidit.
*The traveller handed over the money **to the robbers**.*

vir donum **uxori** emit.
*The man bought a gift **for his wife**.*

It is not always necessary to use the prepositions "to" and "for" to translate this use of the dative into English, e.g.

puer canem **amico** dedit.
The boy gave a dog to his friend.
The boy gave his friend a dog.

fabulam **filiae** narravit.
She told a story to her daughter.
She told her daughter a story.

The idea of "transfer" is also extended to verbs of "taking away" something *from* someone, e.g.

pecuniam **mihi** ademit.   *He took the money away **from me**.*
obsides **hostibus** imperavit.   *He demanded hostages **from the enemy**.*

2 The notion of "to" or "for" helps us to understand why the following verbs govern the dative case, although these prepositions may not appear in the English translation:

imperare (+ *dat.*)	*to order, give orders to*
indulgere (+ *dat.*)	*to indulge, pander to*
minari (+ *dat.*)	*to threaten, offer threats to*
nocere (+ *dat.*)	*to harm, bring harm to*
nubere (+ *dat.*)	*to marry* (lit. "to put on a veil for")
permittere (+ *dat.*)	*to allow, give permission to*
placere (+ *dat.*)	*to please, give pleasure to*
resistere (+ *dat.*)	*to resist, offer resistance to*
servire (+ *dat.*)	*to serve, be a slave to*
studere (+ *dat.*)	*to study, be devoted to*

3 The dative case is used to show "transfer" of FEELINGS or THOUGHTS, e.g.

senatori credidimus.
We believed the senator.

dominus **servo** irascebatur.
The master was angry with the slave.

Compare

confidere (+ *dat.*)	*to trust*	**parere** (+ *dat.*)	*to obey*
favere (+ *dat.*)	*to favour*	**parcere** (+ *dat.*)	*to spare*
ignoscere (+ *dat.*)	*to forgive*	**persuadere** (+ *dat.*)	*to persuade*
invidere (+ *dat.*)	*to envy*	**suadere** (+ *dat.*)	*to urge, advise*

Note: **consulere** (+ *acc.*) = *to consult*
    consulere (+ *dat.*) = *to show concern for, consider the interests of*

4 Many COMPOUND VERBS govern the dative case:

(*a*) most *compounds of esse*, e.g.

> princeps **senatui** aderat.
> *The emperor was present at (attended) the senate.*

> Labienus **exercitui** praefuit.
> *Labienus was in command of the army.*

Compare:	**deesse** (+ *dat.*)	*to be lacking, fail*
	interesse (+ *dat.*)	*to take part in*
	praeesse (+ *dat.*)	*to be in charge of*
	prodesse (+ *dat.*)	*to be of use to, benefit*
	superesse (+ *dat.*)	*to survive*

(*b*) *Other compound verbs* (especially those with the prefixes **ad-, in-, ob-, prae-** and **sub-**) often govern the dative case, e.g.

> **fratri meo** in Via Sacra occurri.
> *I met my brother in the Via Sacra.*

> princeps avunculum meum **classi** praefecit.
> *The emperor put my uncle in charge of the fleet.*

5 The dative may be used with THE GERUNDIVE or with PERFECT PASSIVE FORMS to denote the person by whom something is done (the **agent**), e.g.

is liber **tibi** legendus est.	*That book must be read by you.*
	You must read that book.
in urbem **mihi** eundum est.	*I must go into the city.*
bella **matribus** detestata	*wars abhorred by mothers*

6 The dative case with **esse** expresses POSSESSION, e.g.

mihi sunt multi servi.	*I have many slaves.*

7 Many ADJECTIVES govern the dative case. The prepositions "to" and "for" will usually provide an adequate translation, e.g.

lingua Latina **vobis** utilissima erit.
Latin will be very useful to you.

locus idoneus **castris** erat.
The site was suitable for a camp.

8 For the PREDICATIVE DATIVE see page 13.

EXERCISE A

Translate:
1 Britanni Romanis fortiter resistebant.
2 Caesaris filia Pompeio nupsit.
3 sunt illi senatori magnae divitiae, magnus fundus, multi servi.
4 cur hominibus tam scelestis parcere vultis?
5 viatores itinere defessi cauponae tandem appropinquabant.
6 dum in balneis sum, ille servus vestimenta omnia mihi abstulit.
7 simillimus deo, homini dissimillimus erat Socrates.
8 ei quibus res urbanae non iam placent ruri vitam laeti agunt.
9 Caesar Gallis trecentos obsides imperavit.
10 rex piratis mortem minabatur.
11 cohors septima militibus laborantibus subvenit.
12 mihi et tibi et amicis nostris multa cras explicabit paedagogus.

EXERCISE B

Translate:
1 quia nobis domum redeundum erat, captivos custodibus tradidimus.
2 nobis numquam persuadebis ut hinc in Italiam redeamus.
3 nonne magnae laudi erat Ciceroni illam orationem habuisse?
4 servi improbissimi vestimenta domino pila ludenti abstulerunt.
5 pater meus, decimae legioni praefectus, barbaros identidem vicit.
6 nobis omnibus legenda sunt carmina Q. Horatii Flacci.
7 omnia vobis iam parata sunt; ancillae igitur vobis sunt laudandae.
8 cui hodie in Via Flaminia occurristi? avunculo tuo quidem, qui epistolam ad te scriptam mihi tradidit.
9 cives, rati vicinas gentes sibi esse periculo, urbi murum circumdederunt.
10 qui sibi soli consulit, is sibi soli nocet.

Predicative Dative

1 The dative case of certain nouns is used with a number of verbs (most commonly **esse**) in phrases which are usually best translated by either a verb or an expression such as "an *object* of amazement", "a *means* of assistance" or "*a source* of benefit."

admirationi esse	*to be an object of amazement, to amaze*
auxilio esse	*to be a means of assistance, to help*
bono esse	*to be a source of benefit, to benefit*
curae esse	*to be a matter of concern, to cause anxiety*
decori esse	*to bring distinction, to adorn*
dedecori esse	*to be a cause of shame, to disgrace*
detrimento esse	*to be harmful, to harm*
dolori esse	*to be a cause of grief, to distress*
exemplo esse	*to be an example*
exitio esse	*to bring destruction, to ruin*
honori esse	*to be an honour*
impedimento esse	*to be a hindrance, to hinder*
laudi esse	*to be a credit*
ludibrio esse	*to be an object of ridicule, to be laughed at*
odio esse	*to be an object of hatred, to be hated*
oneri esse	*to be a burden, to weigh down*
periculo esse	*to be a source of danger, to endanger*
praesidio esse	*to be a means of protection, to protect*
saluti esse	*to be the salvation, to save*
subsidio esse	*to be of assistance, to support, to help*
usui esse	*to be of use, to benefit*

2 When used with other verbs (e.g. **mittere, ire, venire, relinquere**), the meaning of the Predicative Dative is often best translated by the English infinitive, e.g.

decimam legionem **subsidio** nostris misit.
He sent the Tenth Legion to help our men.

3 The Predicative Dative **dono** is almost exclusively associated with the verb **dare**, e.g.

libros pueris **dono** dedit.
He gave the boys books as a gift.

4 There is usually another dative to denote the person or object affected, e.g.

ars militaris in acie **militibus** magno usui erat.
Their fighting skill was a great asset to the soldiers in battle.

EXERCISE A

Translate:
1. magno periculo nautis fuit illa tempestas.
2. dux belli sex cohortes auxilio sociis statim misit.
3. haec pecunia parentibus pueri magno usui erit.
4. magnae laudi est Caesari Belgas superavisse.
5. ille homo, quod patriam prodiderat, suis civibus odio fuit.
6. amicis magno ludibrio erat Marcus quod canem timebat.
7. bono omnibus nobis erit victoria Pompeii.
8. equus ligneus urbi Troiae exitio fuit.
9. Caesar praesidio castris ducentos equites, pedites mille reliquit.
10. maximo periculo est senatoribus Romanis in caupona pernoctare.

EXERCISE B

Translate:
1. hos flores Marcus matri heri dono dedit.
2. cum amicos tuos custodibus tradideris, odio iam civibus es.
3. omnes scimus te oneri magistro fore.
4. magno erat tibi dedecori nec panem nec vinum comitibus eo tempore dedisse.
5. putasne me iterum auxilio fore tibi?
6. si legionem subsidio sociis nostris misisses, cladem non accepissemus.
7. tempestas subito coorta exitio compluribus navibus fuit.
8. Iuppiter Stator, cuius erat statua in Capitolio, magnae saluti erat Romanis.
9. cum mihi odio sis, iter tecum Corinthum facere nolam.
10. maximo dedecori erat nostris in Gallia vinci.

Ablative Case

1 The ablative case is frequently used WITH A PREPOSITION. (See pages 23 – 4.) The meaning of the preposition will usually indicate how to translate the phrase.

2 When the ablative case is used WITHOUT A PREPOSITION, it can frequently be translated by the words *from, with, in* or *by*, e.g.

complures captivi **vulneribus** mortui sunt.
*Several prisoners died **from their wounds**.*

miles hostem **gladio** necavit.
*The soldier killed the enemy **with his sword**.*

hostes **virtute** non **fraude** vincemus.
*We shall conquer the enemy **by courage** not **by trickery**.*

nostri **scientia** hostes antecedunt.
*Our men surpass the enemy **in skill**.*

Sometimes, the above prepositions will produce a *literal* translation which can later be improved by using another English preposition.

gladiator **ingenti corpore**
a gladiator of huge physique (lit. "with a big body")

soror **natu** minima
the youngest sister (lit. "least by birth")

agricola servum **trecentis denariis** emit.
The farmer bought the slave for (lit. "with") *300 denarii.*

Compare the following ablatives which are used with verbs of "buying" and "selling":

nihilo, *for nothing*	**magno,** *at a big price*
(lit. "with nothing")	**parvo,** *at a small price*
vili, *cheaply*	**plurimo,** *at a very big price*

3 Any phrase involving the words **locus** or **totus** and expressing PLACE WHERE will usually appear without a preposition, e.g.

loco idoneo, *in a suitable place*
tota urbe, *in the whole city*

4 TIME: When used in Time expressions, the ablative case means "in", "within", "at" or "on", e.g.

duobus diebus veniet.   *He will come in two days.*
prima luce discessit.   *He left at dawn.*

5 There are CERTAIN VERBS governing the ablative case where English translates the ablative by a direct object, e.g.

> miles **gladio** usus est.   *The soldier used his sword.*
> mendicus **cibo** carebat.   *The beggar lacked food.*

Other verbs in this category include:

abutor (3), **abusus sum** (+ *abl.*), *to use up, exhaust*
fruor (3), **fructus sum** (+ *abl.*), *to enjoy*
fungor (3), **functus sum** (+ *abl.*), *to perform*
potior (4), **potitus sum** (+ *abl.*), *to obtain possession of*

vescor (3) (+ *abl.*), *to feed on*
egeo (2) (+ *abl.*), *to need*
indigeo (2) (+ *abl.*), *to need, lack*
nitor (3), **nisus sum** (+ *abl.*), *to lean on*
nudo (1) (+ *abl.*), *to strip of*
spolio (1) (+ *abl.*), *to strip of*
privo (1) (+ *abl.*), *to deprive of*

6 When used WITH A COMPARATIVE adjective/adverb, the ablative may express

(*a*) comparison, e.g.

> **luce** sunt clariora nobis tua consilia omnia.
> *All your plans are clearer to us **than daylight**.*

Note also the following phrases which involve the Ablative of Comparison:

plus solito, *more than usual*
spe celerius, *more quickly than was hoped*
opinione citius, *sooner than expected*

(*b*) the amount of difference, e.g.

> **uno pede** altior sum quam frater.
> *I am a foot taller* (lit. "taller by a foot") *than my brother.*

Compare, **paulo maior,** *a little bigger*   **nihilominus,** *nonetheless*
paucis post diebus, *a few days later.*

7 CERTAIN ADJECTIVES govern the ablative, e.g.

dignus (+ *abl.*), *worthy of*
indignus (+ *abl.*), *unworthy of*

fretus (+ *abl.*), *relying on*
orbus (+ *abl.*), *deprived of*

8 Some ablative words and phrases are best learned as vocabulary items:

sua sponte, *of his own accord*
iure, *rightly*
iniuria, *wrongly, unjustly*
adverso flumine, *upstream*

hoc modo, *in this way*
aequo animo, *calmly*
dextra, *on the right*
sinistra, *on the left*

9 The ABLATIVE ABSOLUTE is discussed on page 30.

EXERCISE A

Translate:
1. muri aedificii magno fragore ceciderunt.
2. nuntius in Graeciam nave celeri navigabit.
3. praedo erat homo risu horribili.
4. neminem sorore tua dulciorem vidi.
5. coniurati ipsi, amicorum auxilio freti, nave effugerunt.
6. Hannibale duce, Carthaginienses trans Alpes ducti erant.
7. sol est multis partibus maior quam luna.
8. leo, uno pede claudus, dolore maximo affectus est.
9. alter consul morbo gravi mortuus est, alter senectute.
10. nonne amicus tuus vita longiore dignus fuit?
11. senator villam magno vendere in animo habebat.
12. dominus servis libertatem, qua nihil est carius, dedit.
13. te dormiente, fur domum intravit.
14. cur adverso flumine natare conaris?
15. nostros amicos tyrannus non modo libertate sed etiam vita ipsa privavit.

EXERCISE B

Translate:
1. solis ortu milites longo agmine profecti sunt.
2. nostri hoc modo castris hostium facile potientur.
3. huic militi novo gladio opus est.
4. hostes, impetu facto, summa vi usi sunt.
5. nobis audientibus, dominus servos feroci voce monuit.
6. rex, cum urbem vi capere non posset, dolo uti constituit.
7. eo ipso tempore cives moenia summis viribus defendebant.
8. solis occasu piratarum dux, homo summa audacia, signum dedit.
9. adulescens, patre nobili natus, parentibus se dignum praebuit.
10. frater meus mihi viribus praestat, quod me est natu maior.
11. tu regem nobilitate totisque divitiis spoliavisti.
12. tum Maharbal Hannibali "vincere scis" inquit "sed victoria uti nescis."
13. cum nostri usu armorum multo meliores essent, hostes impetu destiterunt.
14. Galli lingua, moribus, institutis inter se differunt.
15. clamoribus excitatus, ianitor in viam summa celeritate exiit.

Time Phrases

1 With a preposition or adverb:

    post multos dies   *after many days*
    ante primam lucem   *before dawn*
    abhinc tres dies   *three days ago*
    tribus post diebus   *three days later (afterwards)*

2 Without a preposition or adverb:

  (*a*) The *accusative* case without a preposition is used to indicate *how long* something lasts. The word "for" will usually be used in translation, e.g.

    Graeci Troiam **decem annos** obsidebant.
    *The Greeks besieged Troy **for ten years**.*

  (*b*) The *ablative* case is used to indicate *when* or the period *within which* something happens. The English words "at", "on" or "in" will usually be used in translation; the other words in the sentence, especially the verb, will help to decide which of these three words gives the correct meaning, e.g.

    tribus diebus rediit.   *He returned **in three days**.*
    quinto die advenit.   *He arrived **on the fifth day**.*
    aestate rus redibimus.   ***In summer** we shall return to the country.*
    prima luce profecti sumus.   *We set out **at dawn**.*

EXERCISE A

Translate:
1. Ulixes decem annos per multas terras, multa maria errabat.
2. postero die Caesar legatum cum septima legione praemisit.
3. quattuor abhinc diebus consul cum magno exercitu ab urbe profectus est.
4. Tiberius princeps multos annos Capreis habitabat.
5. aestate Baiis, Romae hieme habitabant multi senatores.
6. tres dies apud Sextum manebam; heri tamen tertia hora inde discessi.
7. tribus ante horis senex in forum descenderat neque ante noctem domum redierat.
8. octo diebus rus redibo; calorem strepitumque urbis Athenarum diutius pati non possum.
9. media nocte dominus e somno excitatus furem capere conatus est.
10. tribus diebus eo regrediemur unde abhinc duos menses profecti sumus.

EXERCISE B

Translate:
1. consule Cicerone, plurimi coniurati Roma in Etruriam confugerunt.
2. quinto post die quam huc pervenerat a servis suis interfectus est.
3. audivi vos paucis diebus ab urbe discessuros esse.
4. Titus tertio post die quam a latronibus verberatus erat in villa sua periit.
5. ille mercator dicebat se domum hieme redire malle, sed Brundisii abhinc tres menses aestate mortuus est.
6. Marcum quinque diebus huc rediturum esse sperabam.
7. puer quindecim annos natus Athenas a patre missus est ut linguam Graecam bene disceret.
8. introductus est eo ipso tempore servus qui se proxima nocte in silva latuisse affirmavit.
9. nos, dum Romam illo anno redimus, piratae aggressi captivos dies triginta detinebant.
10. consul nona hora in forum descendit ut cives de clade duobus ante diebus accepta certiores faceret.

Place

1 As can be seen from pages 22–24, there are numerous prepositions which can be used in expressions of place.

2 The preposition is usually omitted when the expression involves *the name of a town or small island*, or the words **domus, humus** and **rus**:

    (*a*) in the *accusative case*, the meaning of the verb will help you to decide whether the accusative is the *object* of the verb or means "to" the place, e.g.

        Romam servavit.   *He protected Rome.*
        Baias laudabat.   *He praised Baiae.*

but

        Romam festinabat.   *He hurried to Rome.*
        Baias iter fecit.   *He travelled to Baiae.*

    (*b*) in the *ablative case*, motion "from" the place is usually indicated, e.g.

        Carthagine profectus est.   *He set out from Carthage.*
        Athenis expulsus est.   *He was banished from Athens.*
        domo discessit.   *He left home.*

3 In early Latin, there existed a *locative case*, meaning "at" or "in" and applicable to this place-name class of words. Irrespective of the Group to which the noun belonged, the locative case had the ending **-i**, e.g.

    Romae (originally **Romai**)   *at/in Rome*
    Corinthi   *at/in Corinth*
    Carthagini   *at/in Carthage*
    ruri   *in the country*
    humi   *on the ground*
    domi   *at home*

However, in all plural nouns and, as the language developed, in many Group 3 nouns also, this locative meaning was taken over by the ablative case. Accordingly,

    Carthagine may mean *from Carthage* or *at/in Carthage*
    Athenis   may mean *from Athens* or *at/in Athens*.

In this situation, only the verb of the sentence can help the reader arrive at the correct meaning, e.g.

    Gadibus morabatur.   *He stayed at Cadiz.*
    Gadibus discessit.   *He went away from Cadiz.*

EXERCISE A

Translate:
1. Roma statim discede! ruri tutior eris.
2. plurimi coniurati ex urbe Faesulas confugerunt.
3. Carthagine ad Siciliam navigavi; sed domi manere iam volo.
4. Athenis magnus erat clamor strepitusque; multi homines ad theatrum ibant.
5. naves magna tempestate Carthaginem repulsae sunt.
6. ego rus ibo atque ibi manebo, nam mihi placet ruri manere.
7. princeps, postquam Herculaneo discessit, statim Capreas transiit.
8. dum in his locis Caesar moratur, ad eum legati ex castris hostium venerunt.
9. Augustus, qui plurimos annos Romae habitaverat, Nolae mortuus est.
10. naves onerariae, cum Alexandria navigavissent, Melitam ventis adversis vectae sunt.

EXERCISE B

Translate:
1. Athenas multi Romani ibant ut ibi philosophos audirent.
2. patruus meus Mediolano profectus summa celeritate Massiliam petivit.
3. ventum idoneum nactus Caesar Brundisio in Graeciam solvit.
4. Ulixes, cum Troia discessisset, multis post annis Ithacam venit.
5. Hannibal, Romanis ad Cannas magno proelio superatis, Capuam iter fecit neque Romam petivit.
6. ruri aves in arboribus cantantes, Romae nihil nisi clamores ac strepitum audire solemus.
7. spero me Sextum amicum meum duobus diebus Philippis visurum esse.
8. Caesar Roma proficiscitur Neapolim atque inde Brundisium.
9. nescio quare Athenis Corinthum iter facere velit.
10. imperator in Britanniam transgressus, cum Cantium cepisset, tres legiones Londinium duxit.

Prepositions

1 Prepositions followed by the **accusative** case

ad, to, towards, at, near, for, with a view to	ad eam currit.	He runs towards her.
	milites ad Rhenum castra posuerunt.	The soldiers pitched camp near the Rhine.
	ad profectionem omnia parata sunt.	Everything is ready for departure.
	ad ostium Rhodani	at the mouth of the Rhône
	vicos ad quadringentos incendunt.	They set fire to about 400 villages.
	omnes ad unum occisi sunt.	They were all killed to a man.
adversus, against	adversus Gallos	against the Gauls
ante, before (of place and time)	ante oculos imperatoris	before the general's eyes
	ante fundum suum	in front of his own farm
	ante meridiem	before mid-day
apud, at (the house of), in (the works of), near	apud Laecam	at Laeca's (house)
	apud me	at my house
	apud Livium	in the works (writings) of Livy
	apud Rhodanum	near the Rhône
circum, circa, (of place) round, round about	lecti circum mensam ponuntur.	Couches are put round the table.
cis } on this side of **citra**	ei qui cis Rhenum incolunt.	Those who live on this side of the Rhine.
	(cf. Gallia Cisalpina)	(Gaul on this side of the Alps)
contra, against	contra populum Romanum coniurant.	They conspire against the Roman people.
erga, towards, to (usually of feelings)	erga nos benevoli fuerunt.	They were well-disposed towards us.
extra, outside	extra urbem exibimus.	We shall go outside the city.
infra, below	infra dignitatem	beneath one's dignity
inter, between, among	inter crura adstantium canis currit.	The dog runs among the legs of the bystanders.
	inter Iuram et flumen Rhodanum	between the Jura Mountains and the Rhône
	inter nos amamus.	We love one another.
	convivae inter se mussant.	The guests mutter to one another.
intra, inside	intra limen	inside the doorway
iuxta, near	iuxta murum stabat.	He stood near the wall.

ob, on account of, for, because of	quam ob rem eos expulerunt. ob has causas	*For this reason they drove them out.* *for these reasons*
per, through, throughout, during, by means of, along	per provinciam iter fecit. per multos dies nihil edebat. per servum nuntium misit. per Viam Appiam contendebat.	*He marched through the province.* *Throughout (during) many days he ate nothing.* *He sent a message by means of a slave.* *He hurried along the Via Appia.*
post, behind, after	post cenam diu loquebantur. post meridiem impedimenta post legiones collocavit. post hominum memoriam	*They talked a long time after dinner.* *after mid-day* *He positioned the baggage behind the legions.* *within living memory*
praeter, past, beyond, except	praeter oram Etruriae navigavit. nemo praeter mercatores eo ivit. praeter spem	*He sailed past the coast of Etruria.* *No one except merchants went there.* *beyond expectation*
prope, near	prope flumen castra posuit.	*He pitched camp near the river.*
propter, on account of, because of	propter altitudinem maris	*because of the depth of the sea*
super, above, over, beyond	super capita super cetera	*above their heads* *over and above the other factors*
supra, above, beyond	supra portam	*above the gate*
trans, across	trans Rhenum	*across the Rhine*
ultra, beyond	ultra Tiberim	*beyond the Tiber*

2 Prepositions followed by the **accusative** or the **ablative** case

in + accusative, into, to, towards, against	in silvam cucurrit. Gallia est divisa in partes tres. in hostes impetum fecerunt.	*He ran into the wood.* *Gaul is divided into three parts.* *They made an attack on the enemy.*
in + ablative, in, on	in aperto tumulo castra posuit. in urbe permulti habitant.	*He pitched camp on an exposed hill.* *Very many people live in the city.*
sub + accusative, under, close up to	milites victi sub iugum missi sunt. catapultas sub moenia misit.	*The defeated soldiers were sent under the yoke.* *He sent the engines close up to the walls.*
sub + ablative, under	sub arboribus dormiebant. sub hasta vendere	*They were sleeping under the trees.* *to sell by auction* (lit. "under the spear")

3 Prepositions followed by the **ablative case**

a, ab, by, from	exercitus ab Helvetiis pulsus est.	The army was driven back by the Swiss.
	ab urbe discessit.	He departed from the city.
	ab armato hoste populus Romanus condiciones non accipit.	The Roman people does not accept terms from an armed enemy.
	a milibus passuum octo	at a distance of eight miles
	a tergo	from behind, in the rear
	a sinistra parte	on the left side
cum, with, along with	cum hostium equitatu proelium committunt.	They join battle with the enemy cavalry.
	cum impedimentis	(along) with the baggage
	cum cura	with care
de, down from, from, about, concerning	de navibus desiluerunt.	They leapt down from the ships.
	certa de causa	(from) for a particular reason
	de eius adventu certiores facti sunt.	They were informed about his arrival.
	de industria	on purpose, deliberately
e, ex, out of, from, as a result of, in accordance with	ex oppido currebant.	They were running out of the town.
	ex aere simulacrum	a statue (made) out of bronze
	e captivis haec cognovit.	He learned this from prisoners.
	ex clamore	as a result of the shouting
	e legibus	in accordance with the laws
	ex omni parte	on every side
	unus e militibus	one of the soldiers
prae, owing to, in comparison with	prae strepitu audire non potuit.	He couldn't hear because of the din.
	prae nobis beatus est.	He is happy compared with us.
pro, in front of, for, on behalf of, instead of, in return for	pro castris constitit.	He halted in front of the camp.
	pro patria mori	to die on behalf of (for) one's country
	pro munimento	as a defence
	pro multitudine hominum	in proportion to (for) the number of people
sine, without	sine scuto ex acie fugit.	He fled from the battle without his shield.
	sine spe	without hope

EXERCISE A

Translate:
1 totum diem apud fratrem meum mansimus.
2 dum in Graecia iter facit, a latronibus interfectus est.
3 magister pueros multa de regibus Romanis rogabat.
4 Galli Romanos ex loco superiore in flumen celeriter compulerunt.
5 Romani, cum omnia ad profectionem paravissent, subito impetu hostium perturbati sunt.
6 in hostes impetum fecerunt atque in fugam dederunt.
7 meus amicus in Campania iter faciebat solus, sine uxore, nullis comitibus.
8 nemo praeter mercatores ad Britanniam adire solebat.
9 verba imperatoris audiri non poterant prae strepitu ac tumultu.
10 barbari undique ex insidiis a fronte et ab tergo coorti sunt.

EXERCISE B

Translate:
1 Aeneas tempestate actus cum septem navibus ad oram Africae advenit.
2 dux Romanus, castris prope flumen positis, suis quietem unius diei dedit.
3 Galli de Caesaris adventu certiores facti legatos ad eum pacis causa miserunt.
4 hostes circum nos stantes rogabant unde venissemus.
5 servi faces ad urbem inflammandam comparaverant.
6 Christiani certa die ante lucem conveniebant ut carmen Christo cantarent.
7 Caesar, cum hostes post tergum relinquere nollet, propter tempus anni pacem confirmare constituit.
8 ad horam sextam exspectavit dum reliquae naves advenirent.
9 dux praeter Etruriam vectus Massiliam pervenit et ad ostium Rhodani castra posuit.
10 silent leges inter arma. ob eam causam cives saepe de reipublicae salute desperant.

Relative Clauses

1 The noun or pronoun to which a relative pronoun (**qui, quae, quod**) refers is called the *antecedent*. The relative pronoun agrees with its antecedent in *gender* and *number*; its *case* depends on its use in its own clause, e.g.

(*a*) milites, **qui** totum diem contenderant, erant defessi.
*The soldiers, **who** had marched all day, were tired.*

(*b*) milites, **quos** Caesar puniverat, ignavi fuerant.
*The soldiers, **whom** Caesar had punished, had been cowardly.*

The relative pronoun in both of these sentences is masculine plural because the antecedent is **milites**. It is nominative in (*a*) because **qui** is the subject of **contenderant** in the relative clause; it is accusative in (*b*) because **quos** is the direct object of **puniverat** in the relative clause.
Compare:

(*c*) puella, **cuius** mater mortua erat, lacrimabat.
*The girl, **whose** mother had died, was crying.*

(*d*) meus amicus, **cui** pecuniam commisi, me prodidit.
*My friend, **to whom** I handed over the money, betrayed me.*

2 Sometimes, for emphasis, the antecedent comes after the relative clause or is omitted altogether, e.g.

qui non laborat, **is** non manducat.   *He who does not work does not eat.*
qui non laborat, non manducat.

3 Sometimes the antecedent itself, or a superlative adjective agreeing with the antecedent, is incorporated into the relative clause, e.g.

habitamus Athenis, **quam urbem** omnes mirantur.
*We live in Athens, **a city which** all admire.*

venit cum copiis quas **firmissimas** habebat.
*He came with the **strongest forces** he had.*

4 A statement can be greatly strengthened by using the demonstratives **hoc** and **illud** followed by a relative clause to explain the pronoun, e.g.

hoc timeo, **quod** Caesar rex fieri vult.
***This** is what I fear, **that** Caesar wishes to become king.*

5 *Linking qui:* The relative is often used at the beginning of a sentence to provide a link with a person, thing or action in the previous sentence, e.g.

res loquitur ipsa, iudices. **quae** semper valet plurimum.
The facts speak for themselves, gentlemen. ***That*** *always carries conviction.*

leo Androclem non petivit. **quod** ubi vidimus, mirati sumus.
*The lion did not attack Androcles. When we saw **this**, we marvelled.*

6 The verb in a relative clause is normally in the indicative mood; if it is in the subjunctive, then some other idea is present (see pages 103–104 and 111).

EXERCISE A

Translate:
1. omnes, qui orationem eius audiebant, lacrimabant.
2. exercitus, quem in Galliam misimus, ab hostibus victus est.
3. omnes arbores, quae in his agris crescebant, vento deletae sunt.
4. nostri amici, quibus vera dicebamus, nobis non credebant.
5. occasionem, quae tibi data est, noli omittere!
6. agricolae, quorum agri vastati erant, summa ira commoti sunt.
7. pecunia, quam eis commiseramus, a latronibus abrepta est.
8. praemium quod promiserat mihi dare noluit.
9. nomen illius senis, qui solus vivit, nemo scire videtur.
10. vos omnes, qui patriam amatis, debetis hostibus summis viribus resistere. quos repellere facile poteritis.

EXERCISE B

Translate:
1. meam sororem, cuius domus incensa erat, invitavi ut apud me habitaret.
2. omnes captivi, quibus erat nec cibus nec vestis, erant miserrimi.
3. Roma omnibus, qui viderunt, urbs pulcherrima visa est.
4. tandem nautae, qui magnis tempestatibus impediti erant, ad portum pervenerunt.
5. numquam credam homini a quo patria nostra prodita est.
6. dux hostium omnibus pepercit; quod admirationi nobis fuit.
7. templum, quod nostri maiores abhinc multos annos aedificaverant, videre voluimus.
8. qui e pugna fugit, is iterum pugnare poterit.
9. Caesar tertiam cohortem, quae in silvis latebat, subsidio nostris misit. quae res eos servavit.
10. reliquit centurionem et centum milites qui pontem custodirent.

Participles

Tense	Active	Passive
Present	1 port**ans**, port**antis** 2 hab**ens**, hab**entis** 3 mitt**ens**, mitt**entis** 4 aud**iens**, aud**ientis**	
Perfect		1 porta**tus**, **-a**, **-um** 2 habi**tus**, **-a**, **-um** 3 mis**sus**, **-a**, **-um** 4 audi**tus**, **-a**, **-um**
Future	1 porta**turus**, **-a**, **-um** 2 habi**turus**, **-a**, **-um** 3 mis**surus**, **-a**, **-um** 4 audi**turus**, **-a**, **-um**	

N.B. The present participle of **ire** is **iens, euntis**.

1 *Present Participle (Active)*

The present participle indicates an action going on *at the same time* as the main verb. It has endings similar to those of a Group 3 adjective (except that the ablative singular ends in **-e**).

(*a*) It is normally translated by the part of the English verb which ends in *-ing*, e.g.

> abierunt illi **ridentes**.
> *They went away laughing.*

> lupum in silvam **intrantem** conspeximus.
> *We caught sight of the wolf going into the wood.*

(*b*) Sometimes a literal translation will not produce satisfactory English, e.g.

> **ei roganti** respondere semper conor.
> *I always try to answer his questions.*

> multi ex **adstantibus** lacrimabant.
> *Many of the bystanders were weeping.*

In these two examples, a noun has been used to translate the present participles.

2 Future Participle (Active)

There are various ways of translating a future participle into English; for example, **missurus** may mean *about to send, going to send, intending to send, determined to send, on the point of sending*, e.g.

una ex ancillis ad tabernam profecta est panem **emptura**.
One of the maids set out for the shop (intending) to buy bread.

3 Perfect Participle (Passive)

(*a*) The perfect participle indicates an action which took place *before* the action described by the main verb, e.g.

Nominative:
coquus **vocatus** a convivis laudatus est.
Having been summoned,
After being summoned,
After he was summoned,   the cook was praised by the guests.
When he had been summoned,
or *The cook was summoned and praised by the guests.*

Accusative: coquum **vocatum** convivae laudaverunt.
The cook was summoned and the guests praised him.
The guests summoned the cook and praised him.
When they had summoned the cook, the guests praised him.
After summoning the cook, the guests praised him.
Having summoned the cook, the guests praised him.

Dative: coquo **vocato** convivae gratias egerunt.
The cook was summoned and the guests thanked him.
The guests summoned the cook and thanked him.

(*b*) A perfect participle is sometimes used where English would use a noun, e.g.

illi **libertatem imminutam** non tulerunt.
*They did not tolerate **the restriction of freedom*** (literally *reduced freedom*).

(*c*) (See also Ablative Absolute on pages 30–31.)

4 Deponents

The present and future participles of deponent verbs are *active in form* and *active in meaning*, e.g.

sequ**ens**, sequ**entis**, *following*
secut**urus, -a, -um**, *about to follow*

The perfect participle is *passive in form* but *active in meaning*, e.g.

secu**tus**, -a, -um, *having followed*

a villa **profectus** fugitivus flumen transire **conans** captus est.
Having set out *from the villa, the runaway slave was caught* ***trying*** *to cross the river.*

Ablative Absolute

1 When a noun (or pronoun) and a participle are linked together in the ablative case, the usage is called the Ablative Absolute. It is called this because the participial phrase is "free-standing" and has no grammatical connection with the rest of the sentence. The participle may be in any of the three tenses, e.g.

Present:

oratore loquente, cives tacebant.
While the orator was speaking, the citizens did not speak.

Perfect:

oratore locuto, cives inter se loquebantur.
After the orator had spoken, the citizens talked among themselves.

Future:

oratore locuturo, cives conticuerunt.
Since the orator was going to speak, the citizens fell silent.

2 Sometimes a noun will produce a good translation of an Ablative Absolute, e.g. **oratore locuto,** *after the orator's speech.* Compare

Augusto mortuo, Tiberius princeps factus est.
On the death of Augustus, Tiberius became emperor.

militibus progredientibus, hostes terga dederunt.
During the advance of the troops, the enemy turned and fled.

3 The verb **esse** has no present participle. It is therefore necessary to supply the word "being" when translating literally certain Ablative Absolute phrases such as

Caesare duce   *under the leadership of Caesar*
         (lit. "Caesar being leader")

me custode	*while I am on guard* (lit. "me being on guard")
inscia matre	*without mother's knowledge* (lit. "mother not knowing")

EXERCISE A

Translate:
1. pater epistola scripta cubitum ivit.
2. adstantes rogavi ubi incendium esset.
3. dominus ad urbem profecturus servos diligenter laborare iussit.
4. poculis in mensa positis, servi in culinam festinaverunt.
5. milites nostri urbem obsessam et captam incenderunt.
6. pater puerum domo exiturum in cubiculum redire iussit.
7. mihi roganti servi nihil responderunt, sed abierunt ridentes.
8. hostes e loco superiore in nostros progredientes tela coniciebant.
9. puella libros amissos petere coepit.
10. nuntio appropinquanti pater meus "quid novi?" inquit.

EXERCISE B

Translate:
1. ancillae e somno excitatae servos in atrio loquentes audiverunt.
2. barbari eodem usi consilio oppida vicosque omnes incenderunt.
3. senex filiis ad se vocatis valedixit moriturus.
4. omnes pueri vestimentis exutis paulisper morati in aquam frigidam desiluerunt.
5. nostri Gallos impeditos et inopinantes aggressi magnam partem eorum conciderunt.
6. voces magnae domum nocte regredientium nos e somno excitaverunt.
7. leone viso, in speluncam confugi metu tremens; postea animo recuperato domum quam celerrime cucurri.
8. sene dormiente, servi in viam exierunt ridentes ac cantantes.
9. Caesar multas naves comparare coepit in Britanniam navigaturus.
10. Pyramus gladio stricto se vulneravit atque ad terram cecidit moriens.

Infinitives

Tense	Active	Passive
Present	1 portare 2 habere 3 mittere 4 audire	portari haberi mitti audiri
Perfect	1 portavisse 2 habuisse 3 misisse 4 audivisse	portatus esse habitus esse missus esse auditus esse
Future	1 portaturus esse 2 habiturus esse 3 missurus esse 4 auditurus esse	portatum iri habitum iri missum iri auditum iri

N.B. The present infinitive active of some irregular verbs does not end in -re: **velle, nolle, malle**, and **esse** and its compounds, including **posse**.

1 There are several verbs which are very commonly followed by the present infinitive, e.g.

    laborare noluit.   *He refused to work.*
    proficisci constituit.   *He decided to set out.*
    dormire non potest.   *He is unable to sleep.*

2 Passive forms of **dicere** and **videre** are frequently used with infinitives of all tenses, e.g.

    discessisse dicitur.   *He is said to have gone away.*
    profecturi esse videntur.   *They seem to be on the point of leaving.*
    relicti esse videmur.   *We seem to have been abandoned.*
    laudari videbaris.   *It seemed you were being praised.*
    mox redituri esse dicuntur. *It is said they intend to return soon.*

3 *Historic Infinitive*

Present infinitives (often several in succession) are used by Latin authors to heighten the excitement of a passage, especially when they wish to create a feeling of urgency or to give the reader some idea of the speed at which events occurred. These *Historic Infinitives* should be translated as if they were past tenses of the indicative. The subject of a Historic Infinitive is in the nominative case.

Pliny uses Historic Infinitives in the following passage taken from his description of the eruption of Vesuvius. He is describing how his mother wanted him to leave her behind since he, being much younger, would be able to escape more easily without her:

> tum mater **orare, hortari, iubere** quoquo modo fugerem.
> *Then my mother pleaded, urged, ordered me to flee by whatever means I could.*

The Historic Infinitives convey the urgency of her entreaties. Compare the piling up of Historic Infinitives by Pliny to convey the excitement and the rapid sequence of events leading up to a ghost's appearance before the philosopher, Athenodorus:

> initio silentium, dein concuti ferrum, vincula moveri. ille non tollere oculos, non remittere stilum, sed offirmare animum auribusque praetendere. tum crebrescere fragor, adventare et iam ut in limine, iam ut intra limen audiri. respicit, videt agnoscitque narratam sibi effigiem.
>
> *At first, there was silence, then iron clanked and chains rattled. The philosopher did not lift his eyes and did not stop writing, but kept concentrating (on what he was doing) and shut his ears. Then the noise grew louder and drew nearer, and it could be heard now as if it were in the doorway, now as if it were inside the room. He looked up, and saw and recognised the ghost he had been told about.*

Note how Pliny reverts to the indicative at the end of the passage.

4 For *Accusative and Infinitive*, see page 34.

EXERCISE

Translate:
1 domum redire nolebat, nam ruri habitare malebat.
2 dux prima luce navem solvere constituit.
3 quis latrones in vincula conici iussit?
4 Vergilius poeta Brundisii mortuus esse dicitur.
5 rex primo nihil metuere, nihil suspicari.
6 cur servos meridie in agris laborare coegisti?
7 tempestas multas naves in saxa depulisse videtur.
8 uxor senatoris Roma Baias discessura esse videtur.
9 pueros linguam Latinam docere saepe conati sumus.

10 quod revera facere vultis, id sine dubio potestis.
11 piratae in oram Italiae egressi esse dicebantur.
12 denique hostes iam undique fusi. tum spectaculum horribile in campis patentibus: sequi, fugere, occidi, capi. equi atque viri afflicti, ac multi vulneribus acceptis neque fugere posse neque quietem pati, niti modo ac statim concidere.
(Sallust, *Jugurtha* 101)

Accusative and Infinitive

1 The Accusative and Infinitive (known also as Indirect Statement) is normally introduced by such verbs as "to say", "to know", "to believe." In translating, it may be found helpful to insert the word "that" after the introductory verb, e.g.

> puto **pueros esse** molestissimos.
> *I think (that) the boys are very troublesome.*
>
> credisne **servum** in horto **laborare**?
> *Do you believe (that) the slave is working in the garden?*
>
> scimus **patrem** iratissimum **esse**.
> *We know (that) father is very angry.*

2 In the above examples, all the infinitives are present tense. Perfect and future infinitives are also found, e.g.

> audio **Caesarem** Gallos **vicisse**.
> *I hear that Caesar has defeated the Gauls.*
>
> audio **Gallos** a Caesare **victos esse**.
> *I hear that the Gauls have been defeated by Caesar.*
>
> senator dicit **nuntium** mox ab urbe **perventurum esse**.
> *The senator says that a messenger will soon arrive from the city.*

Note that, since the subject of the Accusative and Infinitive clause is in the accusative case, the perfect infinitive passive and the future infinitive active are also in the accusative, agreeing with the subject in number and gender (e.g. **victos esse** and **perventurum esse** above).

3 When the verb of "thinking", "knowing", "saying", etc. is in a past tense, the Latin infinitive remains unchanged but must be translated differently. Compare the following sentences with those in the previous two sections:

> putavi pueros **esse** molestissimos.
> *I thought that the boys **were** very troublesome.*

credebasne servum in horto **laborare**?
*Did you believe that the slave **was working** in the garden?*

audivi Caesarem Gallos **vicisse**.
*I heard that Caesar **had defeated** the Gauls.*

audivi Gallos a Caesare **victos esse**.
*I heard that the Gauls **had been defeated** by Caesar.*

senator dixit nuntium mox ab urbe **perventurum esse**.
*The senator said that a messenger **would** soon **arrive** from the city.*

4 When **se** or **suus** appears in the Accusative and Infinitive clause, it usually refers to the subject of the main verb of "saying", "thinking", etc., e.g.

senator dixit **se suos** amicos in urbe vidisse.
The senator said that he had seen his friends in the city.

In this sentence, "he" and "his" both refer to the senator. If the references had been made to someone else, **eum** would have been used instead of **se**, and **eius** instead of **suos**.

5 When the Accusative and Infinitive is introduced by **negare**, this verb is commonly translated as *say that . . . not*, e.g.

Caesar negavit se captivos necavisse.
Caesar said that he had not killed the prisoners.

Compare **nego quemquam** (*I say that no one*), **nego quidquam** (*I say that nothing*), **nego ullum** (*I say that no*), **nego .... umquam** (*I say that.... never*), **nego .... usquam** (*I say that.... nowhere*).

6 With verbs used impersonally (see p. 57), only the infinitive is expressed, e.g.

scimus acriter **pugnari**. *We know that a fierce battle is going on.*

EXERCISE A

Translate:
1 mater dicit ancillas neglegentes esse.
2 pueri credebant omnia aedificia ruinas esse.
3 omnes putaverunt triclinium pulcherrimum esse.
4 convivae sciunt se coquum laudare debere.
5 consul promisit se vinum optimum omnibus convivis daturum esse.
6 dominus dixit servum diligentissime laboravisse.
7 negavit se umquam in Italia fuisse.
8 adstantes responderunt senem domum portatum esse.

9 uxori dicam eam omnia optime egisse.
10 uxori dixi eam omnia optime egisse.
11 puella dixit se quam diutissime in urbe moratam esse.
12 negavi me quidquam e cista cepisse.

EXERCISE B

Translate:
1 medico respondit filium aegrum cibum libenter sumere.
2 paedagogus negat se fabulas pueris narrare velle.
3 Galli promiserunt duces suos ad Caesarem venturos esse.
4 milites nostri speraverunt se urbem mox capturos esse.
5 Marcus negavit quidquam se pugnare esse coacturum.
6 hostes superati se obsides daturos esse promiserunt.
7 hoc audito, nuntius respondit exercitum in unum locum esse coactum.
8 uxor mea negat eum sibi umquam persuasurum esse ut pecuniam tradat.
9 tu dissimulabas te mandata matris audivisse; ego simulabam me librum legere.
10 captivi nihil consulibus dixisse videbantur.
11 Hannibal credebat se Romanos victurum esse.
12 Hannibal credebat se Romanos victuros esse.

Direct Questions

A. The most common ways of asking Direct Questions in Latin are:

1 The sentence may begin with a *question word*, e.g.

quis hoc fecit? *Who has done this?*
ubi habitat? *Where does he live?*

The commonest question words in Latin are:

Pronouns/Adjectives

qualis, -is, -e?	*of what kind?*
quis?	*who?*
quid?	*what?*
quantus, -a, -um?	*how great?*

Adverbs

cur? (quare?)	*why?*
quomodo?	*how?*
quo?	*where . . . to?*
quando?	*when?*

quot? *(indec.)*	*how many?*	quotiens?	*how often?*
qui, quae, quod?	*what? (adjective)* *which?*	ubi?	*where?*
		unde?	*where . . . from?*
uter, utra, utrum?	*which (of two)?*		

2 **-ne** attached to the end of the first word in the sentence indicates a question in which the first word carries the main emphasis of the question, e.g.

librum**ne** legisti? *Have you read the **book**?*
legist**ine** librum? *Have you **read** the book?*

3 nonne (**non** + **ne**) or **num**, as the first word in the sentence, indicates the answer the questioner would like to receive, even though the opposite answer may be given, e.g.

nonne librum legisti? *Haven't you read the book?*
You've read the book, haven't you?
Surely you've read the book?

num librum legisti? *You haven't read the book, have you?*
Surely you haven't read the book?

In the first example, the questioner would like to receive the answer "Yes"; in the second, the answer "No".

4 an (= *or*) and **annon** (= *or not*) introduce the second part of a double question, e.g.

custos**ne** urbis **an** direptor et vexator esset Antonius?
Would Antony be a guardian or a plunderer and scourge of the city?

es**ne** servus **annon**?
Are you a slave or not?

5 utrum introduces double questions. It is derived from the neuter singular of **uter, utra, utrum** = *which of two*, and later came to mean "whether", although this word is normally omitted in English, e.g.

utrum pro ancilla me habes **an** pro filia?
(Whether) do you regard me as a slave or as a daughter?

utrum enim defenditis **an** impugnatis plebem?
Are you then defending or attacking the plebs?

6 Sometimes the **utrum** part of a double question is suppressed, and the question begins with **an**, e.g.

an servi esse parati estis?
(Would you like to be free) or are you prepared to be slaves?

This use of **an** often introduces a farcical alternative, with the force of **num**, e.g.

> quae sunt perdita consilia? **an** ea quae pertinent ad libertatem populi Romani reciperandam?
> *What are (those) unprincipled policies? Those pertaining to the recovery of the freedom of the Roman people? (Surely not?)*

7 It is also possible to have a question indicated by nothing other than the pitch of the voice, e.g.

> quo fugient socii? ad senatum venient?
> *Where will our friends take refuge? Will they come to the senate?*

8 When the subjunctive appears in a Direct Question, it is probably a Deliberative Question, i.e. the questioner is thinking aloud or expressing some doubts, e.g.

> quid facit?   *What is he doing?*
> quid faciat?   *What is he to do?*
>
> quid faciebat?   *What was he doing?*
> quid faceret?   *What was he to do?*

B. ANSWERS

In Latin, there are no specific words for "Yes" and "No". These ideas are expressed in various ways:

1 Repetition of the question verb (with change of person, where necessary), or other significant word, e.g.

> reddidistine librum?   *Have you returned the book?*
> reddidi. (non reddidi.)   *Yes. (No.)*

2 Adverbs such as **etiam, sic, ita** or **sane** (sometimes strengthened by **quidem, vero** or **enimvero**) often mean "Yes", e.g.

> huic ego "studesne?" inquam. respondit "etiam."
> *I said to him "Are you at school?" He replied "Yes."*

3 Adverbs such as **minime** and **non** (sometimes strengthened by other adverbs) can mean "No", e.g.

> "sed cessas?" "minime quidem!"
> *"You're loitering, aren't you?" "No, I'm not!"*

38

4 immo (*on the contrary*) is used when the reply is the opposite of what is expected, e.g.

"numquid, Simo, peccatum est?" "immo, maxime."
"Surely no harm has been done, Simo?" "On the contrary, a great deal of harm has been done."

EXERCISE

Translate:
1 num constituisti mare hieme transire?
2 qualia in Sicilia scelera admisit Verres?
3 quid cives eo tempore faciebant?
4 quid cives facerent? quo confugerent?
5 utrum vi et armis an virtute ac prudentia Romani omnes gentes superaverunt?
6 cum epistolam scribis, utra manu uteris?
7 nonne tibi gratias egerunt? immo, me maxime culpaverunt.
8 herine huc venire eos iussisti? heri.
9 utrum pecuniam vobis reddiderunt annon?
10 num piratae Caesarem impune ceperunt?

Indirect Question

1 When a subordinate clause is introduced by a question word (e.g. **quis, quid, cur, quando**) and has its verb in the subjunctive, the verb in the subordinate clause is normally translated by the corresponding tense of the indicative. Such clauses tend to depend on a verb of "asking" or a verb that implies "asking oneself", e.g.

eum rogavi quis esset.
I asked him who he was.

nescio cur non pervenerit.
I do not know why he has not arrived.

mirabar quando perventurus esset.
I wondered when he would arrive.

The conjunction **num** (*whether* or *if*) may also be used to introduce the subordinate clause, e.g.

rogavit num quid audivissem.
He asked if I had heard anything.

2 Double Indirect Questions may be asked in several ways:

(*a*) The most straightforward way is
utrum . . . an . . ., *whether . . . or . . .*, e.g.

miror **utrum** domum redire velit **an** diutius manere malit.
I wonder if he wants to return home or prefers to remain longer.

(*b*) instead of **utrum**, **-ne** may be attached to the first word of the first clause, e.g.

incerti erant copias**ne** adversus hostem educere **an** castra defendere praestaret.
They were uncertain whether it was best to lead their troops out against the enemy or to defend the camp.

(*c*) **utrum . . . necne** means *whether . . . or not*, e.g.

scisne **utrum** venire in animo habeat **necne**?
Do you know if he intends to come or not?

3 When **se** or **suus** appears within the Indirect Question, it will usually refer to the subject of the main verb, e.g.

puer rogavit cur se punirem.
The boy asked why I was punishing him.

4 Note that Indirect Questions may often be translated into English by a noun rather than a clause, e.g.

scimus quot sint discipuli.
We know the number of the pupils.

vidi quantus esset exercitus.
I saw the size of the army.

cognovi quando pervenisset.
I learned the time of his arrival.

sciebamus quo iret.
We knew his destination.

EXERCISE A

Translate:
1 scire volo ubi soror mea sit.
2 nemo scit cur hoc feceris.
3 speculatores cognoscere conati sunt quot essent hostes.

4 cur mihi non dixisti unde homo venisset?
5 patrem rogavi num ad ludos iturus esset.
6 intellegere non possum cur servi hodie laborare nolint.
7 consul cognoscere volebat quando collega ad Italiam rediturus esset.
8 consulem rogavi num ad urbem rediturus esset.
9 omnes sciunt quam ferociter contra hostes pugnaverimus.
10 eum rogabo quo eat.

EXERCISE B

Translate:
1 nemo scit num fur captus sit.
2 non intellego quare pater tuus hoc facere constituerit.
3 nescivimus utrum hostes urbem cepissent necne.
4 dic mihi cur Romam redire velis.
5 nonne audivisti verane an falsa tibi dixerit?
6 rogavit ubi se et filium eius vidissemus.
7 mirabar utrum magister nos ipse esset puniturus an domum missurus.
8 Caesar dixit se cognoscere velle qualis et quanta esset insula.
9 cognoscere non poteramus ubi senex aurum celavisset.
10 Corneliam rogabo ut mihi dicat quid acciderit.

Indirect Command

1 When a Latin verb of "ordering" or "asking" (see list below) is followed by a clause introduced by **ut** with its verb in the subjunctive, the **ut** clause is normally translated by the infinitive in English, e.g.

senem rogavimus **ut** domi **maneret**.
*We asked the old man **to stay** at home.*

tyrannum orabimus **ut** mulieribus **parcat**.
*We shall beg the tyrant **to spare** the women.*

When the clause is introduced by **ne** it may usually be translated as *not to ...*, e.g.

servos monebo **ne** vinum in culina **bibant**.
*I shall warn the slaves **not to drink** wine in the kitchen.*

dux milites hortatus est **ne** arma **deponerent**.
*The general urged the soldiers **not to lay down** their arms.*

2 Sometimes it is not possible to translate the **ut** or **ne** clause by an infinitive. For example, study the difference between:

(a) coquo imperavit ut in atrium veniret.
   He ordered the cook to come into the atrium.

(b) imperavit ut coquus arcesseretur.
   He gave orders that the cook be sent for.

In (a), the order is issued to the cook personally; in (b), the orders are issued to someone else (not specified). In this latter type of command, "that" is often used to introduce the Indirect Command clause, but the infinitive may also sometimes be used, e.g. *He ordered the cook to be sent for.*

3 In double Indirect Commands, translate **neque, neve** or **neu** (introducing the second clause) as *and not*, e.g.

Catilinae imperavit ut ex urbe abiret **neve umquam** regrederetur.
*He ordered Catiline to leave the city **and never** return.*

4 When **se** or **suus** appears within the Indirect Command clause, it usually refers to the subject of the main verb, e.g.

mihi persuasit ut **sibi** pecuniam darem.
He persuaded me to give him the money.

5 Verbs which commonly introduce Indirect Commands include:

decernere, *to decree*	**persuadere** (+ *dat.*), *to persuade*
petere, *to ask*	**postulare,** *to demand*
hortari, *to urge*	**praecipere** (+ *dat.*), *to order, instruct*
imperare (+ *dat.*), *to order*	**precari,** *to pray, beg*
invitare, *to invite*	**rogare,** *to ask*
monere, *to warn, advise*	**scribere,** *to write*
obsecrare, *to beseech*	**suadere** (+ *dat.*), *to urge*
orare, *to beg*	

EXERCISE A

Translate:
1. heri agricolae persuasimus ut nos per agros ambulare sineret.
2. puellae a patre monitae sunt ne prope flumen luderent.
3. vos oro ne hoc consilium capiatis.
4. legatis consules praecipient ut extra Curiam maneant.
5. rex custodes monuerat ut totum diem vigilarent.
6. consul suos hortabatur ne ex acie fugerent.
7. magister ludi pueros monuit ut vera dicerent.
8. mercator nobis suasit ut se defenderemus.
9. mulieres lacrimantes obsecraverunt ut sacerdos se ad templum deduceret.
10. parentes pueri nos rogabant ne ex ludo eum mitteremus.
11. dux postulavit ut captivi statim liberarentur.
12. frater meus mihi persuasit ne se ad forum sequerer.

EXERCISE B

Translate:
1. nemo umquam nobis persuadebit ut cives Romanos hostibus tradamus.
2. servi dominum monebant ut salutem fuga peteret.
3. magistratus lictoribus praeceperat ut, adstantibus repulsis, viam sibi facerent.
4. alii ex circumstantibus milites hortati sunt ne vi uterentur.
5. viator iratus postulavit ut caupo sibi pecuniam redderet.
6. matronae sacerdotem precatae sunt ut sibi permitteret ut in templo paulisper manerent.
7. mercator piratas orat ut sibi parcant neve se in mare desilire cogant.
8. imperator rogavit ut patres triumphum sibi pararent.
9. cives nuntium orabant atque obsecrabant ut se certiores de proelii eventu faceret.
10. ad fratrem meum scribam ne Romam hoc anno regrediatur.
11. complures mendici a senatoribus petebant ut panem sibi darent; moniti tamen sunt ne hunc peterent neve prope Curiam inambularent.
12. decrevit senatus ut consules viderent ne quid respublica detrimenti caperet.

Purpose

1 ut or **ne** followed by a verb in the *subjunctive* is used to express the purpose of the main verb, i.e. the *aim* or *intention* with which someone did something. In such sentences, **ut** is usually translated by *to* or *so that*, e.g.

> puer arborem ascendit **ut** milites **videret**.
> *The boy climbed the tree **to see** the soldiers.*

> puer de arbore descendit **ut** milites se **viderent**.
> *The boy came down from the tree **so that** the soldiers **would see** him.*

The negative **ne** may be translated in several ways: *so that . . . not, in case, to avoid, to prevent*, e.g.

> puer arborem ascendit **ne** milites se viderent.
> *The boy climbed the tree* { *in case the soldiers saw him.*
> *so that the soldiers would **not** see him.*
> *to prevent the soldiers seeing him.* }

> puer arborem ascendit **ne** a militibus videretur.
> *The boy climbed the tree **to avoid** being seen by the soldiers.*

When a part of **quis, quis, quid** appears after **ne**, translate as *so that no one (nothing)* or *in case anyone (anything)*, e.g.

> aurum celavit **ne quis** id inveniret.
> *He concealed the gold **so that no one** might find it.*

When **neve** or **neu** appears in a Purpose clause, translate *and not* or *or*, e.g.

> servus aufugit ne puniretur **neve** caederetur.
> *The slave ran away to avoid being punished **or** killed.*

2 *The Relative Pronoun* (**qui, quae, quod**) followed by a verb in the *subjunctive* is also used to express purpose, especially after verbs implying motion (e.g. **mittere** and **venire**) and verbs of choosing and appointing (e.g. **deligere** and **creare**), e.g.

> duae legiones advenerunt **quae** castra **defenderent**.
> *Two legions arrived **to defend** the camp.*

> legatos delegerunt **qui** pacem **peterent**.
> *They chose ambassadors **to sue for** peace.*

> cives arma poscunt **quibus** moenia **defendant**.
> *The citizens are demanding arms* { ***with which to defend** the walls.*
> *so that they may defend the walls with them.* }

Sometimes the antecedent is omitted, e.g.

> dux misit qui haec Caesari nuntiarent.
> *The general sent (men) to report this to Caesar.*

> venerunt qui se excusarent.
> *People came to apologise.*

3 **quo** is used instead of **ut** if the Purpose clause contains a comparative adjective or adverb, e.g.

> milites manipulos laxaverunt **quo facilius** gladiis uti possent.
> *The soldiers opened up their ranks **so that** they could use their swords **more easily**.*

4 A *gerund* or *gerundive* used with **ad** or **causa** may also express purpose, e.g.

> Caesar **ad cohortandos milites** decucurrit.
> *Caesar ran down **to encourage the soldiers**.*

> **ad eas res conficiendas** biennium eis satis esse videbatur.
> *Two years seemed to them to be enough **to complete these preparations**.*

> *milites* **praedandi causa** e castris egressi sunt.
> *The soldiers went out of the camp **to gather booty**.*

5 The *supine* is found expressing purpose only after verbs of motion or verbs implying motion, e.g.

> principes legatos miserunt pacem **rogatum**.
> *The chieftains sent envoys **to ask** for peace.*

> Hannibal patriam **defensum** revocatus est.
> *Hannibal was recalled **to defend** his homeland.*

6 The *future participle* is occasionally used to express purpose, the participial phrase almost invariably appearing at the end of the sentence, e.g.

> Galli Clusium venerunt legionem Romanam **oppugnaturi**.
> *The Gauls came to Clusium **intending to attack** the Roman legion.*

7 When **se** or **suus** appears in a Purpose clause, it usually refers to the subject of the main clause, e.g.

> hoc fecit ut **se suosque** servaret.
> *He did this to protect himself and his men.*

EXERCISE A

Translate:
1. senator ad urbem descendit ut librum emeret.
2. piratae in portum navigaverunt ut naves nostras incenderent.
3. incolae portas clauserunt ne hostes oppidum caperent.
4. poeta Athenas iter faciet ut templa pulchra spectet.
5. nuntius epistolam incendit ne tyrannus omnia cognosceret.
6. Caesar equites praemisit qui hostium castra circumvenirent.
7. mox servi ex agris ambulabunt ut sub arboribus quiescant vel dormiant.
8. complures mercatores advenerant qui bona civibus venderent.
9. miles in fossa iacebat ne ab hostibus caperetur.
10. cives prope rostra stabant quo facilius consulis orationem audirent.
11. avunculus meus navem conscendit multis civibus laturus auxilium.
12. fur in arbore alta latebat ne quis se conspiceret.

EXERCISE B

Translate:
1. pueri ad flumen descenderunt natandi ac piscandi causa.
2. Hannibal venenum sumpsit ne a Romanis caperetur.
3. Lacedaemonii legatos Athenas miserunt qui de pacis condicionibus agerent.
4. nonnulli ex militibus in agros vicinos frumentatum erant missi.
5. nos omnes diligenter laborabamus quo celerius opus conficeremus.
6. procul hostes ad pontem interrumpendum progredientes videbamus.
7. eadem legio in hoc vico hiemandi causa iterum considet.
8. nos e nave egressi sumus eo consilio ut ad urbem iter faceremus.
9. Athenas missi sunt qui leges illius urbis describerent.
10. legati Mileto Athenas venerunt auxilii petendi causa.
11. Romani nocte appropinquaverunt, ab tergo Gallicam invasuri aciem.
12. heri mane domo clam discessi ne parentes rogarent quo irem.
13. sacerdos templum vel ad precandum vel ad deam colendam nocte intravit.
14. imperator magnam praedam suis promittebat quo fortius in acie pugnarent.
15. cum hostes appropinquarent, rex custodes circum regiam collocavit ne quid detrimenti sibi accideret.

EXERCISE C

Translate:
Caesar, postquam ex Menapiis in Treveros venit, duabus de causis Rhenum transire constituit; quarum una erat, quod auxilia contra se Treveris miserant; altera, ne ad eos Ambiorix receptum haberet. his constitutis rebus, paulum supra eum locum quo ante exercitum traduxerat facere pontem instituit. nota atque instituta ratione, magno militum studio paucis diebus opus efficitur. firmo in Treveris ad pontem praesidio relicto ne quis ab his subito motus oreretur, reliquas copias equitatumque traduxit. Ubii, qui ante obsides dederant atque in deditionem venerant, purgandi sui causa ad eum legatos mittunt qui doceant neque auxilia ex sua civitate in Treveros missa neque ab se fidem laesam. petunt atque orant ut sibi parcat ne, communi odio Germanorum, innocentes pro nocentibus poenas pendant.

Caesar, Bellum Gallicum VI.9

Result

The words

tam, *so*   **tantus,** *so great, so much*
tot, *so many*   **tantum,** *so much*
totiens, *so often*   **adeo,** *to such an extent, so*
talis, *such, of such a kind*   **ita,** *in such a way, so*

are often followed by an **ut** clause expressing Result. The verb in the Result Clause is in the subjunctive, e.g.

iter **tam** periculosum est **ut** proficisci **timeamus**.
The route is so dangerous that we are afraid to set out.

tanti erant fluctus **ut** naves portum capere non **possent**.
The waves were so big that the ships could not reach the harbour.

servus dominum **adeo** timebat **ut aufugerit**.
The slave feared his master so much that he ran away.

adeo mihi **non** subvenerunt **ut** inimicis me **tradiderint**.
Instead of helping me they handed me over to my enemies. (lit. "to such an extent did they not help me . . .")

The impersonal expression **tantum abest ut** (lit. "it was so far distant"), which introduces a pair of Result clauses, could also have been used to convey this meaning:

tantum afuit ut mihi subvenirent ut inimicis me tradiderint.
Instead of helping me, they handed me over to my enemies.

For Result clauses introduced by **qui**, see page 103, note 3.

EXERCISE A

Translate:
1 cena talis erat ut eam edere non possemus.
2 tam superbus est dominus ut omnes servi eum timeant.
3 ita se gerebat princeps ut omnes cives eum contemnerent.
4 tam calidus erat dies ut cuncti ad litus quam celerrime iter facerent.
5 tanta erat ferocitas militum Romanorum ut barbari brevi se receperint.
6 ad Circum eo die tot homines convenerunt ut permulti spectaculum videre non possent.
7 adeo aegrotabat ut medicum arcessiverit.
8 tam feroces erant leones ut ne custodes quidem eis appropinquarent.
9 tanta erat vis pulveris ut nemo eum aufugientem conspiceret.
10 eum falsa dicentem totiens audivi ut ei numquam crediturus sim.

EXERCISE B

Translate:
1 liberi adeo pericula viae non timebant ut omnibus nobis essent magnae admirationi.
2 tam tristi vultu mecum est locutus ut eum aegrotare crederem.
3 talis, ut vides, est ille homo ut nemo nisi stultissimus ei confidat.
4 tot et tantis me beneficiis oneravisti ut gratias tibi maximas debeam.
5 cives tanta voce clamant ut nemo exaudiri possit.
6 totiens me reprehendit magister ut nunc in ludo neque dormiam neque tempus teram.
7 ille dominus tantum pecuniae a servis postulare solet ut nemo ex eis libertatem petiverit.
8 mortuo rege, tanto erant dolore affecti cives ut ubique esset ululatus, fletus, luctus.
9 adeo te cives non amant ut odio eis sis.
10 tamdiu hic in vinculis captivus retineor ut mortem iam libenter obeam.

Fearing

1 Verbs of Fearing are found introducing clauses which begin with **ne** (translated *that*) and whose verbs are in the subjunctive, e.g.

puer timet **ne** in aquam **cadat**.
*The boy fears **that** he **will fall** into the water.*

Caesar metuebat **ne** Galli castra Romana **oppugnarent**.
*Caesar feared **that** the Gauls **would attack** the Roman camp.*

timebant **ne** unus ex custodibus urbem hostibus **prodidisset**.
*They feared **that** one of the guards **had betrayed** the city to the enemy.*

nos timemus omnes **ne** nuntius ad tempus **non adveniat**.
*We are all afraid **that** the messenger **will not arrive** in time.*

2 Note that, after a verb of Fearing, the tenses of the subjunctive are usually translated as follows:

present subjunctive: *will*   perfect subjunctive: *have*
imperfect subjunctive: *would* pluperfect subjunctive: *had*

3 When **ut** is found introducing a Fearing clause, translate it by *that . . . not*, e.g.

verebantur Romani **ut** socii sibi **subvenirent**.
*The Romans feared **that** their allies **would not help** them.*

4 The perfect participle **veritus** (from the verb **vereor** (2), **veritus sum**, *to fear*) would be expected to have a past-tense meaning, but it is usually translated as *fearing*.

5 When **se** or **suus** appears in a Fearing clause, it usually refers to the subject of the main verb, e.g.

verebantur ne piratae **se** caperent.
*They feared that the pirates would capture **them**.*

6 Verbs of Fearing are also found with the present infinitive in both Latin and English, e.g.

pueri speluncam intrare timebant.
The boys were afraid { to enter / of entering } the cave.

EXERCISE A

Translate:
1. senex timet ne servi vinum bibant.
2. senex timet ne servi vinum biberint.
3. senex timebat ne servi vinum biberent.
4. senex timebat ne servi vinum bibissent.
5. metuo ne tu hoc opus hodie non conficias.
6. verebar ne pater me Romam secum non duceret.
7. vereor ut testis vera dixerit.
8. viator metuebat ne pecuniam suam in via amisisset.
9. vereor ne Poeni nostros proelio navali vicerint.
10. captivus timebat ne effugere non posset.

EXERCISE B

Translate:
1. num times ne caupo te media nocte necet?
2. timemus ne barbari, impetu facto, castra nostra capiant.
3. mater adulescentis, verita ne filius numquam domum rediret, eum foras exire vetuit.
4. nos omnes verebamur ne hostes pontem captum delevissent.
5. coniurati timuerunt ne comprehensi in vincula conicerentur.
6. verebamur ne consules, mutato consilio, ab Hannibale vincerentur.
7. Ariovistus dixit se vereri ne per insidias ab eo circumveniretur.
8. verebantur Britanni ne, omni pacata Gallia, exercitus noster in se traduceretur.
9. periculum est ne nostri ab hostibus vincantur.
10. vereor ut servi satis diligenter laboraverint.

Time Clauses

The following are the conjunctions which most commonly introduce Time clauses:

*cum, *when, whenever*
ubi, *when, whenever*
ut, *when*
ubi primum, *as soon as*
cum primum, *as soon as*
ut primum, *as soon as*
simulac, *as soon as*
simulatque, *as soon as*

antequam, *before, until*
priusquam, *before, until*
postquam, *after*
*dum, *while, as long as, until*
quamdiu, *as long as*
donec, *until*
quoad, *as long as, until*
quotiens, *as often as, whenever*

*See also notes on **cum** (pages 88–9) and **dum** (page 91).

1 When the verb in the Time clause is in the *indicative*, *time only* is being expressed, e.g.

ubi domum **rediero**, statim cubitum ibo.
When I return home, I shall go to bed immediately.

consul, **ut** Curiam **intravit**, a patribus salutatus est.
When the consul entered the Senate-house, he was greeted by the senators.

pueri, **dum natabant**, delphinum spectabant.
While the boys were swimming, they were watching the dolphin.

simulatque nos **viderunt**, fugerunt.
As soon as they saw us, they fled.

2 When the verb in the Time clause is in the *subjunctive*, usually *something more than time* (e.g. purpose or intention) is implied. This happens expecially with

antequam, *before, until*   dum, *until*
priusquam, *before, until*   quoad, *until*

e.g.

custodes portas clauserunt **antequam** hostes urbem **ingrederentur**.
*The guards closed the gates **before** the enemy **could enter** the city.*

paucos moratus est dies **dum** se copiae ab Corcyra **adsequerentur**.
*He delayed a few days **for** the forces from Corcyra **to catch** (him) **up**.*

lupus exspectabat **dum dormitarent** canes.
*The wolf was waiting **for** the dogs **to doze off**.*

3 Differences of tense between Latin and English:

(a) **dum dormio,** fur vestimenta arripuit.
*While I **was sleeping,** the thief stole my clothes.*

(b) **cum** ludos **videbo,** laetus ero.
*When I **see** the games, I shall be happy.*

cum eum **videro,** eum salutabo.
*When I **see** him, I shall greet him.*

In both of these examples, Latin shows that the "seeing" has not happened yet by using the future or future perfect tense.

(c) The conjunctions **cum, quotiens** and **ubi** mean *whenever* when they are found with the following combination of indicative tenses:

perfect in Time clause   + present in main clause
pluperfect in Time clause + imperfect in main clause
e.g.
servi, **cum** dominum **conspexerunt,** strenue laborant.
***Whenever** the slaves **see** their master, they work hard.*

quotiens eum cantantem **audiveram,** ridebam.
***Whenever I heard** him singing, I used to laugh.*

(d) The present tense is used with **iam, iam diu, iam pridem** and **iam dudum** to indicate past actions that have continued into the present time, e.g.

iam pridem effugere **conamur.**
*We **have been trying** to escape for a long time (and we are still trying).*

Compare:
iam diu effugere **conabamur.**
*We **had been trying** to escape for a long time (and we were still trying).*

4 antequam and **priusquam** are sometimes split up, especially when the main verb is negative, e.g.

non **prius** abibo **quam** tu vera dixeris.
*I shall not go away **until** you tell the truth.*

5 postquam may also be split up, especially when a definite interval of time is mentioned, e.g.

poeta tribus **post** diebus **quam** ex Graecia redierat mortuus est.
*Three days **after** he (had) returned from Greece, the poet died.*

Exercise A

Translate:
1. custodes, ubi hostes conspexerunt, portas clauserunt.
2. custodes, ubi hostes impetum fecerant, portas claudebant.
3. custodes, cum hostes conspexissent, portas clauserunt.
4. custodes, cum portas clauderent, hostes conspexerunt.
5. custodes, cum primum hostes conspexerunt, portas clauserunt.
6. custodes, ut hostes conspexerunt, portas clauserunt.
7. custodes, postquam hostes conspexerunt, portas clauserunt.
8. custodes tribus post horis quam portas clauserant hostes conspexerunt.
9. custodes vix portas clauserant cum hostes conspexerunt.
10. custodes, simulac hostes conspexerunt, portas clauserunt.
11. custodes portas non prius claudent quam hostes conspexerint.
12. hostes impetum fecerunt antequam portae a custodibus clausae sunt.
13. hostes impetum fecerunt antequam portae a custodibus clauderentur.
14. custodes exspectabant donec hostes impetum fecerunt.
15. custodes exspectabant donec hostes impetum facerent.
16. dum custodes portas claudunt, hostes impetum fecerunt.
17. dum custodes portas claudebant, hostes impetum faciebant.
18. hostes impetum fecerunt priusquam custodes portas clauserunt.
19. hostes impetum fecerunt priusquam custodes portas clauderent.
20. quamdiu portae custodiebantur, hostes impetum facere nolebant.

Exercise B

Translate:
1. mercatores navem conscendebant cum tempestas magna coorta est.
2. nostri proelium non prius committent quam dux signum dederit.
3. piratae, cum captivum laete cantantem audiverant, valde ridebant.
4. non prius lupum videram.
5. non prius lupum videram quam illa bestia me ferociter petiit.
6. cum Athenis studerem, multas epistolas a patre accepi.
7. adstantes undique concurrerunt antequam fur per viam aufugeret.
8. paucis post diebus quam coniurati novum consilium ceperant, consul omnia cognovit.
9. non prius ex urbe abibo quam nuntium tuum accepero.
10. non prius ex urbe abii quam nuntium tuum accepi.

Conditional Sentences

1 *With the Indicative:*

si tu vales, ego gaudeo.
If you are well, I am pleased.

si id fecit, erravit.
If he did that, he made a mistake.

si falsa dicis, punieris.
If you are lying, you will be punished.

si id feceris, poenas dabis.
If you do that, you will be punished.

nisi celerius curremus, furem non capiemus.
If we do not run faster, we shall not catch the thief.

When the verb in the **si/nisi** clause is in the future or future perfect indicative (i.e. if it refers to the future), English uses the present tense to translate the verb in the **si/nisi** clause.

When the verb in the **si/nisi** clause is in any other tense of the indicative, it may be translated into the same tense in English.

2 *With the Subjunctive:*

si id dicas, erres.
If you were to say that, you would be wrong.

nisi canis latravisset, furem non cepissemus.
If the dog had not barked, we would not have caught the thief.

si rex essem, omnes me timerent.
If I were king, all men would fear me.

Note the pattern when the verbs are in the subjunctive:

Present subjunctive in both clauses: "**were to** . . . , **would**"
Imperfect subjunctive in both clauses: "**were** (now) . . . , **would** (now)"
Pluperfect subjunctive in both clauses: "**had** . . . , **would have**".

Different tenses may be used in the two clauses:

si talia verba tibi dixissem, amici non essemus.
If I had said that sort of thing to you, we should not (now) be friends.

3 *Mixed Indicative and Subjunctive:*

Occasionally, the verb of the **si/nisi** clause is in the subjunctive, and the main verb in the indicative.

> (*a*) This occurs mainly with verbs of "ability" (**possum**) or "obligation" (**debeo, oportet,** gerundive):
>
> nisi anseres clangorem fecissent, arx **capi potuit**.
> *If the geese had not cackled, the citadel **could have been taken**.*
>
> In this kind of sentence there is an ellipsis in the statement: "The citadel was capable of being captured (and it would have been captured), if the geese had not cackled."
>
> Compare:
> nos servare **potest**, si vellet.
> *He could save us if he wanted to.*
>
> si me revera amares, mihi parcere te **oportuit**.
> *If you really loved me, you ought to have spared me.*
>
> nisi ex Italia effugisset, **puniendus fuit**.
> *If he had not escaped from Italy, he would have had to be punished.*
>
> (*b*) **si** + present or imperfect subjunctive (often in the form **si forte**) can often mean *in case, in the hope that* or *to see if*, especially following a verb of "trying" or "waiting", e.g.
>
> omnia faciam si forte viam salutis invenire possim.
> *I'll make every effort to see if I can find a path to safety.*
>
> clamabant si quis se audiret.
> *They kept shouting in the hope that someone would hear them.*

4 *Alternative Conditions:*

These are introduced by

sive ... sive ... or
seu ... seu ...

> seu sol lucet seu pluit, semper in agris laborant servi.
> *Whether the sun is shining or it is raining, the slaves always toil in the fields.*
>
> sive vera dixisset sive falsa, nemo ei credidisset.
> *Whether he had told the truth or lied, no one would have believed him.*

EXERCISE A

Translate:
1. si illum adiuvisti, certe patriam prodidisti.
2. si in forum descenderis, fortasse senatores in Curiam intrantes videbis.
3. nisi his viatoribus cibum dederitis, fame peribunt.
4. si forte lupum videam, quam celerrime aufugiam.
5. si media aestate navigaret, nec venti nec fluctus eum impedirent.
6. nisi matri paruisses, a patre culpatus esses.
7. si mihi in hoc discrimine subveniant, gratias maximas eis agam.
8. rex, nisi miles eum fefellisset, magnum praemium ei dedisset.
9. si fidem servavisti, cur civibus rem explicare times?
10. si cras ad Circum ire vultis, iam cubitum ire necesse est.
11. nisi mecum in forum descendisset, illud spectaculum non vidisset.
12. si revera patriam amares, hostes non adiuvares.

EXERCISE B

Translate:
1. si apud me usque ad mediam noctem manere habes in animo, servum plus cibi parare iubebo.
2. nisi praedonibus magnam pecuniam promisissent, in mare sine dubio coniecti essent.
3. si eam dolore oppressam videam, opem libenter ei feram.
4. ad Curiam statim festinavi si forte consulem viderem.
5. si quid novi audivisset, nobis rem totam narravisset.
6. sive pro lege in senatu orationem habebis sive tacebis, omnibus Pompeio favere videberis.
7. ille servus, si domino falsa dixit, supplicio dignus est.
8. nisi ad alteram fluminis ripam tranasses, in numero captivorum nunc esses.
9. sive hostes impetum in urbem statim fecerint sive eam obsidere constituerint, vos oportebit eam defendere.
10. etiamsi hostes impetum fecissent, te oportuit in statione manere.
11. coniuratus, si de periculo ab amicis moneatur, ex urbe clam nocte egrediatur.
12. nisi consulatum tanto studio petiisset, vitam beatam ruri agere potuit.

Impersonal Verbs

1 (a) The passive is used impersonally in the 3rd person singular when the writer wishes to emphasise *the action rather than the person or persons involved*, e.g.

acriter pugnatur	*There is a fierce battle.* / *The battle is raging fiercely*
tandem ad urbem **perventum est.**	*At last the city was reached.* / *At last they reached the city.*
hostibus ferociter **resistebatur.**	*Fierce resistance was offered to the enemy.* / *The enemy were fiercely resisted.*
ad urbem **concursum est.**	*There was a rush to the city.*
nobis **laborandum est.**	*We must work.* (See page 62.)

(b) Verbs which govern the dative case are used impersonally in the passive, e.g.

militibus imperatum est.	*The soldiers were ordered.*
hostibus a custodibus **resistebatur.**	*The enemy were resisted by the guards.*
tibi numquam **credetur.**	*You will never be believed.*
legibus a nobis **parendum est.**	*The laws must be obeyed by us.*

In these examples, the noun or pronoun in the dative usually becomes the subject in English.

(c) In Indirect Statement, the impersonal passive is in the infinitive, e.g.

dicunt acriter **pugnari.**	*They say that a fierce battle is raging.*
scimus nobis laborandum **esse.**	*We know that we must work.*

2 The following verbs/expressions are commonly used impersonally:

(a) **accidit,** *it happens* **restat,** *it remains*
 fit, *it happens* **ex quo factum est,** *the result was*
 evenit, *it turns out* **fieri potest,** *it is possible*
 sequitur, *it follows* **fieri non potest,** *it is impossible*

accidit ut Cicero adesset. 　　*It happened that Cicero was there.*
　　　　　　　　　　　　　　Cicero happened to be there.

fieri potest ut pervenerint. 　　*It is possible that they have arrived.*

restat ut respondeamus. 　　*It remains for us to reply.*

(b) The impersonal verbs **interest** and **refert** (both meaning "it is of importance") are used with the genitive of nouns and 3rd person pronouns, or with the ablative singular feminine of the possessive adjectives **mea, tua, nostra, vestra** (originally agreeing with the **re** of **refert**), e.g.

Caesaris interest ad castra celeriter pervenire.
It is important to Caesar to reach the camp quickly.

nostra refert ad castra celeriter pervenire.
It is important to us to reach the camp quickly.

(c) **licet,** *it is allowed* 　　**oportet,** *it behoves (... ought)*
　　placet, *it pleases* 　　**constat,** *it is well known*
　　decet, *it is fitting*

tibi licet exire. 　　　　　　　*You are allowed to go out.*
mihi placet manere. 　　　　*I decide to remain.*
puellas oportet festinare. 　　*The girls ought to hurry.*
puellas oportebat festinare. 　*The girls ought to have hurried.*
eum decet captivos liberare. *It is right for him to free the captives.*

constat Romanos Carthaginem delevisse.
It is well known that the Romans destroyed Carthage.

In these examples, the noun or pronoun in the accusative or dative case usually becomes the subject in English.

(d) **me miseret,** *I pity* 　　　　　　**me pudet,** *I am ashamed of*
　　me paenitet, *I am sorry, regret* 　**me taedet,** *I am tired of*
　　me piget, *I loathe*

te miseret liberorum. 　　　　　*You pity (are sorry for) the children.*
eum paenitet sceleris. 　　　　　*He regrets his wickedness.*
puerum pudet ignaviae. 　　　　*The boy is ashamed of his laziness.*
milites taedet bellum gerere. 　*The soldiers are tired of waging war.*

In these examples, the noun or pronoun in the accusative case becomes the subject in English, and the infinitive or the noun in the genitive indicates what caused the particular feeling.

(e) Note that there is a group of impersonal verbs which deal with the weather and time, e.g.

pluit, *it is raining* 　　　　**lucet,** *it is becoming light*
ningit, *it is snowing* 　　**advesperascit,** *it is growing dark*
tonat, *there is thunder*

EXERCISE A

Translate:
1. hodie pluit; heri pluebat; cras fortasse pluet.
2. vos domum redire oportet, nam advesperascit.
3. utrimque diu et acriter pugnatum est.
4. liberos parentibus semper parere decet.
5. inter omnes constat Ciceronem rem publicam servavisse.
6. interdiu plaustra in urbis viis agere non licebat.
7. accidit ut omnes fere naves in portu delerentur.
8. nuntiatum est exercitum Romanum magna pugna esse victum.
9. cum gladiatores in arenam venissent, ab omnibus spectatoribus clamatum est.
10. fieri potest ut nuntius vera dixerit.
11. ad urbem prima luce perventum est.
12. me epistolas scribere non taedet; nonne te nihil facere pudet?
13. ab omnibus civibus ad Curiam undique concursum est.
14. inter omnes constabat Catilinam contra rem publicam coniuravisse.

EXERCISE B

Translate:
1. divitibus saepe invidetur; proditori numquam credetur; parentibus a liberis olim parebatur.
2. custodibus imperatum erat ne sine captivo regrederentur.
3. domi manere te oportet quod tibi in urbem soli descendere non licet.
4. cives putant consulem ipsum orationem in senatu habere oportuisse.
5. quamquam iam advesperascebat, mihi placuit Ostia proficisci.
6. constat Hannibalem venenum sumpsisse ne a Romanis caperetur.
7. nuntius dixit ad urbem diripiendam signo dato concursum esse.
8. legatis hostium a senatu comiter responsum est.
9. hos praedones ad mortem heri duci oportuit.
10. omnium civium interest leges servare.
11. regibus expulsis, Romanis placuit ut imperium duobus consulibus traderetur.
12. huic mendico persuaderi non potest ne pecuniam ab adstantibus peteret.
13. creditur tyrannum scelerum paenitere; numquam tamen ei ignoscetur.
14. nonne legibus ab omnibus bonis semper parendum est?

Gerunds and Gerundives

The Gerund and Gerundive can be recognised by the letters **-and-**, **-end-** or **-und-** in the stem.

I The GERUND is a noun which has the same endings as a neuter singular noun of Group 2. The gerund is found:

1 in the ACCUSATIVE CASE AFTER **ad**, expressing Purpose, e.g.

> pueri ad litus **ad natandum** descenderunt.
> *The boys went down to the beach **to swim**.*

> libri **ad studendum** necessarii sunt.
> *Books are necessary **for studying**.*

2 in the GENITIVE CASE,

> (*a*) with **causa**, expressing Purpose, e.g.
>
> > pueri ad litus **natandi causa** descenderunt.
> > *The boys went down to the beach **to swim**.*

> (*b*) depending on another noun or on an adjective which governs the genitive, e.g.
>
> > puer artem **natandi** a fratre didicit.
> > *The boy learned the art **of swimming** from his brother.*
> >
> > mater pueri omnia **cognoscendi** avida erat.
> > *The boy's mother was eager **to learn** everything.*
> >
> > tempus **redeundi** est.
> > *It is time **to return** (**for returning**).*

3 in the ABLATIVE CASE, e.g.

> omnes **vivendo** discimus.   *We all learn **by living**.*

Note that a gerund is translated into English by the infinitive or by a verbal noun ending in "-ing".

II The GERUNDIVE is an adjective which has the same endings as Group 1/2 adjectives. It has two main uses:

A. Latin authors tend to avoid using a gerund governing an object in the accusative case; instead, they usually prefer to use a gerundive phrase:

1 *(a)* in the ACCUSATIVE CASE AFTER **ad**, expressing Purpose, e.g.

> **ad urbem capiendam** milites misit.
> *He sent soldiers **to capture the city**.*
>
> **ad equos emendos** huc venerunt.
> *They have come here **to buy horses**.*

(b) in the ACCUSATIVE CASE governed by certain verbs (e.g. **curare, suscipere** and **tradere**), e.g.

> nautae **navem reficiendam** curaverunt.
> *The sailors attended to **the repair(ing) of the ship**.*

2 in the GENITIVE CASE,

(a) with **causa**, expressing Purpose, e.g.

> **libri legendi causa**   *to read a book*
> **civium servandorum causa** *to save the citizens*

(b) depending on another noun or on an adjective which governs the genitive, e.g.

> ars **epistolae scribendae**   *the art **of writing a letter***
> peritus **belli gerendi**   *skilled **in waging war***
>
> iam tempus est **discipulorum dimittendorum**.
> *Now it is time **to dismiss the pupils**.*

3 in the ABLATIVE CASE, e.g.

> **de epistolis scribendis**   *about writing letters*

When translating these gerundive phrases, the simplest technique is to translate the gerundive as if it were a gerund, and to treat the noun as its direct object.

B. The gerundive is also found with the verb **esse** expressing the idea of "obligation" or "necessity". When used in this way, the gerundive is translated *must be, should be, ought to be, had to be* or *will have to be*, depending on the tense of **esse**, e.g.

> urbs **defendenda** est.
> *The city must be (ought to be, should be) defended.*
>
> moenia erant **custodienda**.
> *The walls had to be guarded.*

vinum tibi non **bibendum** est.
The wine must not be drunk by you.
You must not drink the wine.

Note how the last example can be translated in two ways. In the second version, the dative **tibi** has become the subject of an active verb in English. This will be the normal method of translation when the neuter of the gerundive is used impersonally, e.g.

surgendum **mihi** est.   *I ought to get up.*
mox **nobis** proficiscendum erit.   *We will have to set out soon.*
militibus fortius est pugnandum. *The soldiers must fight more bravely.*

Note also that the person "by whom" something is done is expressed by the dative case with the gerundive. When the verb itself governs the dative, however, the normal **a** + ablative is used, e.g.

magistro **a discipulis** parendum est.
{ *The teacher must be obeyed by the pupils.* }
{ *The pupils must obey the teacher.* }

EXERCISE A

Translate:
1 nostri fortiter pugnando hostes facile vicerunt.
2 studiosissimus erat puer natandi.
3 multi adulescentes studendi causa Athenas ire solebant.
4 filius Catonis artem legendi a patre didicit.
5 milites ex castris ad agros vastandos exierunt.
6 incolae muros ascenderunt ad urbem defendendam.
7 legati pacis petendae causa ad castra hostium a consule missi sunt.
8 Caesar idoneam ad navigandum tempestatem nactus tertia fere vigilia solvit.
9 Caesar legatis respondit diem se ad deliberandum sumpturum esse.
10 urbs nobis capienda et delenda est.
11 fures in vincula coniciendi erant.
12 medicus tibi statim arcessendus erit.

EXERCISE B

Translate:
1. cupidus erat domum quam celerrime redeundi.
2. oratoris audiendi studiosus erat iuvenis.
3. nuntius ad hostium ducem de captivis redimendis mittendus est.
4. ei qui ad rem publicam delendam coniuraverunt capitis sunt condemnandi.
5. nobis nunc est domum proficiscendum.
6. milites clamabant praedam inter se aeque dividendam esse.
7. pontem in flumine faciendum curavit.
8. Caesar Volusenum ad haec cognoscenda esse idoneum arbitratus est.
9. consul urbem diripiendam atque incendendam suis tradidit.
10. hostibus conspectis, explorator sensit sibi ad castra quam primum esse redeundum.
11. simul militibus et de navibus desiliendum et in fluctibus consistendum et cum hostibus erat pugnandum.
12. inter omnes constat legibus ab omnibus bonis civibus parendum esse.

Correlatives

1 Correlatives are pairs of corresponding words (e.g. **tot** ... **quot** ...; **tantus** ... **quantus** ...) which are used to express a comparison or similarity, e.g.

tantam pecuniam habeo **quantam** tu.
*I have **as much** money **as** you.*

talis erat nubes **qualem** numquam antea videramus.
*The cloud was **such as** we had never seen before.*

eandem fabulam mihi narravisti **ac** puer.
*You have told me **the same** story **as** the boy.*

pirata mortem **ita** obiit **ut** vitam egerat.
*The pirate met death **in the same way as** he had lived his life.*

eo profectus est **quo** ceteri viatores.
{ *He set out for the place to which the other travellers (had gone).* |
{ *He set out for **the same place as** the other travellers.* |

tot captivi sunt in castris **quot** milites.
*There are **as many** prisoners in the camp **as** soldiers.*

2 The correlative clause is sometimes put before the main clause, without altering the meaning, e.g.

quot sunt milites in castris, **tot** sunt captivi.
There are as many prisoners in the camp as soldiers.

3 The correlatives

quo ... eo ... } *the more ... the more ...*
quanto ... tanto ...

express proportion when followed by comparative adjectives or adverbs, e.g.

quo saepius urbem visito, **eo magis** ruri habitare malo.
The more often I visit the city, the more I prefer to live in the country.

4 The following is a list of common correlatives. Note that the second of the corresponding words is often translated by *as*:

tam ... quam ... , *so (as) ... as ...*
talis ... qualis ... , *such ... as ...*
tantus ... quantus ... , *as much (great) ... as ...*
tot ... quot ... , *as many ... as ...*
totiens ... quotiens ... , *as often ... as ...*
idem ... ac ... } *the same ... as ...*
idem ... qui ...
ibi ... ubi ... , *there ... where ...*
eo ... quo ... } *to the place ... (to) where ...*
illuc ... quo ...
inde ... unde ... , *from the place ... from where ...*
hinc ... unde ... , *from this place ... from where ...*
ita ... ut ... } *just ... as ... , in the same way ... as ...*
sic ... ut ...
tum ... cum ... , *at the time ... when ...*
non aliter ... ac ... , *not otherwise than, exactly as*

EXERCISE A

Translate:
1. miles tam fortis est quam leo.
2. tamdiu gaudent agricolae quamdiu lucet sol.
3. pater meus tot annos natus est quot avus tuus.
4. eisdem litteris non utebantur Romani quibus Graeci.
5. Romani Hannibalem non totiens proelio vicerunt quotiens Romanos Hannibal.
6. quamdiu hostes ibi morabantur, tamdiu nostri castris se continebant.
7. Quintus Horatius Flaccus duodecim fere annos ibi mansit ubi natus erat.
8. quo diligentius laborabis, mi amice, eo magis laudaberis.
9. quot arbores succisae sunt, tot serentur.
10. ille puer talis esse videtur quales sunt comites.
11. quo diutius quis vivit, eo prudentior fit.
12. inter omnes constat ducem nostrum tam prudentem esse quam fortem.

EXERCISE B

Translate:
1. quotiens aves cantantes audio, totiens me vivere gaudeo.
2. ille senator talis non est qualem eum esse putas.
3. nulli homines tam crudeles sunt quam eius gentis.
4. quot homines se venturos esse promiserant, tot aderant.
5. non erat Romanis tanta classis quanta Carthaginiensibus.
6. Clodius eo iam profectus erat quo Milo appropinquabat.
7. magister ludi negavit quemquam tam molestum esse quam me.
8. eo omnes mortales iter aliquando faciunt, unde quemquam redire negant.
9. quotiens vos nobis auxilio fuistis, totiens nos vobis.
10. cives tanta maestitia affecti sunt quanta numquam prius.
11. quanto maior urbs Roma est hoc oppido, tanto maior est fundus meus quam tuus.
12. ut seritur, ita metitur.

Days, Months and Years

I The Calendar

1 The Romans had calendars which were usually engraved in stone. Among other things, they listed the festivals which recurred annually – the days on which business might be transacted (**dies fasti**) and the days on which business might not be transacted (**dies nefasti**).

They had a week consisting of eight days, indicated on calendars by the letters A to H, but there were no special names for the days of the week corresponding to our Sunday, Monday, etc. For seven of the days in the week, the Roman farmer worked on his farm; on the eighth, he went to the market in the nearby town. Since these market-days occurred at intervals of eight days (i.e. every ninth day according to the inclusive reckoning of the Romans), they were called **nundinae**.

The day itself (from sunrise to sunset) was divided into twelve hours (**horae**); and the night (sunset to sunrise) was made up of four watches (**vigiliae**). The length of hours and watches naturally varied according to the season of the year.

2 In each month, there were three special days from which the Romans calculated all dates:

Kalendae, -arum (*f.pl*), *the Kalends*, which were always the 1st day of the month.
Nonae, -arum (*f.pl*), *the Nones*, which usually fell on the 5th of the month.
Idus, Iduum (*f.pl*), *the Ides*, which usually fell on the 13th day of the month.

But "In March, July, October, May,
       Nones are the 7th, Ides the 15th day."

The *names of the months are adjectives* which agree either with the word **mensis** ("month") or with one of the above fixed dates:

Ianuarius	Iulius
Februarius	Augustus
Martius	September
Aprilis	October
Maius	November
Iunius	December

Until they were renamed in honour of Julius Caesar and Augustus respectively, July was called **mensis Quin(c)tilis** and August was called **mensis Sextilis**.

II Dates

Actual dates were expressed in various ways:

1 (*a*) The *ablative case* indicates that the date coincides with one of the special days, e.g.

Kalendis Aprilibus   *1st April*
Nonis Februariis   *5th February*
Idibus Martiis   *15th March*

Compare **eo die**, *on that day.*

(*b*) **pridie** + *accusative* indicates the day before one of the special days, e.g.

pridie Kalendas Maias, *30th April* (lit. "on the day before 1st May")
pridie Idus Octobres, *14th October*

(*c*) **postridie** + *accusative* is used by some authors to indicate the day immediately after one of the special days, e.g.

postridie Nonas Iulias, *8th July*

(*d*) a phrase beginning **ante diem** (abbreviated to **a.d.**) is used to express all other dates, e.g.

a.d.iv (ante diem quartum) **Kalendas Decembres**, *28th November* (lit. "on the fourth day before the Kalends of December")

Originally, this would have been **die quarto ante Kalendas Decembres**, where **die quarto** is in the ablative case expressing "time when". Gradually, **ante** came to be placed at the beginning of the phrase, causing the ablative to be changed to accusative.

2 When calculating, you should use "inclusive reckoning", i.e. count backwards, including the special day in the reckoning (cf. French *quinze jours*, a fortnight), e.g.

a.d.viii Idus Martias means **7 days before** the Ides of March (8th March)
a.d.iv Nonas Apriles means **3 days before** the Nones of April (2nd April)

When calculating from Kalends, subtract 2 from the figure shown and count back from the last day in the month. (This is to take account of inclusive reckoning and the first day of the next month.) For example, if the date is **a.d.ix** Kalendas Decembres, subtract 7 from 30, giving 23rd November.

III Years

1 These were originally indicated by the names of the consuls for that year (in the ablative case – "time when"), e.g.

Sulla et Pompeio consulibus
In the consulship of Sulla and Pompeius
In the year when Sulla and Pompeius were consuls (88 BC)

2 Later writers often reckoned from the date traditionally given for the foundation of Rome (753 BC). The letters **A.U.C. (anno urbis conditae** or **ab urbe condita)** were followed by the number of years from that date, e.g.

A.U.C septingentesimo tricesimo sexto
in the 736th year from the founding of the city.

When converted into an English date, this will be **BC** since the number given is less than 753. To find the date BC, subtract *735* (not 736, because of inclusive reckoning) from 753, i.e. 18 BC.

The date will be **AD** if the number of the Roman year is greater than 753. In calculating the English date, do *not* use inclusive reckoning; there was no Year Zero since AD 1 followed immediately after 1 BC. For example, A.U.C. DCCCXLIII is the 843rd year after the founding of the city. Since 843 minus 753 is 90, the date is AD 90.

EXERCISE

Translate:
1. pater meus ex Bithynia a.d.iv Id.Iul. rediit.
2. Vergilius Idibus Octobribus natus est.
3. vento secundo usi, a.d.xiv Kal.Sept. ad Britanniam navigavimus.
4. Valerius Corneliam in matrimonium a.d.iv Non. Iun. duxit.
5. Caesar nactus idoneam ad navigandum tempestatem tertia fere vigilia navem solvit.
6. ipse hora circiter diei quarta cum primis navibus Britanniam attigit.
7. amicus meus Athenis Romam a.d.xiii Kal. Iun. profectus est.
8. Cicero mortem a.d.vii Id.Dec. obiit.
9. speravit se Athenas pridie Kalendas Apriles perventurum esse.
10. A.U.C. CCXLV, Tarquinio expulso, Brutus et Collatinus consules primi creati sunt.
11. Romani maximam cladem ab Hannibale A.U.C. DXXXVIII Cannis acceperunt.
12. Augustus princeps a.d.ix Kal.Oct. A.U.C. DCXCI natus est.
13. Nolae a.d.xiv Kal.Sept. A.U.C. DCCLXVII mortuus est.
14. C. Claudio Marcello L. Cornelio Lentulo consulibus, Caesar flumen Rubiconem transgressus exercitum Romam duxit.
15. L. Gellio Cn. Cornelio Lentulo cos., Spartacus tres imperatores Romanos acie superavit.

Roman Names

In the earliest days, most Romans had only two names, the **nomen** of the clan or **gens** to which they belonged, and their personal name (**praenomen**) by which they would be addressed by relatives and friends.

Later, as families divided, branches of the same **gens** were distinguished by a third name (**cognomen**), e.g.

Gaius: praenomen (personal name)
Iulius: nomen (name of the **gens**)
Caesar: cognomen (branch of the Julian **gens**)

The **cognomen** frequently started off as a nickname given to one member of the family, and it was handed down to his descendants as part of their name, even though the nickname did not apply to them personally, e.g.

P. Ovidius **Naso**	*"big nose"*
L. Domitius **Ahenobarbus**	*"bronze beard"*
M. Iunius **Brutus**	*"the stupid one"*
C. Licinius **Calvus**	*"bald"*

A few Romans, who had earned some special distinction, were granted a fourth name (**agnomen**) which was usually connected with the events that had made them famous. For example, P. Cornelius Scipio, who conquered the Carthaginians in North Africa, was called P. Cornelius Scipio Africanus.

It is interesting that, when General Montgomery was granted a peerage after his victory over Rommel at El Alamein in the Second World War, he took the title of "Lord Montgomery of Alamein." Likewise, T.E. Lawrence became known as Lawrence of Arabia because of his exploits in the Middle East in the First World War.

It is usual in Latin books to find the praenomen abbreviated. This is not the same as our practice of giving someone's initials since each Latin abbreviation stands for one particular name:

App.	= Appius	**L.**	= Lucius	**S(ex).**	= Sextus
A.	= Aulus	**M.**	= Marcus	**Ser.**	= Servius
C.	= Gaius	**M'.**	= Manius	**Sp.**	= Spurius
Cn.	= Gnaeus	**P.**	= Publius	**T.**	= Titus
D.	= Decimus	**Q.**	= Quintus	**Ti(b).**	= Tiberius

Girls were normally given the feminine form of the father's nomen, e.g.

The daughter of M. Túllius Cicero was called Tullia.
The daughter of C. Julius Caesar was called Julia.

What happened if there was more than one daughter? The comparative adjectives **Maior** (elder) and **Minor** (younger) after the main name could draw the distinction between two daughters, and **Tertia** could be used if there was a third daughter. Diminutives such as **Tulliola** might also be used.

Part II: Translation

Preamble

Part I deals with what could be described as the more traditional way of explaining Latin constructions. In translation, however, difficulty sometimes arises, not because the student is ignorant of these constructions, but because certain key words (**cum, dum, quam, quod**, etc.) may have multiple meanings or usages.

Part II analyses these various usages and concludes with a discussion of certain techniques designed to help students to narrow the range of options when dealing with these and other problems in reading Latin, and thus arrive at the correct sense of the Latin.

The general advice may be summarised as follows:

1 Try to grasp the meaning of the sentence as you read the Latin words *in the order in which they are written*, not in the order in which they would appear in an English sentence.

2 When you meet any of the key words, suspend judgment until later words provide clues to help you decide what the key word means.

3 When you have read the whole sentence, try to narrow the range of possibilities for the key words by testing each of the meanings/usages in turn until you identify the one that makes best sense.

4 Having ascertained the meaning of the Latin, decide on the best way to translate the sentence into idiomatic English.

Case Recognition

1 Coincident Endings

One of the positive advantages of a highly inflected language is the considerable help which the different endings give in identifying the case and function of nouns and adjectives. For such a system to be foolproof, however, each ending would have to be unique; in other words, each ending would not only be restricted to one noun-group, but would apply to one, and only one, number/case within that group. Examination of the Tables of Noun and Adjective Groups (pages 142–143) shows that this is not so in Latin. In the following list of the commonest "coincident endings", the words used in the examples are the pattern nouns used in the Tables:

Ending **-a**

	Group 1 Singular	**Group 2** Neuter Plural	**Group 3** Neuter Plural	**Group 4** Neuter Plural
Nom.	puell**a**	bacul**a**	nomin**a**	corn**ua**
Acc.	—	bacul**a**	nomin**a**	corn**ua**
Abl.	puell**a**	—	—	—

Ending **-ae**

| | **Group 1** ||
	Singular	Plural
Nom.	—	puell**ae**
Gen.	puell**ae**	—
Dat.	puell**ae**	—

Ending **-es**

| | **Group 3** || **Group 5** ||
	Singular	Plural	Singular	Plural
Nom.	mil**es**	milit**es** voc**es**	di**es**	di**es**
Acc.	—	milit**es** voc**es**	—	di**es**

N.B. There are a few nouns like **miles** which end in -es in the nominative singular as well as in the nominative and accusative plural, e.g.
pedes, -itis (*m*); **eques**, -itis (*m*); **hospes**, -itis (*m*); **comes**, -itis (*m*); **rupes**, -is (*f*); **nubes**, -is (*f*).

Ending **-is**

	Group 1 Plural	**Group 2** Plural	**Group 3** Singular	
Nom.	—	—	civ**is**	—
Gen.	—	—	civ**is**	voc**is**
Dat.	puell**is**	serv**is**	—	—
Abl.	puell**is**	serv**is**	—	—

N.B. In the accusative plural of Group 3 nouns, the ending **-is** is sometimes found instead of **-es**.

Ending **-us**

	Group 2 Singular	**Group 4** Singular	**Group 4** Plural
Nom.	serv**us**	man**us**	man**us**
Acc.	—	—	man**us**
Gen.	—	man**us**	—

N.B. Certain neuter nouns of Group 3 end in **-us** in the nominative and accusative singular, e.g. **tempus, onus, opus**.

Ending **-um**

	Group 2 Singular		**Group 3** Plural	**Group 4** Singular	**Group 4** Plural
Nom.	—	bacul**um**	—	—	—
Acc.	serv**um**	bacul**um**	—	man**um**	—
Gen.	—	—	voc**um**	—	manu**um**

Ending **-i**

	Group 2 Singular	**Group 2** Plural	**Group 3** Singular	**Group 4** Singular	**Group 5** Singular
Nom.	—	serv**i**	—	—	—
Gen.	serv**i**	—	—	—	die**i**
Dat.	—	—	voc**i**	manu**i**	die**i**

N.B. The coincident endings of adjectives correspond to the Group 1–3 noun endings listed above, except that, in most adjectives of Group 3, the dative and ablative singular both end in **-i**.

2 Recognising Groups

It is clear from the above list that case recognition is immensely simplified if the student possesses the basic information about the Group to which the noun in question belongs. Accordingly, all nouns are presented in the following way:

Nom. Sing.   Gen. Sing.   Gender
tempus   **tempor*is***   neuter

The *genitive singular ending* identifies the group number, as follows:

Group 1	Group 2	Group 3	Group 4	Group 5
puell**ae**	serv**i**	voc**is**	man**us**	di**ei**

When the genitive singular ending is removed, the remaining part of the noun is known as the *stem*, e.g.

tempus, tempor*is*   stem: **tempor-**

and it is to the stem that most endings are attached.

3 Case Clues

The clues which help the reader to identify the cases of nouns are:

(*a*) the Group Number information (i.e. Nom. Sing., Gen. Sing. and Gender);
(*b*) the position of the noun in the sentence;
(*c*) the context.

(*a*) Sometimes the *Group Number information* will by itself give the right answer, e.g.

pueri vocem matris audiunt.

Here, **vocem** can be only accusative, and **matris** is unmistakably genitive. However, **pueri** could be genitive singular or nominative plural. If it was genitive, **pueri** would probably be placed next to **matris**. Since it is not, **pueri** must be the subject of the plural verb **audiunt**.

(*b*) Sometimes the *order and position* of words will help, e.g.

vocem puellae **pueri** audiunt.

Both **puellae** and **pueri** could be either genitive singular or nominative plural. The position of the two words makes it clear that **vocem** and **puellae** are to be taken together.

73

(c) Sometimes, only the *context* will determine the meaning, e.g. the following sentence has two possible meanings:

vocem **puellae** mater audit.

The mother hears the girl's voice.
The girl's mother hears the voice.

Without the context, it is impossible to state which of these meanings is correct.

EXERCISE

Translate the following sentences which exemplify coincident endings:
1 bacula multa puella portat.
2 servus manus magnas habet.
3 omni puellae tempus est sonitus audire cantus.
4 me delectat sonitus dulcis vocis tuae.
5 equi voci domini parent.
6 sine metu impetus sustinere hostium pulchrum est.
7 virgini pulchrae pulchros flores miles dat.
8 gladius non baculum virorum fortium telum est.
9 instructa acies milites Punicos terruit.
10 miles omnes res audiverat.
11 est militis sapientis mandatis imperatoris parere.
12 nobis videtur esse imperatoris prudentis captivis parcere.

Agreement of Adjectives

The ending of an adjective is determined by the noun with which it agrees. For example, in the sentence

multos servos, multas ancillas, multa plaustra habet dominus,

since **servos** is a masculine noun in the accusative plural, **multos** has a masculine accusative plural ending.

Similarly, **multas** is feminine accusative plural agreeing with **ancillas**, and **multa** is neuter accusative plural agreeing with **plaustra**.

There are certain clues which enable the reader to decide with which noun an adjective agrees. These are:

1 clues of agreement (i.e. gender, number, case);
2 the position of the adjective in the sentence;
3 the context.

Study the following examples:

1 (*a*) *All three agreement clues* present:

    dominus **bonas** puellas laudat. *The master praises the good girls.*

    Since **dominus** and **puellas** differ in gender, number and case, **bonas** is clearly to be taken with **puellas**.

(*b*) *Only two agreement clues present:*

    domina **bonas** puellas laudat. *The mistress praises the good girls.*

    Although **domina** and **puellas** have the same gender, they differ in number and case.

(*c*) *Only one agreement clue present:*

    dominam **bonum** servum culpare veto.
    I tell the mistress not to blame the good slave.

    Here, the *gender* only is decisive.

    dominam **bonas** puellas culpare veto.
    I tell the mistress not to blame the good girls.

    Here, only the *number* is decisive.

2 When agreement clues are absent, the position of the word in the sentence will often help:

    vilicum vetamus **bonum** servum verberare.
    We tell the overseer not to beat the good slave.

3 Sometimes, only *sense* (based on the context) will decide the meaning.

    puellam **veterem** ancillam culpare veto.
    I tell the girl not to blame the old maid-servant.

The fact that adjectives indicate, by their endings, agreement with their nouns in gender, number and case, permits Latin writers to put adjectives before or after their nouns, and even to separate adjective and noun altogether. This flexibility enables writers to emphasise particular words, e.g. to heighten dramatic tension. A Latin sentence in which no special emphasis is intended usually follows the order: subject, object, verb, as in sentence (*a*) below. However, the emphasis is radically altered by changing the positions of the same four words in the other sentences:

    (*a*) Marcus puellam pulchram amat.   *Marcus loves the beautiful girl.*
    (*b*) **pulchram** puellam Marcus amat.   *It's the **beautiful** girl that Marcus loves.*
    (*c*) **amat** Marcus pulchram puellam.   *Marcus **loves** the beautiful girl.*

EXERCISE

Translate the following sentences. Where you think that the word order suggests a special emphasis, try to bring this out in the translation.

1 puella pulchra Marcum amat.
2 puerum pulchra puella amat.
3 pulchrum puerum puella amat.
4 amat puellam pulchram puer.
5 formam pulchram puellae laudat mater.
6 mater puellae pulchrae formam laudat, mentem culpat.
7 vilicus Britannicus miseros servos Graecos verberat.
8 Graecos culpat servos vilicus Britannicus.
9 felices servi domini boni numquam poenas dant.
10 domini boni servi vita bona est.

Dative or Ablative?

In the following Groups, the dative and ablative cases are not differentiated by their endings:

	Group 2 Singular	Groups 1 and 2 Plural	Group 4 Neut. Sing.	Groups 3, 4 and 5 Plural
Dat.	servo	puellis servis	cornu	civibus manibus diebus
Abl.	servo	puellis servis	cornu	civibus manibus diebus

How are you to tell which case is used in a particular sentence? Latin will usually provide clues to help you decide (e.g. Predicative Dative or Ablative with a comparative). The following procedure will fit most other situations:

1 Is the noun *preceded by a preposition*? If it is, the noun will be in the ablative case because no preposition governs the dative case.

2 If there is no preposition, does the noun refer to a *person* or a *thing*?

(a) If it refers to a *thing*, it is likely to be ablative case – either "instrumental" ablative or Ablative Absolute, e.g.

baculo lupum verberat.   *He strikes the wolf with a stick.*
baculo arrepto, lupum reppulit.   *Having grabbed a stick he drove off the wolf.*

(b) If it refers to a *person*, it is likely to be Dative or an Ablative Absolute. Suspend judgment until you see whether it is followed by

(i) a participle, e.g.

coquo vocato, convivae cenam laudaverunt.
When the cook was summoned, the guests praised the dinner.

(ii) a verb governing the dative case, e.g.

coquo dominus praemium **dedit**.
The master gave a reward to the cook.

(iii) an adjective governing the dative or ablative, e.g.

coquo utilis   *useful to the cook* (dative)
coquo fretus   *relying on the cook* (ablative)

EXERCISE A

Translate:
1 dominus illum servum magno pretio emit.
2 servi dominum virgis verberabant.
3 servus domino pecuniam reddidit.
4 servus domino conspecto statim aufugit.
5 servus domino conspecto statim auxilio venit.
6 visne equo an raeda ad urbem vehi?
7 gladiator spectatoribus magna voce clamavit.
8 latrones fustibus viatorem aggressi sunt.
9 omnibus bonis patriam defendere necesse est.
10 adstantes lapidibus cadentibus oppressi sunt.

EXERCISE B

Translate:
1 ducem victorem clamoribus cantuque per vias deduxerunt.
2 rates magnae ripae vinculis alligatae sunt.
3 imperator hostibus visis septimam legionem impetum facere iussit.
4 imperator militibus laborantibus cohortem decimam subsidio misit.
5 consul Romanus Britannis reginaeque eorum superatis haec imperavit.
6 captivi vinculis ac verberibus cruciati sunt.
7 consul pro certo habebat suos fortiores esse hostibus.
8 amico meo persuadebo ut verbis non armis se defendat.
9 Horatius gladio stricto hostibus obviam ivit.
10 vilicus clamoribus auditis servis imperavit ut pueris subsidio statim irent.

Word Building

Words may be built up or have their meanings changed by an addition at either end of the word.

Prefixes

An addition at the beginning of a word is called a *prefix*, e.g. **ire**, *to go;* **abire**, *to go away.*

(*a*) Prefixes added to Adjectives/Adverbs:

The most common of these are:

in-, *not*	e.g. **dignus**, *worthy*	**indignus**, *unworthy*
per-, *very*	e.g. **multi**, *many*	**permulti**, *very many*
prae-, *very*	e.g. **altus**, *high*	**praealtus**, *very high*

(*b*) Prefixes added to Verbs/Nouns:

a-, ab-, abs-, *away, from*
ad-, *towards, to*
ante-, *before*
circum-, *around*
con-, *along with, together* (or simply emphasising the verb)
de-, *down, down from*
dis-, di-, *away, apart, in different directions*
e-, ex-, *out, out of*

in-, *into, in, on*
inter-, *between*
per-, *through* (or simply emphasising the verb)
prae-, *in front, ahead*
praeter-, *past, beyond*
pro-, prod-, *forward*
re-, red-, *back, again*
sub-, *under, below, up to*
trans-, tra-, *across*

It will be noted that many of these are common prepositions.

(*c*) Consonantal change:

Some prefixes undergo a change (often for ease of pronunciation) when they are added to verbs which begin with certain consonants:

(i) **ad-**. The -d- tends to change to the consonant that follows it, e.g.

accurro (from ad-curro)
affero (from ad-fero)
aggredior (from ad-gredior)
appeto (from ad-peto)
allatum (from ad-latum)
arrogo (from ad-rogo)
attuli (from ad-tuli)

This type of change is called *assimilation* (**ad** + **similis**), a word which is itself a good example of assimilation.

(ii) **in-** and **con-**. The same kind of change can take place with **in-** and **con-** before certain consonants, e.g.

illatum	(from **in-latum**)	**collatum**	(from **con-latum**)
immitto	(from **in-mitto**)	**committo**	(from **con-mitto**)
irruo	(from **in-ruo**)	**corruo**	(from **con-ruo**)

Note that **in-** and **con-** become **im-** and **com-** before **-b-** or **-p-**, e.g.

impono (from **in-pono**)
compello (from **con-pello**)

(iii) **ex-** becomes **ef-** in front of words beginning with **f-**, e.g.

effero (from **ex-fero**)

(iv) **ab-** becomes **au-** in front of verbs beginning with **f-**, e.g.

aufero (from **ab-fero**)
aufugio (from **ab-fugio**)

(*d*) Sometimes the simple word undergoes a vowel-change when a prefix is added to it, e.g.

facere, *to make*	reficere, *to remake, repair*
amicus, *a friend*	inimicus, *an enemy*
tenere, *to hold*	retinere, *to hold back*
claudere, *to shut*	includere, *to shut in*

Suffixes

An addition to the end of a word is called a *suffix*. Common examples of Latin suffixes are:

(*a*) The suffix **-or**:

(i) added to the present stem of a verb means *the state of, the act of* or *the result of*, e.g.

amor *the state of loving*, i.e. *love* (from **amare**)
dolor *the act of grieving*, i.e. *grief* (from **dolere**)
terror *the result of terrifying*, i.e. *fear* (from **terrere**)

(ii) added to the supine stem means *the person who does something*, e.g.

amator, *the person who loves, lover* (from **amatum**, the supine of **amare**)
captor, *the person who captures, captor* (from **captum**, the supine of **capere**)
defensor, *the person who defends, defender* (from **defensum**, the supine of **defendere**)

(b) The noun suffix **-arius** means *the person who handles/deals with something*, e.g.

raedarius, *the person who drives a carriage,* i.e. *a coachman*
lignarius, *the person who deals with wood,* i.e. *a joiner, carpenter*

(c) The noun suffix **-arium** means *a place for*, e.g.

librarium, *a place for books,* i.e. *a library*

(d) The adjective suffixes **-abilis** and **-ibilis** mean

(i) *able to be -ed,* e.g.

navigabilis, *able to be sailed (on)*
credibilis, *able to be believed*

(ii) *able to do something,* e.g.

terribilis, *able to terrify, terrifying*

(e) The adjective suffix **-osus** means *full of,* e.g.

periculosus, *full of danger*

(f) There are various diminutive suffixes: **-ulus, -olus, -ellus,** e.g.

parvus, *small;* **parvulus,** *tiny*
filia, *daughter;* **filiola,** *little daughter*
liber, *book;* **libellus,** *pamphlet*

(g) The verb suffix **-sco** means *I grow, I become,* e.g.

senesco, *I grow/become old*
pubesco, *I become an adult*

Compound Words

Not all compounds are formed from the addition of a prefix or suffix. Other combinations include

(a) words formed from a noun + a verb, e.g.

agricola (ager, field + **colere,** to till), *farmer*
causidicus (causa, a case + **dicere,** to speak), *lawyer*
signifer (signum, standard + **ferre,** to carry), *standard-bearer*
tibicen (tibia, flute + **canere,** to sing), *flute-player*
particeps (pars, part + **capere,** to take) *sharing in*
manumittere (manu + **mittere,** to send from one's hand) *to free (a slave)*
animadvertere (animum + **ad** + **vertere,** to turn one's mind towards), *to notice*

(b) verbs formed from an adverb + a verb, e.g.

> **maledicere** (**male** + **dicere**, to speak evilly), *to abuse, curse*
> **satisfacere** (**satis** + **facere**, to do enough), *to satisfy*

(c) words formed from an adjective + noun, e.g.

> **meridies** (**medius**, middle of + **dies**, day). *mid-day*
> **flavicomus** (**flavus**, yellow + **comae**, hair), *flaxen-haired*
> **triennium** (**tres**, three + **annus**, year) *a period of three years*
> **magnanimus** (**magnus**, great + **animus**, mind), *great-hearted, noble*

N.B. See also Latin Word Families on page 84.

EXERCISE I

Prefixes and Verbs

(a) *To find the meaning, break the following verbs down into simple prefix and simple verb:*

convenire	adducere	postponere	extorquere
redire	permanere	desilire	aufugere
provolare	interrumpere	praetercurrere	reddere
auferre	redintegrare	conicere	traducere

(b) *To find the meaning, break the following verbs down into simple prefix and simple verb, noting the assimilation:*

appropinquare	colloqui	irrumpere	collocare
diffidere	effundere	assumere	corrumpere
immittere	dissolvere	afferre	alloqui

(c) *To find the meaning, break the following verbs down into simple prefix and simple verb, noting where assimilation has occurred or a vowel change has taken place when the prefix is added:*

accipere	sustinere	deficere	exigere
corripere	exprimere	inicere	decidere
includere	colligere	surripere	incipere

EXERCISE 2

Prefixes and Adjectives

In this exercise, the meanings of the prefixes are:

(a) **per-**, very
(b) **in-, im-, ig-**, not
(c) **prae-**, very

Give the meanings of:

(a) permulti	(b) praevalidus	(c) inutilis	imprudens
perpauci	praeclarus	incautus	imperitus
permagnus	praegrandis	incertus	impius
perterritus	praedurus	iniquus	immemor
perangustus	praedulcis	insolitus	improbus
perfacilis	praegravis	intrepidus	improvisus
perfrigidus	praepotens	inimicus	ignotus
permotus	praecelsus	infelix	ignobilis

EXERCISE 3

Suffixes

(a) *Work out the meanings of these Latin nouns ending in* **-or**:

emptor	sponsor	error	cursor
timor	rector	spectator	victor
horror	clamor	pudor	tremor
successor	lusor	obsessor	auditor

(b) *Give the meanings of the following nouns ending in* **-arius**:

retiarius	bestiarius	legionarius	sicarius
sagittarius	lecticarius	argentarius	aquarius
essedarius	librarius	pullarius	falcarius

(c) *Give the meanings of the following nouns endings in* **-arium**:

caldarium	tepidarium	frigidarium	librarium
Lararium	Tabularium	aerarium	vivarium

(d) *Give the meanings of the following adjectives ending in* **-bilis**:

amabilis	memorabilis	laudabilis	stabilis
incredibilis	horribilis	irrevocabilis	legibilis
possibilis	navigabilis	reprehensibilis	mobilis
notabilis	tolerabilis	sensibilis	flebilis
mirabilis	flexibilis	innumerabilis	mutabilis

(e) *Give the meanings of the following adjectives ending in* **-osus**:

lacrimosus	pretiosus	saxosus	spatiosus
animosus	otiosus	verbosus	maculosus
formosus	luctuosus	tenebrosus	formidulosus

(f) *Give the meanings of these Latin verbs ending in* **-sco**:

convalesco	evanesco	inveterasco	maturesco
ingravesco	languesco	conticesco	cresco
crebresco	adolesco	advesperascit	nigresco
aegresco	consuesco	illucescit	quiesco

EXERCISE 4

Compounds

What are the meanings of the following compound words?

aquilifer	malevolus	liquefacio	artifex
somnifer	beneficus	stupefacio	belliger
mortifer	aquaeductus	princeps	praeceps

Latin Word Families

Even in one's native language, one constantly encounters new words. The safest way to discover their meanings is to turn to a dictionary. But that is not always possible, and other ways have to be found to deal with the situation. The most common devices are

(a) using the context, i.e. using the other available information to guess the meaning of the unknown word; and

(b) relating the unknown word to words already known.

This section shows how Word Families (i.e. words which have the same basic roots) can help in deducing the meanings of unknown words, e.g.

Noun	Verb	Adjective	Adverb
libertas *freedom* **liberatio** *release* **libertus** *freedman*	**liberare** *to free*	**liber** *free* **liberalis** *generous*	**liberaliter** *freely, generously*
nomen *name*	**nominare** *to name*	—	**nominatim** *by name, one by one*
onus *load*	**onerare** *to load*	**onerosus** *heavy* **onustus** *laden*	—
propinqui *relatives*	**appropinquare** *to draw near*	**propinquus** *near*	**prope** *near*
pars *part*	**partire** *to share*	**particeps** *taking part*	**partim** *partly*
equus *horse* **eques** *horseman* **equitatus** *cavalry*	**equitare** *to ride*	**equinus** *of horses* **equester** *of a horseman*	—

saevitia	saevire	saevus	saeviter
ferocity	*to rage*	*savage*	*ferociously*
amor	amare	amabilis	amabiliter
love	*to love*	*lovable*	*amiably*
amator		amicus	amanter
lover		*friendly*	*lovingly*
amicitia			
friendship			
memoria	memini	memor	memoriter
memory	*I remember*	*mindful*	*from memory*
	memorare	memorabilis	
	to mention	*memorable*	
dubitatio	dubitare	dubius	dubie
doubt	*to doubt*	*doubtful*	*doubtfully*

Within the word family, it is often possible to recognise whether a particular word is a noun, verb, adjective or adverb.

(*a*) The following are common NOUN ENDINGS:

-tia,   e.g. **avaritia**, *greed*
-tio,   e.g. **ratio**, *method, reason*
-tudo, e.g. **amplitudo**, *bulk, size*
-tas,   e.g. **civitas**, *state*
-tor,   e.g. **victor**, *conqueror*
-sor,   e.g. **tonsor**, *barber*

(*b*) The following are common ADJECTIVE ENDINGS:

-idus, e.g. **timidus**, *fearful*
-inus, e.g. **porcinus**, *of a pig*
-alis, e.g. **mortalis**, *mortal*
-elis, e.g. **fidelis**, *faithful*
-ilis, e.g. **virilis**, *manly*
-osus, e.g. **periculosus**, *dangerous*

(*c*) Examples of ADVERB ENDINGS are:

-ter, e.g. **audacter**, *boldly*
-iter, e.g. **fortiter**, *bravely*
-e,   e.g. **stulte**, *stupidly*
-o,   e.g. **subito**, *suddenly*
-tim, e.g. **gradatim**, *gradually*

EXERCISE I

Here are some examples of word families, consisting of adjectives, nouns and adverbs. Complete the groups, and give the meanings of the nouns and the adverbs.

	Adjective	Noun	Adverb
(a)	**brevis,** *short* **crudelis,** *cruel* **felix, -icis,** *lucky* **celer, -eris,** *swift* **gravis,** *heavy* **atrox, -ocis,** *harsh* **alacer, -cris,** *swift* **utilis,** *useful*	**brevitas,** *shortness*	**breviter,** *briefly*
(b)	**fortis,** *brave* **turpis,** *disgraceful* **similis,** *like* **acer, acris,** *keen*	**fortitudo,** *bravery*	**fortiter,** *bravely*
	altus, *high* **longus,** *long* **latus,** *wide* **rectus,** *right* **sollicitus,** *anxious*	**altitudo,** *height*	**alte,** *on high*
(c)	**tristis,** *sad* **laetus,** *joyful* **stultus,** *foolish* **avarus,** *greedy* **piger (pigri),** *lazy*	**tristitia,** *sadness*	**triste,** *sadly*
	sapiens, -ntis, *wise* **diligens, -ntis,** *diligent* **prudens, -ntis,** *wise* **constans, -ntis,** *resolute*	**sapientia,** *wisdom*	**sapienter,** *wisely*

EXERCISE 2

Here are examples of word families in which the adjectives end in either **-idus** *or* **-osus**. *Fill in the gaps.*

Noun	Verb	Adjective	Adverb
timor, fear	**timere,** to fear	**timidus,** timid	**timide,** timidly
—	**placere,** to please		
	splendere, to shine		
		frigidus, cold	
			lucide, brightly
tumor, swelling			
		stupidus, amazed	—
calor, heat			
	horrere, to shudder		
studium, enthusiasm	**studere,** to study	**studiosus,** studious	**studiose,** eagerly
	dolere, to grieve		—
		laboriosus, laborious	
	iocari, to jest		

EXERCISE 3

In the grid below, only one member of the word family is given. Fill in the gaps. The root is underlined to give you a clue to the other words.

Noun	Verb	Adjective	Adverb
bellum **bellator**			
	fidere		
		cupidus	
servus **servitus**			
navis			—
senex **senator**			
	pernoctare		

cum

cum may be a preposition or a conjunction.

1 PREPOSITION. If **cum** is a preposition, it will be followed immediately or closely by a word in the ablative case, e.g.

    cum puero

or **cum** domini irati **servis**

2 CONJUNCTION. The context of the passage and the mood of the verb in the clause introduced by **cum** will usually provide the necessary clues:

  (*a*) (i) When **cum** is followed by a verb in the *indicative mood*, it expresses *time only*. (The time sense is sometimes reinforced by **tum** in the main clause.) Translate by *when*, e.g.

cives, **cum** hostes impetum **fecerint**, moenia defendent.
When the enemy attack (literally *will have attacked*), *the citizens will defend the walls.*

tum clamores audivi **cum surgebam**.
I heard the shouts just when I was getting up.

vix domum adveneram **cum** clamores **audivi**.
I had scarcely arrived home when I heard the shouts.

(ii) **cum primum** followed by a verb in the indicative mood means *as soon as*, e.g.

cum primum domum **rediit**, cubitum ivit.
As soon as he returned home, he went to bed.

(iii) **cum** followed by a verb in the pluperfect indicative usually means *whenever*, e.g.

pueri, **cum** taurum **conspexerant**, aufugiebant.
Whenever they saw *a bull, the boys used to (would) run away.*

Note that, in present time, the perfect and present tenses would replace pluperfect and imperfect respectively, e.g.

pueri, **cum** taurum **conspexerunt**, aufugiunt.
Whenever they see *a bull, the boys run away.*

(b) When **cum** is followed by a verb in the *subjunctive mood*, it can mean *when*, *since* or *although*. Usually only the context will decide which of these meanings is correct (although it is worth noting that the "when" meaning occurs only with *past* tenses of the subjunctive). The reader should therefore suspend judgment until the meaning of the rest of the sentence is known.

dominus, **cum** omnia **cognovisset**, servos culpavit.
When the master learned the whole story, he blamed the slaves.

cum custodes **dormirent**, unus ex captivis effugit.
When the guards were sleeping, one of the prisoners escaped.

discipuli, **cum** ignavi **sint**, poenas dabunt.
Since the pupils are lazy, they will be punished.

cum senator multos inimicos **haberet**, neminem timebat.
Although the senator had many enemies, he feared no one.

(c) When they have a common verb, **cum . . . tum . . .** may sometimes mean *both . . . and . . .* or *not only . . . but also . . .* , e.g.

movit patres conscriptos **cum** causa **tum** auctor.
Both the motion and its proposer influenced the senators.

EXERCISE A

Translate:
1. cum ego Romae habitabam, tu Athenis studebas.
2. cum tres horas navigavissemus, oram Italiae videre poteramus.
3. cum valde aegrotarem, medicum arcessere constitui.
4. nostri, cum diu et fortiter pugnavissent, tamen ab hostibus victi sunt.
5. cum primum ad urbem rediero, ad Curiam ibo.
6. cum Romam venerat, amicos suos visitabat.
7. pueri, cum molestissimi fuissent, e domo excedere a patre vetiti sunt.
8. cum captivi per oppidum a militibus ducerentur, ex adstantibus complures aquam eis dederunt.
9. quae cum ita sint, novum consilium capere nobis necesse est.
10. cum discipuli ludum sero intraverunt, magister eos punire solet.

EXERCISE B

Translate:
1. consul, cum primum Curiam ingressus est, rem senatoribus explicavit.
2. cum eos accusare ausus sis, nemo tibi credet.
3. cum amico tuo in forum ingressus, eum multa de rebus urbanis rogavi.
4. cum amico tuo in foro occurrissem, eum multa de rebus urbanis rogavi.
5. dominus, cum voces servorum audiverat, eos tacere iubebat.
6. in lecto tu iacebas cum ego in Campo Martio me exercebam.
7. cives, cum nullam salutis spem haberent, pacem petere coacti sunt.
8. cum in litore ambularemus, complures pueros pila ludentes vidimus.
9. cum me adiuvare velis, ego solus opus conficere malo.
10. viatores urbi iam appropinquabant, cum fumum flammasque conspexerunt.
11. Romani cum copiis tum argento superiores erant.
12. piratarum dux captivum, cum cantare destitisset, in mare desilire iussit.

dum

The conjunction **dum** has a number of meanings, e.g. *while, as long as, until, provided that*.

Both the *context* and the *mood of the verb* (indicative or subjunctive) in the clause introduced by **dum** will provide clues as to the meaning of the conjunction.

1 When **dum** is followed by a verb in the *indicative*, it expresses *time only*, and will usually be translated by *while, as long as* or, sometimes, *until*, e.g.

> **dum** per viam **ambulabam**, amicum meum quaerebam.
> *While I was walking along the street, I kept looking for my friend.*
>
> amicum meum quaerebam **dum** eum **conspexi**.
> *I kept looking for my friend until I caught sight of him.*
>
> **dum** cives legibus **parebunt**, res publica erit tuta.
> *As long as the citizens (will) obey the laws, the state will be safe.*
>
> **dum** per viam **ambulo**, amico meo occurri.
> *While I was walking along the street, I met my friend.*

In the last example, although **dum** is followed by a verb in the present tense, English translates this verb by a past tense. This happens when the action of the main verb (here **occurri**) takes place within the longer period of activity described by the **dum** clause.

2 **dum** followed by a verb in the *subjunctive mood* means

(*a*) *until*, when there is an underlying idea of purpose or intention, e.g.

> hic manebo **dum** tu vera mihi **dicas**.
> *I shall remain here until you tell me the truth.*
>
> senatores exspectabant **dum** consul **adveniret**.
> *The senators were waiting for the consul to arrive* (literally *until such time as the consul should arrive*).

(*b*) *so long as* or *provided that* (the strengthened form **dummodo** also occurs in this sense), e.g.

> oderint **dum metuant**.
> *Let them hate so long as they fear.*
>
> te adiuvabimus **dummodo ne** huc **redeas**.
> *We shall help you provided that you do not return here.*

Note that the negative in this use is **ne** (not **non**).

EXERCISE A

Translate:
1. dum tu aberis, amicum tuum ad cenam cotidie invitabo.
2. de multis rebus, dum Athenis habitabam, certior fiebam.
3. custodes, dum hostes impetum faciebant, urbem fortiter defendebant.
4. custodes exspectabant dum hostes impetum facerent.
5. diu et acriter pugnatum est dum nox proelio finem dedit.
6. dummodo hostes arma tradant, pacem faciemus.
7. consul paulisper moratus est dum collegam consuleret.
8. vixit, dum vixit, bene.
9. dum ego praetor in Sicilia sum, nemo me furti accusavit.
10. domi manebimus dum revenias.

EXERCISE B

Translate:
1. dum milites pabulantur, hostes subitum impetum fecerunt.
2. servo in templo manere licebit dum dominus eius e foro redeat.
3. dum tu domi cum patre meo maneas, ego Brundisium cras proficiscar.
4. dum haec Romae geruntur, Caesar in Britanniam navigare constituit.
5. dum Romani de his rebus agebant, Saguntum a Poenis obsidebatur.
6. in foro mansi dum advesperavit.
7. ruri manere in animo habeo dum frater reveniat.
8. dum haec geruntur, nuntiatum est hostes haud procul abesse.
9. Caesar, dum reliquae naves convenirent, ad horam nonam in ancoris exspectavit.
10. dum anima est, spes esse dicitur.

ut

Although there are many uses of **ut**, more often than not there will be a strong clue to guide you towards its meaning or use.

I. OBVIOUS CLUES:

1 (*a*) If the verb is in the *indicative*, translate **ut** by *when* or *as*, e.g.

> pauci, **ut videtur**, pro patria arma sumere volunt.
> *Few men, (as) it seems, are willing to take up arms for their country.*

> puer, **ut** taurum **conspexit**, quam celerrime aufugit.
> *When the boy caught sight of the bull, he ran off as quickly as possible.*

(*b*) When there is *no verb*, **ut** introduces a phrase which either reinforces what has been said or, more commonly, modifies it slightly, e.g.

> haec, **ut in secundis rebus**, segniter otioseque gesta sunt.
> *This was done in a slow and leisurely way, as (was natural) in favourable circumstances.*

> inde perventum est ad frequentem, **ut inter montanos**, populum.
> *After that they reached a district that was thickly populated for a mountain region.* (lit. *considering it was*)

2 When the verb is in the *subjunctive*:

(*a*) Following such words as **tam, tantus, ita, adeo** (see page 47) the **ut** clause expresses *Result*. Translate **ut** by *that*, e.g.

> **tanta** erat civium multitudo **ut** in mediam urbem pervenire non **possem**.
> *So great was the number of citizens that I could not reach the city-centre.*

(*b*) Depending on a verb of "ordering", "telling", "begging", "urging", "persuading", etc. (see pages 41–2), the **ut** clause expresses an *Indirect Command* and is generally translated by an infinitive in English, e.g.

> Caesar principibus Gallorum **imperavit ut** obsides **traderent**.
> *Caesar ordered the Gallic chiefs to hand over hostages.*

> lacrimantes regem **oraverunt ut** sibi **parceret**.
> *In tears they begged the king to spare them.*

It is not always possible, however, to use the infinitive in English, e.g.

> orator **obsecrabat ut** reus **absolveretur**.
> *The orator pleaded that the accused be acquitted.*

(c) Following part of the verb **vereri**, translate **ut** as *that . . . not*, e.g.

> **veritus sum ut** milites me servarent.
> *I feared that the soldiers would **not** protect me.*

(d) **ut** clauses follow certain expressions such as:

> **accidit ut . . .** , *it happens/happened that . . .*
> **fieri potest ut . . .** , *it is possible that . . .*
> **ex quo factum est ut . . .** , *the result of this was that . . .*

> (See pages 57–8 for a fuller list of these.)

II. NO OBVIOUS CLUE

If none of the obvious clues mentioned above is present, the **ut** clause will most likely express Purpose (see page 44) and it will normally be translated by the infinitive, e.g.

> mane profecti sumus **ut** fugientes **persequeremur**.
> *We set off in the morning to pursue the fugitives.*

> cras collem ascendemus **ut** solem orientem **spectemus**.
> *We shall climb the hill tomorrow to watch the sunrise.*

III. **ut** CLAUSE/PHRASE PRECEDING MAIN VERB

Sometimes an **ut** clause/phrase appears early in a sentence, preceding the verb on which it depends. When this happens, the three most likely possibilities are:

(a) It is a phrase with no verb or a clause with an indicative verb (see I(1) above), e.g.

> tibi, **ut** mihi **videtur**, domum redeundum est.
> *As it seems to me, you should return home.*

(b) It is used with its correlative **ita**, e.g.

> **ut** seritur, **ita** metitur.
> *As one sows, so does one reap.*

(c) It introduces an Indirect Command or a Purpose clause, e.g.

> hic contra **ut** paulum **exspectaret** manu significat.
> *He however gestured with his hand that he should wait a little.*

> **ut** hostes **averteret**, Hannibal Hannonem adverso flumine misit.
> *To distract the enemy, Hannibal sent Hanno upstream.*

> In this sort of situation, the best possible advice is to suspend judgment to see how the sentence unfolds.

EXERCISE A

Translate:
1. pueris imperavi ut in horto manerent.
2. tam grave erat vulnus ut miles moveri non posset.
3. Catulus Romam rediit ut consulatum peteret.
4. Hannibal, ut omnes bene sciunt, exercitum trans Alpes in Italiam duxit.
5. canis tam celeriter cucurrit ut eum capere non possemus.
6. cives ad portam processerunt ut imperatorem redeuntem salutarent.
7. rex legatis persuasit ut undecim obsides traderent.
8. pater, ut cotidie solebat, epistolas scribebat.
9. tanta erat vis fluctus ut malum navis fregerit.
10. Hannibal, ut legatos Romanos appropinquare vidit, venenum sumpsit.
11. hostes pontem interrumpunt ut nostros impediant.
12. nemo est tam fortis ut mortem non timeat.
13. nos oraverunt ut opus quam celerrime conficeremus.
14. collem ascenderamus ut solem orientem spectaremus.

EXERCISE B

Translate:
1. rex milites ad flumen misit ut Caesarem transire prohiberet.
2. consulibus persuasum est ut exercitum quam celerrime colligerent.
3. hi gladiatores tantam virtutem praestare solent ut multa milia hominum ad spectaculum veniant.
4. ut aquam ingressi sunt nostri, tum hostes ex silvis eruperunt ut in eos laborantes impetum facerent.
5. tot milites necati sunt ut pacis condiciones petere cogamur.
6. misero poetae imperatum est ut sine mora Roma discederet.
7. Labienus, ut erat ei praeceptum, proelio abstinebat.
8. huc non missus es ut tempus teras.
9. ut timorem eorum leniret, consul cives in forum vocavit.
10. ut finem loquendi fecit consul, surrexit Clodius.
11. amicos ut se tanto ex periculo eriperent vehementer orabat.
12. dux piratarum captus facetam, ut in tali tempore, orationem habuit.
13. Antonius Ciceronem adeo oderat ut non solum eum sed etiam amicos eius interficere vellet.
14. adeo verebantur servi ne capti punirentur ut perpauci effugere conarentur.

ne

Latin uses **ne** with a *subjunctive* verb in various ways:

1 Depending on verbs of "ordering", "asking", "begging", "warning", etc. (see p. 41), **ne** introduces an *Indirect Command* and is usually translated by *not to*, e.g.

> vilicus servos **monuit ne** ex agris **errarent**.
> *The farm manager warned the slaves not to wander from the fields.*

2 Depending on verbs of "fearing" (see p. 49), **ne** is translated by *that*, e.g.

> vilicus **timet ne** servi ex agris **errent**.
> *The farm manager is afraid that the slaves will wander from the fields.*

> vilicus **timebat ne** servi ex agris **errarent**.
> *The farm manager feared that the slaves would wander from the fields.*

3 A **ne** clause, which does not depend on verbs of the types mentioned in notes 1 and 2 above, commonly expresses *Purpose*. (See page 44.) Used in this way, **ne** may be translated *so that . . . not, in case, to avoid, to prevent*, e.g.

> vilicus portam clausit **ne** servi **aberrarent**.
> *The overseer closed the gate* { *so that the slaves wouldn't wander off.*
> *in case the slaves wandered off.*
> *to prevent the slaves wandering off.*

> servi diligentissime laborabant **ne** a vilico **reprehenderentur**.
> *The slaves worked extremely hard to avoid being reprimanded by the farm manager.*

4 ne is also used as a negative (meaning "not"):

(*a*) with the present subjunctive, e.g.

> **ne** ex agris **erremus**!
> *Let us not wander from the fields!*

> **ne** servi ex agris **errent**!
> *May the slaves not wander from the fields!*

Note that in this use (sometimes called *Jussive*) **ne** does not depend on any main verb.

(*b*) with the perfect subjunctive to express a negative order in the 2nd person, e.g.

> **ne clamaveris!** *Don't shout!*

N.B. When **ne** is followed closely by **quidem** (the two together enclosing the significant word), these words mean *not . . . even*, e.g.

ne ego **quidem** tibi credo. *Not even I believe you.*

EXERCISE A

Translate:
1 timebam ne pater me culparet.
2 diligenter laborabant servi ne vilicus se culparet.
3 vobis saepe imperabam ne per silvam ambularetis.
4 ne quis effugeret, custodes pervigilare iussi sunt.
5 ne eis tantam pecuniam tradamus.
6 captivus, ne interficeretur, rem totam militibus narravit.
7 ne hodie in forum descendamus. vereor enim ne patruo occurramus.
8 metuebant omnes ne a praedonibus interficerentur.
9 ne pater nos colloquentes audiret, ianuam statim clausi.
10 ne servus quidem tantam ignominiam ferre solet.

EXERCISE B

Translate:
1 imperator, veritus ne hostes secundo vento uterentur, omnes portus custodiri iussit.
2 timent magnopere illi ne capitis damnentur.
3 ne patrem vexaveris! quotiens te monuimus ne eum vexes?
4 ne omnibus odio sitis, desinite talia loqui.
5 ne tyrannum fallere conemur! vereor enim ne nos puniat.
6 suos hortatus ne se reciperent neve se dederent in aciem duxit.
7 ne parentibus dedecori sis, labora semper diligentissime.
8 iam diu metuebam ne in carcerem conicerer.
9 quotiens, quaeso, tibi suasi ne tali homini confideres?
10 ne inimicis quidem morte esse dignus videbatur ille homo.

quod

1 INTERROGATIVE ADJECTIVE

The most easily recognised use of **quod** is as a neuter interrogative adjective, e.g.

> **quod** praemium sperat Caecilius?
> ***What*** *reward does Caecilius hope for?*

> **quod** nomen tibi est?
> ***What*** *is your name?*

2 RELATIVE PRONOUN

quod may be the neuter singular of the relative pronoun, e.g.

> flumen **quod** per fines Aeduorum fluebat, Caesar transire constituit.
> *Caesar decided to cross the river **which** flowed through the territory of the Aedui.*

> id, **quod** vides, monumentum antiquissimum est.
> ***What*** *(literally that which) you see is a very ancient monument.*

Sometimes there is an inversion of clauses so that the relative pronoun appears *before* its antecedent, e.g.

> **quod** ea nocte cognovit, **id** ne uxori quidem patefecit.
> ***What*** *he learned that night he did not reveal even to his wife.*

Sometimes the antecedent **id** is omitted altogether, e.g.

> **quod** tu fecisti, nemo culpare potest.
> *No one can criticise **what** you have done.*

Sometimes the antecedent is incorporated in the relative clause, e.g.

> **quod** monumentum vides, est antiquissimum.
> *The monument which you see is very old.*

3 CONJUNCTION

(*a*) **quod** often introduces a Causal clause which may either follow or precede the main clause, e.g.

> nocte ex urbe discessit **quod** inimicos timebat.
> *He left the city at night **because** he feared his enemies.*

> nostri, **quod** hostes numero superiores erant, se castris continebant.
> ***Because*** *the enemy were superior in number, our men confined themselves to the camp.*

(b) Further examples of this use of **quod** are found in such phrases as **idcirco quod,** *for the (simple) reason that* and **propterea quod,** *for the following reason, namely that.*

In the above examples, the verb in the **quod** clause is in the indicative mood.

(c) Sometimes, the clause has a *subjunctive* verb, indicating that the reason is *alleged* rather than *actual*, e.g.

Milonem reum fecerunt **quod** Clodium **interfecisset.**
*They brought Milo to trial **on the grounds that he had killed** Clodius.*

(d) **quod** occurring as the first word in a sentence may be a "linking relative", referring to a noun or statement in the previous sentence. Translate *it/this/that*. (See page 26.)

e.g. hostes ad vallum currebant.   **quod** cum vidisset . . .
*The enemy ran towards the rampart. When he saw **this** . . .*

EXERCISE A

Translate:
1 illam domum emere noluit quod rimosum erat tectum.
2 quod aedificium spectatis, pueri?   Tabularium spectamus quod antiquissimum nobis videtur.
3 frater meus, quod patriam iterum visere volebat, mecum in Italiam iter fecit.
4 idcirco mihi odio es quod parentes meos totiens fefellisti.
5 id oppidum quod sub montibus iacet olim pulcherrimum totius regionis fuit.
6 quod heri in senatu audivimus, id nemini dicemus.
7 quod te ego et uxor amamus, ad sponsalia filiae nostrae invitaberis.
8 iudices, quod cives innocentes persaepe damnavissent, a populo contemnebantur.
9 portum petebant nautae quod cibus et vinum deficiebant.
10 nonnulli, quod mortem timent, mortem sibi consciscunt.

EXERCISE B

Translate:
1 scutum quod stulte abieci in flumine est inventum.
2 quod scutum stulte abieci, id in flumine invenit amicus meus.
3 quod tibi heri dixi, noli alteri communicare.

4 praedo, quod opus erat ei pecunia, senem crudeliter necavit.
5 quod tibi admirationi est, id a nobis cotidie in urbe videtur.
6 quod tu cives totiens decepisti, gaudeo quod iudices te damnaverunt.
7 idcirco, ut credo, illum hominem laudas quod multam pecuniam, magnam auctoritatem habet.
8 quod vehiculum conducere vis? quod heri conduxisti, id hodie non video.
9 in vincula coniectus est quod consilia sociorum hostibus nuntiasset.
10 quod hic natus sum, hic et mori malo.

quam

1 quam IMMEDIATELY PRECEDING AN ADJECTIVE OR ADVERB will usually introduce an exclamation or a question. Translate as *How . . .* (or sometimes, in exclamations, as *What a . . . !*).

e.g. **quam ferociter** latrant hi canes!
How fiercely these dogs are barking!

quam mirabilem fabulam!
What a wonderful story!

quam celeriter huc rediisti?
How quickly did you return here?

nuntium rogavi **quam celeriter** huc rediisset.
I asked the messenger how quickly he had returned here.

2 quam IMMEDIATELY PRECEDING A FEMININE NOUN IN THE ACCUSATIVE SINGULAR may be an interrogative adjective introducing a question. Translate as *what* or *which*. (See pages 36–37.)

e.g. **quam fabulam** miles tibi narravit?
What story did the soldier tell you?

nescio **quam fabulam** miles tibi narraverit.
I do not know what story the soldier told you.

3 quam FOLLOWING A SINGULAR FEMININE NOUN OR PRONOUN may be the accusative singular feminine of the relative pronoun. Translate as *whom* or *which*. (See page 26.)

e.g. haec est **navis quam** cras conscendemus.
This is the ship which we will board tomorrow.

For the relative appearing before its antecedent ("inverted relative"), see page 98.

4 quam OCCURRING AS THE FIRST WORD IN A SENTENCE may be a "linking relative", referring to a singular feminine noun in the previous sentence. Translate as *her/it* or *this/that*. (See page 26.)

e.g. raeda lente appropinquabat. **quam** ubi audivi, respexi.
The coach was approaching slowly. When I heard it, I looked round.

One common use of a Linking Relative is the phrase **quam ob rem**, *therefore* (literally, *because of this*).

5 quam FOLLOWING A COMPARATIVE ADJECTIVE OR ADVERB means *than*,

e.g. nemo cantat **dulcius quam** soror tua.
No one sings more sweetly than your sister.

senex **infirmior** erat **quam** qui e lecto surgeret.
The old man was too weak (literally weaker than who . . .) to get up from his bed.

quam may also mean *than* when used with certain verbs or expressions that suggest *comparison* or *preference*,

e.g. te **quam** eum adiuvare **malo**.
I prefer to help you (rather) than him.

nihil **aliud quam** pacem peto.
I seek only (literally nothing other than) peace.

6 quam PRECEDING A SUPERLATIVE ADJECTIVE OR ADVERB means *as . . . as possible*. (See page 145.)

e.g. haec templa **quam saepissime** visitare conamur.
We try to visit these temples as often as possible.

Sometimes, a part of the verb **posse** is retained,

e.g. **quam maximum potuit** numerum militum collegit.
He gathered as large a number of soldiers as possible.

7 quam USED WITH ITS CORRELATIVE **tam** will usually be translated as *as*. (See page 64.)

e.g. nonne nostri **tam** fortes sunt **quam** hostes?
Surely our men are as brave as the enemy?

8 The conjunctions **priusquam, antequam** and **postquam** are often split up so that **quam** appears as a separate word. (See page 52.)

e.g. non **prius** abibo **quam** omnia cognovero.
I shall not go away until I learn everything.

paucis **post** horis **quam** navigaveramus, tempestas coorta est.
A few hours after we had sailed, a storm arose.

EXERCISE A

Translate:
1 quam celeriter ad urbem pervenisti, mi amice!
2 quam longa erat illa oratio quam Cicero heri apud senatum habuit!
3 multo tutius est hic manere quam per urbis vicos nocte ambulare.
4 nihil aliud respondit quam haec verba: "civis Romanus sum."
5 quam honestam vitam egit ea mulier quam vos nunc accusatis!
6 quam in regionem proficisci in animo habent amici vestri?
7 si tam strenuus es quam frater, cur non tu quoque illum montem ascendere vis?
8 nonne ianuam prius clausisti quam cubitum ivisti?
9 transfuga se hostibus dedere maluit quam a suis trucidari.
10 nesciebamus quam in insulam pervenissemus.

EXERCISE B

Translate:
1 numquam mihi persuadebis Graecos tam fortes esse quam Romanos.
2 quam celerrime ad urbem contendit ut amicum adiuvaret.
3 ille orator eadem ratione dicendi utitur quam a Cicerone didicit.
4 decimo post die quam rus ad villam redierat, morbo gravissimo periit.
5 quam diligentissime laborabant discipuli ne a magistro reprehenderentur.
6 ille prudentior mihi videtur quam qui dolo servorum fallatur.
7 quam benigne nos semper accipit patruus tuus! quam saepissime igitur ad villam eius iter faciemus.
8 Catilina nihil aliud facere volebat quam rem publicam evertere.
9 nulla femina erat pulchrior quam Atalanta. quam ubi Hippomenes vidit, statim amavit.
10 consul timidior erat quam qui patriam defenderet. quam ob rem omnibus civibus odio fuit.

qui + Subjunctive

The Relative Pronoun is used with the subjunctive in a number of ways:

1 PURPOSE: with the present or imperfect subjunctive, especially common after such verbs as **ire, venire** and **mittere**, e.g.

> custodes **missi sunt qui** nuntium **comprehenderent**.
> *Guards were sent to arrest the messenger.*
>
> viator gladium habet **quo** se **defendat**.
> *The traveller has a sword with which to defend himself.*

See also "Purpose" on pages 44–45.

2 CAUSAL: with any tense of the subjunctive to explain the cause or reason underlying an action, e.g.

> Cicero, **qui** coniuratorum consilia **sciret**, rem publicam servavit.
> *Seeing that (since) he knew the conspirators' plans, Cicero saved the state.*

Sometimes, in this use, **quippe** accompanies the relative pronoun, e.g.

> ancillae, **quippe quae** falsa **dixissent**, castigatae sunt.
> *The maidservants were scolded since they had told lies* **or** *for telling lies).*

3 CONCESSIVE: Occasionally, **qui** may be translated as *although*, e.g.

> consul, **qui aegrotaret,** tamen ad Curiam ivit.
> *Although he was ill, the consul went to the Senate.*

4 RESULT: with almost any tense of the subjunctive, **qui** = **ut is**, e.g.

> domina non erat **tam** stulta **quae** servo **crederet**.
> *The mistress was not so stupid as to believe the slave.*
>
> dignus sum **qui** domum **mittar**.
> *I deserve to be sent home.* (literally *I am worthy so that (as a result) I should be sent home.*)

5 GENERIC: the relative clause describes a "type" of person (or thing) or a "class" of people ("generic" is derived from the Latin word **genus, generis** (*n*), meaning *class* or *type*), e.g.

> sunt **qui credant** te multa scelera admisisse.
> *There are some who believe that you have committed many crimes.*
>
> Caesar non **erat is qui** periculum **timeret**.
> *Caesar was not the (sort of) man to fear danger.*

In this use, when the main clause contains a negative (especially **nemo**), **qui . . . non** may become **quin**, e.g.

nemo erat **quin** tibi **confideret**.
There was no one who did not trust you.

In certain clauses, **quin** (= **qui . . . non**) may be translated as *without*, e.g.

nemo hos versus umquam audivit **quin lacrimaret**.
No one ever heard these lines without weeping.

EXERCISE A

Translate:
1 praemissi sunt septem speculatores qui portus explorarent.
2 servo pecuniam dedit qua panem et vinum emeret.
3 ego non sum qui divitias honestati praeponam.
4 praedo, quippe qui socios fefellisset, timebat ne nocte interficeretur.
5 arma vobis libenter praebebo quibus patriam defendatis.
6 sunt permulti qui pro patria omnia pati parati sint.
7 Gallorum principes, qui consilia Caesaris cognovissent, castra media nocte movere constituerunt.
8 arma, quae essent inutilia, abiecit Hector.
9 quis erat quin Romanos timeret?
10 uxor tua non est digna quae talia patiatur.

EXERCISE B

Translate:
1 erant qui Caesarem esse regem velle existimarent.
2 dicit se indignum esse qui talem puellam uxorem ducat.
3 illi nautae, qui secundum ventum essent nacti, huc brevissimo tempore advenerunt.
4 nemo huius hominis scelera cognovit quin eum contemneret.
5 postridie eius diei ad imperatoris castra venerunt qui pacem ac permutationem obsidum peterent.
6 praetor, qui templa diripuisset, omnibus bonis civibus odio erat.
7 custodes huc brevi advenient qui te in vincula coniciant.
8 sunt nonnulli qui te dignum esse summo supplicio putent.
9 nostri, omnibus rebus paratis quibus castra hostium oppugnarent, prima luce profecti sunt.
10 nemo res gestas divi Augusti legit quin eum admiretur.

quin

1 **quin** with an *indicative* verb means *Why . . . not?*, e.g.

   quin domum mecum **venis**?
   Why don't you come home with me?
   Why not come home with me?

   quin conscendimus equos?
   Why don't we mount our horses?
   Why not mount our horses?

2 **quin** with a *subjunctive* verb:

   (*a*) After a verb of "preventing" or "hindering", translate **quin** as *from -ing*, e.g.

   nihil patrem **deterrebit quin** rus **proficiscatur**.
   Nothing will prevent my father from leaving for the country.

   nostri vix **impediri** poterant **quin** flumen **transirent**.
   Our men could scarcely be stopped from crossing the river.

   (*b*) After a verb of "doubting", translate **quin** as *that*, e.g.

   quis **dubitat quin** vera **dixeris**?
   Who doubts that you told the truth? (i.e. No one is in any doubt.)

   non **dubium** erat **quin** falsa **diceret**.
   There was no doubt that he was lying.

   (*c*) In most other instances, **quin** means *who . . . not* (= **qui non**), *that . . . not* (= **ut non**) or *without -ing*, e.g.

   nemo est **quin sciat**.
   There is no one who does not know. (i.e. Everyone knows.)

   nulla fuit civitas **quin** Caesari **pareret**.
   There was no community which did not submit to Caesar.

   quis est **quin** ei **credat**?
   Who is there who does not believe him? (i.e. There is no one who does not believe him.)

   nemo est **tam** prudens **quin** interdum **erret**.
   No one is so wise that he does not sometimes make a mistake.

   numquam eum vidi **quin riderem**.
   I never saw him without laughing.

105

(*d*) There are certain stock phrases which are best learned as complete vocabulary items, e.g.

fieri non potest quin vera dixerit.
It is impossible that he has not told the truth. (i.e. *He must have told the truth.*)

facere non possum quin te rideam.
I cannot help laughing at you.

nulla causa est quin tibi credam.
There is no reason why I should not believe you.

nihil praetermittemus quin patriam defendamus.
We shall leave no stone unturned to defend our country.

nullum diem praetermitto quin aliquid novi discam.
I let no day pass without learning something new.

haud multum afuit quin caderem.
I almost fell. (literally *It was not far away from my falling.*)

EXERCISE A

Translate:
1. quis dubitat quin Hannibal omnium ducum peritissimus fuerit?
2. eo die nemo fuit omnium militum quin vulneraretur.
3. nemo est quin sciat Ciceronem summum oratorem haberi.
4. facere non possum quin tibi irascar.
5. haud multum afuit quin fame perirem.
6. non dubito quin frater tuus librum optimum scripserit.
7. fieri non potest quin Verres illud scelus nefarium admiserit.
8. tyrannus nihil praetermittebat quin inimicos cruciatu puniret.
9. nemo tam improbus est quin patriam contra barbaros defendere cupiat.
10. facere non possumus quin putemus illum captivum mentiri.

EXERCISE B

Translate:
1. non dubium erat quin Britanni, multitudine navium perterriti, a litore discessissent.
2. quis est qui tyrannum deterreat quin leges violet?
3. haud multum aberat quin urbs Roma a Poenis caperetur.
4. nulla causa est quin cives nostri cibum pecuniamque his pauperibus dent.

5 nullum fere tempus intermiserunt quin trans Rhenum legatos mitterent.
6 Cato numquam dubitavit quin Carthago esset delenda.
7 neque erat quisquam quin nostros rem bene gesturos esse existimaret.
8 signifer non dubitavit se ex navi proicere atque in hostes aquilam ferre.
9 Caesar scripsit non esse dubium quin totius Galliae plurimum possent Helvetii.
10 non abest suspicio quin Orgetorix ipse sibi mortem consciverit.

The Subjunctive in Main Clauses

1 PRESENT TENSE:

   (*a*) Expressing a WISH, COMMAND or EXHORTATION, e.g.

sis felix!	*May you be fortunate!*	(Wish)
Caesar **adveniat**!	*Let Caesar come!*	(Command)
statim **proficiscamur**!	*Let us set out at once!*	(Exhortation)
utinam Caesar **veniat**!	*I wish Caesar would come!*	(Wish)

The negative is **ne**, e.g.

ne dominus hoc **audiat**! *May the master not hear this!*
Don't let the master hear this!

   (*b*) Expressing CONCESSION, e.g.

sit fur, at est dux bonus. *A thief he may be, but he is a good leader.*

   (*c*) In CONDITIONAL SENTENCES, e.g.

si pater nos videat, nos **puniat**.
If father were to see us, he would punish us.

Sometimes the "if" clause is omitted or suppressed, e.g.

quis tibi **credat**? *Who would believe you* (if you were to say that)?

   (*d*) In a DELIBERATIVE QUESTION (i.e. when the speaker is thinking aloud or expressing some doubts), e.g.

quid faciam? *What am I to do?*

(e) POTENTIAL SUBJUNCTIVE (i.e. when the speaker expresses an opinion in a polite, tentative way), e.g.

*velim abire.   *I should like to go away.*
ausim hoc negare.   *I'd venture to deny this.*

*Cf. French "je voudrais".

This use is also found with **malim**, *I should prefer*, and **nolim**, *I should not like*.

2 IMPERFECT TENSE:

(a) Expressing a WISH, e.g.

(utinam) Caesar **adesset**!   *I wish Caesar were here (now).*
   Would that Caesar were here (now)!

(b) In CONDITIONAL SENTENCES, e.g.

si Caesar adesset, nullum periculum **esset**.
If Caesar were here, there would be no danger.

(c) In a DELIBERATIVE QUESTION, e.g.

quid faceret?   *What was he to do?*

(d) POTENTIAL SUBJUNCTIVE, e.g.

crederes eos victos esse.
You would have thought they had been defeated.

mallem domi manere.
I would have preferred to stay at home.

3 PERFECT TENSE:
In a NEGATIVE COMMAND, e.g.

ne existimaveris hoc esse facile!
Do not think this is easy!

4 PLUPERFECT TENSE:

(a) Expressing a WISH, e.g.

(utinam) me **vidisses**!   *I wish you had seen me (then)!*
   Would that you had seen me (then)!

(b) In CONDITIONAL SENTENCES, e.g.

castra, si hostes oppugnavissent, facile **cepissent**.
If the enemy had attacked the camp, they would have captured it easily.

The Subjunctive in Subordinate Clauses

1 Various conjunctions introduce subordinate clauses whose verbs are in the subjunctive. Frequently, there will be a clue in the main clause to help you decide how to translate these subordinate clauses, but one of the main clues will be the conjunction itself:

antequam (See page 51.)
cum (See page 89.)
dum (See page 91.)
facere (See Section 3 of this Note.)
licet (See Section 2 of this Note.)
ne (See pages 96 – 7.)
perinde ac si (See Section 5 of this Note.)
priusquam (See page 51.)
quasi (See Section 5 of this Note.)
question words (See pages 36 – 37, 39 – 40.)
qui (See pages 103–4.)
quin (See pages 105–6.)
quo (See page 45.)
quod (See pages 98–9.)
quominus (See Section 3 of this Note.)
si (See pages 54–5.)
tamquam si (See Section 5 of this Note.)
ut (See pages 93 – 4.)
velut si (See Section 5 of this Note.)

2 **licet**: Although this impersonal verb is used most commonly with the present infinitive, it is also found with the subjunctive in two senses, e.g.

(*a*) **licet abeas.** *You may go away.*

(*b*) **licet** mihi odio **sis**, tamen tibi subveniam.
Even though I hate you, I will still help you.

3 **facere** (sometimes with **ut**, sometimes without **ut**), e.g.

di faciant **ut vincas.**   *May the gods see to it that you win.*
fac **redeas.**   *See to it that you return.*

4 **quominus** (sometimes written as two separate words): When used with verbs of "hindering" and "preventing", translate as *from -ing*, e.g.

nihil te **impedit quominus** eum **adiuves.**
Nothing prevents you from helping him.

5 **perinde ac si, quasi, tamquam si** and **velut si** may be used with the subjunctive when a comparison is made with an untrue situation, e.g.

> se gerit **perinde ac si** rex **esset**.
> *He is behaving exactly as (he would) if he were a king.*

6 Subordinate clauses within Reported Speech (see page 111) will have their verbs in the subjunctive when the subordinate clause is part of what was said or thought. For example, compare the following two sentences:

> nuntiavit legionem decimam, **quam arcessivisset**, mox adventuram esse.
> nuntiavit legionem decimam, **quam arcessiverat**, mox adventuram esse.

In the first example, the relative clause is part of what was announced; in the second, the relative clause is an additional piece of information added by the author.

Reported Speech (Oratio Obliqua)

1 For the simpler uses of reported speech see

Indirect Statement (Accusative and Infinitive)	Page 34
Indirect Question	Page 39
Indirect Command	Page 41

2 Where extended passages of reported speech occur, there is usually only one introductory verb, even though the reported speech may contain different types of construction, e.g.

> (i) Ariovistus ad postulata Caesaris pauca respondit. de suis virtutibus multa praedicavit: transisse Rhenum sese non sua sponte sed rogatum et arcessitum a Gallis; non sine magna spe magnisque praemiis domum propinquosque reliquisse; sedes habere in Gallia ab ipsis concessas, obsides ipsorum voluntate datos; stipendium capere iure belli, quod victores victis imponere consueverint; non sese Gallis sed Gallos sibi bellum intulisse.
>
> Caesar, *Bellum Gallicum* I.44

> *Ariovistus spent little time in replying to Caesar's demands, but he spoke at length about his own merits. (He said that) he had crossed the Rhine not of his own accord but at the request and invitation of the Gauls. (He pointed out that) he had left his home and his relatives only because of the prospect of rich rewards. (He added that) the areas of Gaul which he held had been given voluntarily by the Gauls themselves, as had the*

hostages. (He stated) that the tribute he was exacting was what a victor would normally impose on a defeated nation according to the rights of war. (He reminded Caesar that) it was the Gauls who had attacked him and not vice versa.

In the above translation, introductory verbs have been inserted within brackets to indicate how each part of the reported speech might have been structured; but English, like Latin, would more naturally omit these.

The above example contains only Indirect Statements. The following examples begin with an Indirect Command:

(ii) cohortatus est ne perturbarentur incommodo: non virtute neque in acie vicisse Romanos, sed artificio quodam et scientia oppugnationis.

Caesar, *Bellum Gallicum* VII.29

He urged them not to be too downhearted. (He reminded them that) the Romans had won not because of their superior bravery in battle but because of a certain skill and knowledge of assault tactics.

(iii) Ariovistus postulavit ne quem peditem ad colloquium Caesar adduceret: vereri se ne per insidias ab eo circumveniretur; uterque cum equitatu veniret; alia ratione se non esse venturum.

Caesar, *Bellum Gallicum* I.42

Ariovistus demanded that Caesar should not bring any infantry to the meeting. (He said that) he was afraid that Caesar would lay a trap for him. (He insisted that) each of them should come with a cavalry escort. (He maintained that) he would not come at all if these conditions were not met.

3 If a SUBJUNCTIVE is found in a passage of reported speech, it may be because:

(*a*) it is the normal use, e.g. where a certain conjunction is regularly followed by the subjunctive, as in Purpose, Result, Fearing, etc., e.g.

dixit milites esse tam fessos ut non iam resistere **possent**.
He said that the soldiers were so tired that they could resist no longer.

See also example 2(iii) above, where **adduceret** is in an Indirect Command; **circumveniretur** is in a Fearing clause; and **veniret** is another Indirect Command.

(*b*) it is the verb of a subordinate clause which is part of what was actually said or thought e.g.

obsides daturos **quae**que **imperasset** sese facturos polliciti sunt.
They promised to give hostages and do what he had ordered.

111

Note, however, that the indicative is retained in clauses which represent an author's comment and are not part of the original statement:

Caesar, cum septimam legionem (**quae** iuxta **constiterat**) item urgeri ab hoste vidisset, ...

When Caesar saw that the Seventh Legion (which had taken up its position nearby) was also being hard pressed by the enemy, ...

4 The above points are well illustrated by the following passages:

(*a*) Helvetii legatos ad Caesarem mittunt, cuius legationis Divico princeps fuit, qui bello Cassiano dux Helvetiorum fuerat. is ita cum Caesare egit: si pacem populus Romanus cum Helvetiis faceret, in eam partem ituros atque ibi futuros Helvetios, ubi eos Caesar constituisset atque esse voluisset; sin bello persequi perseveraret, reminisceretur et veteris incommodi populi Romani et pristinae virtutis Helvetiorum.

Caesar, *Bellum Gallicum* I.13

The Helvetii sent to Caesar a delegation led by Divico who had been their general in the war in which they had beaten Cassius. He told Caesar that, if the Roman people made peace with the Helvetii, the latter would go and settle wherever he decided and wished them to be; but if he persisted in hounding them with war, he should remember the courage the Helvetii had already shown and the previous defeat they had inflicted on the Romans.

(*b*) ad haec Ariovistus respondit: ius esse belli ut, qui vicissent, eis quos vicissent, quemadmodum vellent, imperarent; item populum Romanum victis non ad alterius praescriptum sed ad suum arbitrium imperare consuesse; si ipse populo Romano non praescriberet quemadmodum suo iure uteretur, non oportere sese a populo Romano in suo iure impediri. Aeduos sibi, quoniam belli fortunam temptassent et armis congressi ac superati essent, stipendiarios esse factos. magnam Caesarem iniuriam facere, qui suo adventu vectigalia sibi deteriora faceret. Aeduis se obsides redditurum non esse. quod sibi Caesar denuntiaret se Aeduorum iniurias non neglecturum, neminem secum sine sua pernicie contendisse. cum vellet, congrederetur; intellecturum, quid invicti Germani exercitatissimi in armis virtute possent.

Caesar, *Bellum Gallicum* I.36

In response to this Ariovistus replied that it was an accepted principle in war for the victors to impose any conditions they wished on those they had conquered. This was the practice the Roman people habitually followed in ruling conquered nations in the way they decided rather than according to instructions drawn up by someone else. If he (Ariov-

istus) *did not dictate to the Romans how they should use these rights, they should not interfere with him in exercising his rights. The Aedui had to pay him tribute because they had risked going to war and had lost. Caesar was doing him a great injustice by coming to Gaul and reducing his revenues. He would not return the hostages to the Aedui. As to Caesar's threat to do something about the wrongs the Aedui were suffering, no one had ever gone to war against him without coming to grief himself. Let him attack whenever he liked; he would learn what the Germans, who were superbly trained and had never been defeated, could achieve by their courage.*

EXERCISE

Translate:

1 legatis respondit diem se ad deliberandum sumpturum: si quid vellent, ad Idus Apriles reverterentur.

Caesar, *Bellum Gallicum* I.7

2 biduo post Ariovistus ad Caesarem legatos mittit: velle se de his rebus agere cum eo; ut aut iterum colloquio diem constitueret aut, si id minus vellet, e suis legatis aliquem ad se mitteret.

Caesar, *Bellum Gallicum* I.47

3 qua re animadversa, Ambiorix pronuntiari iubet ut procul tela coniciant neu propius accedant, et quam in partem Romani impetum fecerint cedant; levitate armorum et cotidiana exercitatione nihil eis noceri posse; rursus se ad signa recipientes insequantur.

Caesar, *Bellum Gallicum* V.34

4 quem cum Scipio rogaret quis et cuius filius esset et cur in castris fuisset, se Numidam esse dixit, nomine Massivam; se, orbum a patre relictum, apud regem Numidarum eductum esse et cum avunculo Masinissa, qui cum equitatu auxilio Carthaginiensibus venisset, in Hispaniam transiisse; se eo die, quamquam propter aetatem a Masinissa prohibitus esset pugnam inire, armis equoque sumpto in aciem exiisse; ibi prolapso equo se ab Romanis captum esse.

Livy, XXVII. 19.8

5 Dumnorix omnibus primo precibus petere contendit ut in Gallia relinqueretur, partim quod insuetus navigandi mare timeret, partim quod religionibus impediri sese diceret. posteaquam id obstinate sibi negari vidit, omni spe impetrandi adempta, principes Galliae

sollicitare, sevocare singulos hortarique coepit ut in continenti remanerent: metu territare; non sine causa fieri ut Gallia omni nobilitate spoliaretur; id esse consilium Caesaris ut, quos in conspectu Galliae interficere vereretur, hos omnes in Britanniam traductos necaret.

Caesar, Bellum Gallicum V.6

6 Nasica ausus est monere consulem ne hostem manibus emitteret: vereri ne, si nocte abeat, sequendus maximo labore ac periculo in intima Macedoniae sit; se magnopere suadere, dum in campo patenti hostem habeat, adgrediatur nec oblatam occasionem vincendi amittat.

Livy XLIV.36

7 tribuni militum nihil temere agendum neque ex hibernis iniussu Caesaris discedendum existimabant: re frumentaria non premi; interea et ex proximis hibernis et a Caesare conventura subsidia; postremo quid esset levius aut turpius quam auctore hoste de summis rebus capere consilium?

Caesar, Bellum Gallicum V.28

se and suus

The various parts of **is, ea, id** and of **se** may all be translated by *him, her, it* or *them*. Likewise, **eius/eorum** and the various cases of **suus, sua, suum** may be translated by *his, her, its* or *their*.

In one sense, therefore, these words should present no difficulty when translating from Latin to English. However, an English sentence which contains more than one of these words is very often ambiguous. For example, in the sentence "*He asked why we had wounded him*", it is not clear whether "he" and "him" refer to the same person or to different people. In Latin, the degree of ambiguity is reduced, since Latin has two ways of translating that English sentence:

(*a*) rogavit cur **se** vulneravissemus.
(*b*) rogavit cur **eum** vulneravissemus.

In (*a*), the reflexive pronoun **se** tells us that "he" and "him" refer to the same person.

In (*b*), the use of **eum** shows that "he" and "him" refer to different people.

The following "rules" should help you.

1 In a *simple sentence* or a *main clause*, **se** and **suus** refer to the subject of the clause in which they appear, whereas **is, ea, id** and **eius/eorum** refer to someone else, e.g.

> senatores **se** laudaverunt.
> *The senators praised themselves.*

> senatores **eos** laudaverunt.
> *The senators praised them* (i.e. other people).

> incolae bona **sua** servaverunt.
> *The inhabitants saved their (own) possessions.*

> adstantes bona **eorum** servaverunt.
> *The bystanders saved their* (i.e. other people's) *possessions.*

2 In *subordinate clauses*, **se** and **suus** sometimes refer to the subject of their own clauses, sometimes to the subject of the main clause.

(*a*) In subordinate clauses which indirectly report someone's "words", "thoughts" or "intentions" (see Reported Speech on page 110), **se** and **suus** usually refer to the subject of the main verb, e.g.

  (i) Indirect Statement (Accusative and Infinitive):

  > captivus dixit **se** innocentem esse.
  > *The prisoner said that he* (the prisoner) *was innocent.*

  > captivus dixit **eum** innocentem esse.
  > *The prisoner said that he* (someone else) *was innocent.*

  (ii) Indirect Question:

  > servus rogavit cur vilicus **se** puniret.
  > *The slave asked why the overseer was punishing him* (the slave).

  (iii) Indirect Command:

  > captivi nos oraverunt ut **sibi** parceremus.
  > *The prisoners begged us to spare them* (the prisoners).

  (iv) Purpose:
  > cives arma sumpserunt ut **se** et **suos** liberos servarent.
  > *The citizens took up arms to protect themselves and their children.*

  (v) Fearing:
  > discipuli timebant ne magister **se** punirent.
  > *The pupils feared that the teacher would punish them* (the pupils).

(b) In other subordinate clauses (e.g. Relative, Causal, Time, Concession, Result), **se** and **suus** generally refer to the subject of the clause in which they appear, e.g.

pueros, qui me ad urbem **secum** duxerunt, laudavi.
I praised the boys who took me to the city with them.

cum pueri **se** servare non possint, nos **eos** defendemus.
Since the children cannot save themselves, we shall defend them.

viatores, ubi ad **suam** villam venerunt, tandem quiescere poterant.
When the travellers came to their own estate, they were at last able to rest.

tot hostes impetum faciebant ut nostri vix **se** defendere possent.
So many enemies were attacking that our men were scarcely able to defend themselves.

3 However, when a subordinate clause of the type mentioned in 2(b) occurs within Reported Speech, **se** and **suus** tend to refer to the subject of the main verb. Note the difference between

(a) consul dixit milites, qui **secum** pugnavissent, fortissimos fuisse.

(b) consul dixit milites, qui **cum eo** pugnaverant, fortissimos fuisse.

In (a), the subjunctive **pugnavissent** along with **secum** shows that the relative clause was part of what the consul had said. (See page 111.) His original words were *"The soldiers who fought **with me** were very brave."*

In (b), the indicative **pugnaverant** along with **cum eo** shows that the relative clause was not part of his remarks. All he said was *"The soldiers were very brave."*

4 Although the above notes describe what normally happens, there are exceptions to these "rules", e.g.

scimus **eos se** defensuros esse.
scit **eos se** defensuros esse.

In the first sentence, there is no ambiguity. It must mean *We know that they will defend themselves.*

The second sentence, however, could mean

either *He knows that they will defend themselves.*
or   *He knows that they will defend him.*

In the last resort, only the context will decide which is correct.

EXERCISE

Translate:
1. Caesar suos omnes iussit se sequi.
2. regem multis lacrimis obsecravit ut sibi et suis amicis parceret.
3. puer adeo se laudabat ut omnes eum contemnerent.
4. Caesar suis suadebat ne impetum eorum timerent.
5. dux suos hortatus est ne hostibus occasionem sui circumdandi darent.
6. Romani legatos ad regem miserunt qui ab eo peterent ne suum inimicissimum adiuvaret.
7. Pompeius, ubi equites suos pulsos vidit, ad se servandum ex acie excessit.
8. Paetus amico dixit se omnes libros, quos pater suus sibi reliquisset, ei daturum esse.
9. puer a suo fratre petivit ut secum per totum diem maneret.
10. Tarquinius sic Servium diligebat ut is filius eius vulgo haberetur.

Translation

When we are reading something or listening to someone speaking, we can often anticipate how a sentence will develop. This is noticeable, for example, in a theatre when the audience anticipates the end of a joke and begins to laugh before the comedian has completed it.

Of course, this does not happen all the time, but it happens more freqently than we sometimes realise. In fact, clues abound in English. For example, in a sentence which begins "He prevented . . . ", we can be almost certain that it will continue ". . . someone from doing something." In the same way, "We decided . . ." will usually continue ". . . to do something", and "They questioned . . . is likely to continue "someone about something." Similarly, "I wondered . . ." could be followed by a variety of words ("who", "what", "where", "when", "why", etc.), but these have all one thing in common, i.e. they are all question words. In other words, there are clues which enable us to anticipate the likely development of the sentence.

It is quite easy to do this in English because English relies so much on word order for its meaning. However, we have every reason to believe that the Romans, in reading or listening to Latin, must also have built up the meaning of a sentence as it unfolded and that they did not "jump about" in the sentence, picking out first the subject, then the verb, then the object, and so on. That is an English way of thinking; and, if the Romans had thought in that way, they would have put the words in that order. (Indeed, that is what did eventually happen in some Medieval Latin writing, as you will see in the note on page 137.)

Clues in Latin

Because Classical Latin is not structured like English, it is important that we read it in the order in which it appears, building up information as we go, until we complete the picture at the end of the sentence. The longer and more complex the sentence is, the more essential it is to tackle it systematically, suspending judgment until the sentence – and sometimes even the paragraph – has been read right through. In a classroom situation, the ideal arrangement is for the teacher to read the passage aloud to the class, thus revealing the word-grouping and sentence-structure. But, even where the student is working on his/her own, it is still advisable to read the Latin passage through several times. With each reading, a little more of the sense should emerge, just like focusing in on an object till the image is sharp.

What sorts of clues are available in Latin to help us do this?

(*a*) Case endings and verb endings, e.g.

patres timet: The singular verb ending shows that **patres** is not the subject.

(*b*) Adjective agreement, e.g.

flores pulchros mihi . . .: The accusative ending of **pulchros** would suggest that **flores** is also accusative, and the sentence is likely to have a pattern such as: **flores pulchros mihi dedit.**

(*c*) Cases governed by prepositions, e.g.

when we meet **ad, post** or **per**, we should be looking out for a noun or pronoun in the accusative case.

Take the phrase **ad hostium castra:** Since **hostium** is genitive it is not governed by **ad; ad** and **castra** go together and, since **hostium** appears between them, it also belongs to this phrase.

Sometimes, several words separate the preposition from its noun, e.g.

> **contra** civium perditorum popularem turbulentamque **dementiam**
> *against the rabble-rousing madness of degenerate citizens*

(*d*) Balance/contrast

The use of coordinating or contrasting conjunctions, far more common in Latin than in English, helps the reader to understand and anticipate what is going to be said. For example, words meaning "and" (**et, -que, ac** and **atque**) join two similar words, phrases or clauses. Similarly, if you meet **non modo . . .**, you can expect **sed etiam** or **verum etiam**. (Compare **aut . . . aut . . .** ; **vel . . . vel . . .** ; **neque . . . neque . . .** ; **et . . . et . . .** ; **cum . . . tum . . .**), e.g.

non solum ab optimis studiis excellentes viri deterriti non sunt **sed ne** opifices **quidem** se ab artibus suis removerunt qui **aut** Ialysi quem Rhodi vidimus non potuerunt **aut** Coae Veneris pulchritudinem imitari.

Not only have outstanding poets not been discouraged from the highest literary endeavours (by the excellence of their predecessors), but not even craftsmen have given up their particular skills because they could not match the beauty of either (the statue) of Ialysus which we saw at Rhodes or the Venus of Cos.

(Cicero, *Orator* 5)

(*e*) One type of balance which is very common in Latin involves several clauses beginning with the same word, e.g.

nihilne te nocturnum praesidium Palati, **nihil** urbis vigiliae, **nihil** timor populi, **nihil** concursus bonorum omnium, **nihil** hic munitissimus habendi senatus locus, **nihil** horum ora vultusque moverunt?

(Cicero, *In Catilinam* I.1)

The repetition of **nihil** indicates a series of similar phrases. In this case, all of them have to be taken with the words **-ne te moverunt**.

(*f*) Clue words like **tam** or **tantus**, anticipating either an **ut** clause (Result) or **quam** or **quantus** (Correlative).

(*g*) Remember that *context* (i.e. the content of what you have already read) is one of the most important clues in any sentence.

Analysing Sentences

To be able to think like a Roman will require a lot of practice! The general strategy which we suggest you should adopt is to tackle Latin sentences in a systematic, analytical way, "suspending judgment" about the final translation until the whole sentence has been read. For example, take the following sentence from Caesar's *Civil War* I.40:

Fabius finitimarum civitatum animos litteris nuntiisque temptabat.

The thought-process for this sentence might run as follows:

(*a*) **Fabius:** a noun, nominative singular masculine, meaning *Fabius*. Since it is the first word in the sentence and nominative, it is likely to be the subject of the sentence. Unless there is another subject, the verb will be singular.

(*b*) **finitimarum:** genitive plural feminine of the adjective **finitimus** (*neighbouring*). Look out for a feminine noun in the genitive plural with which it would agree.

(*c*) **civitatum:** a genitive plural feminine noun, and therefore likely to go with **finitimarum** (*of the neighbouring states*). To which noun is this genitive phrase linked?

(*d*) **animos:** accusative plural (*minds*). As it is not governed by a preposition, it is probably the object of a verb occurring later in the sentence.

(*e*) **litteris:** dative or ablative? It is probably the ablative since the word does not refer to people. (Perhaps it means *by* or *with letters*.)

(*f*) **nuntiisque:** The **-que** links two similar things, in this case **litteris nuntiisque**. (Perhaps it means *by/with letters and messages*.)

(*g*) **temptabat:** singular verb in imperfect tense. Only the context can decide whether it means *was tempting/testing* or *kept tempting/testing*.

(*h*) **animos** is the object of **temptabat** and also the only noun with which **finitimarum civitatum** can be associated.

(*i*) The literal translation is: *Fabius kept testing the minds of the neighbouring states with letters and messages.*

(*j*) Translate: *Fabius kept trying to undermine the loyalty of the neighbouring states by means of letters and messages.*

The above procedure may initially appear very cumbersome; but, after some practice, you will be able to absorb the information without formally analysing in the above manner. It takes far less time to *think* along these lines than it does to articulate it in actual words. The important point is that, by tackling the Latin systematically in this way, instead of approaching it as a kind of puzzle, you are much more likely to arrive at the correct meaning of the sentence, as well as appreciating the characteristics of Latin as a language. You will also begin to recognise the special effects which the author is striving to produce, particularly through word order and sound patterns.

Only when you have mastered this technique will you be in a position to tackle the long, complex sentences which are so common in Latin. For this we suggest a systematic technique which we have called "Overview". (See pages 121–4.)

EXERCISE

First of all, however, practise analysing the following sentences:
1 itaque hesterno die L. Flaccum et C. Pomptinum praetores, fortissimos atque amantissimos rei publicae viros, ad me vocavi.
(Cicero, *In Catilinam*, III.5)

2 flumen Axonam, quod est in extremis Remorum finibus, exercitum traducere maturavit, atque ibi castra posuit.
(Caesar, *B.G.* II.5)

3 equites hostium essedariique acriter proelio cum equitatu nostro in itinere conflixerunt. (Caesar, *B.G.* V.15)

4 comprehensus est in templo Castoris servus P. Clodii, quem ille ad Cn. Pompeium interficiendum collocarat. (Cicero, *Pro Milone* 18)

5 urbem Syracusas maximam esse Graecarum, pulcherrimam omnium saepe audistis. (Cicero, *Verrines* II.iv.117)

6 dum ea Romani parant consultantque, iam Saguntum summa vi oppugnabatur. (Livy XXI.7)

7 cum provinciam Africam proconsulari imperio meus dominus obtineret, ego ibi iniquis eius et cotidianis verberibus ad fugam sum coactus. (Aulus Gellius V.xiv.17)

8 etenim adhuc ita cum illo rege contenderunt imperatores nostri ut ab illo insignia victoriae, non victoriam reportarent. (Cicero, *Pro Lege Manilia* III.8)

9 tertius expeditionum annus novas gentes aperuit, vastatis usque ad Taum (aestuario nomen est) nationibus. (Tacitus, *Agricola* XXII)

10 Aeoliam venit. hic vasto rex Aeolus antro
luctantes ventos tempestatesque sonoras
imperio premit ac vinclis et carcere frenat. (Virgil, *Aeneid* I.52)

11 istae nationes a ceterarum gentium more ac natura dissentiunt. (Cicero, *Ad Fam.* 13)

12 Romulus dicitur ab Amulio ob labefactandi regni timorem ad Tiberim exponi iussus esse. (Cicero, *De Re Publica* 2.2)

Overview

When sentences are longer and more complex, the Analysing technique needs to be developed further, using what we have called "Overview".

The aim of this technique is to reduce the sentence to smaller, manageable units before completing the translation. Where subordinate clauses are clearly recognisable, it is often possible to deal with them one by one until only the main clause remains. It is then far easier to tackle the sentence as a whole. The following complicated sentences should illustrate how the technique works. Note that the Analysis technique discussed above should be employed within each clause.

Example 1

exigua parte aestatis reliqua, Caesar, etsi in his locis, quod omnis Gallia ad septentriones vergit, maturae sunt hiemes, tamen in Britanniam proficisci contendit quod omnibus fere Gallicis bellis hostibus nostris inde sumministrata auxilia intellegebat.

(Caesar, *B.G.* IV.20)

(*a*) The sentence begins with an Ablative Absolute: **exigua ... reliqua**. A rough translation such as *a small part of the summer remaining* is sufficient at this stage.

(*b*) **Caesar** is nominative case but, before we discover the verb it governs, a subordinate clause intervenes: (*Caesar*)

(*c*) The subordinate clause beginning **etsi in his locis** is also interrupted before it is completed: (*although in these parts*).

(*d*) **quod omnis Gallia ad septentriones vergit:** Since there is no antecedent for **quod**, it possibly means *because*: (*because the whole of Gaul faces towards the north*).

(*e*) Return to (*c*) and pick up **etsi in his locis**, but this time omit the **quod** clause. The **etsi** clause may now be translated: *although the winters are early in these parts*; and the **quod** clause added to it: *because the whole of Gaul lies to the north*.

(*f*) Having translated **etsi ... hiemes**, return to **Caesar**, but this time move straight on to **tamen in Britanniam proficisci contendit**, which can be translated *Caesar nevertheless hastened to set sail for Britain*.

(*g*) After the main clause contained in (*f*), there is another **quod** clause which can be simplified by removing the identifiable phrase **omnibus fere bellis Gallicis** (*in almost all the wars in Gaul*).

(*h*) That leaves: **hostibus nostris inde sumministrata (esse) auxilia**, which is an Accusative and Infinitive depending on **intellegebat**: (*because he understood that reinforcements were supplied to our enemies from there*).

(*i*) Now go back and translate the whole sentence:

Only a small part of the summer remained; but, although the winter sets in early in these regions because the whole of Gaul lies to the north, Caesar nevertheless made hasty preparations to cross over into Britain. He did this because he understood that our enemies had received reinforcements from Britain in almost all his Gallic campaigns.

In the early stages of practising this technique, the use of brackets/underlining can highlight the structure of the sentence, as illustrated below:

(exigua parte aestatis reliqua,) Caesar, [etsi in his locis, (quod omnis Gallia ad septentriones vergit,) maturae sunt hiemes,] <u>tamen in Britanniam proficisci contendit</u> [quod (omnibus fere Gallicis bellis) hostibus nostris inde sumministrata auxilia intellegebat.]

Using different colours of highlighting pens would be even more effective.

Example 2

polliceor vobis hoc, patres conscripti, tantam in nobis consulibus fore diligentiam, tantam in vobis auctoritatem, tantam in equitibus Romanis virtutem, tantam in omnibus bonis consensionem, ut Catilinae profectione omnia patefacta, illustrata, oppressa, vindicata esse videatis.

(Cicero, *In Catilinam* I.13)

(*a*) **polliceor**: Expect either an accusative or an Accusative and Infinitive.

(*b*) **vobis**: normal dative with the verb **polliceor**.

(*c*) **hoc**: This is the accusative depending on **polliceor**, but it is not unusual for an Accusative and Infinitive to follow this word, to explain what "this" is.

(*d*) **patres conscripti**: The dative **vobis** makes it likely that this is vocative.

(*e*) **tantam in nobis consulibus fore diligentiam**: An Accusative and Infinitive, as expected. The adjective **tantam** probably points forward to a Result clause or a correlative. Look out for either **ut** or a part of **quantus**.

(*f*) **tantam in vobis auctoritatem**: This balances (*e*). Supply **fore** to complete another Accusative and Infinitive. Orators are fond of Anaphora, i.e. starting successive clauses with the same word. Look out for other clauses beginning with **tantam**.

(*g*) **tantam ... virtutem** and **tantam ... consensionem**: These are also Accusative and Infinitive clauses.

(*h*) **ut**: as expected in (*e*). To get the thread of the sentence, go back to the beginning, but this time omit the second, third and fourth clauses beginning with **tantam** to take you straight from the first Accusative and Infinitive into the Result Clause.

(*i*) **Catilinae profectione**: Why is **profectione** ablative? You cannot tell yet.

(*j*) **omnia patefacta**: nominative or accusative?

(*k*) **illustrata** and **oppressa** seem to be similar to **patefacta**.

(*l*) **vindicata esse**: This completes an Accusative and Infinitive agreeing with **omnia**. You can now go back to (*j*) and (*k*) and note that, since they balance **vindicata esse**, they must stand for **patefacta esse, illustrata esse** and

oppressa esse. On what do these Accusative and Infinitive clauses depend? Remember that you still have not completed the **ut** clause.

(*m*) **videatis:** This is the verb of the Result clause.

Although this is a long sentence, the "bones" (as indicated by bold letters) are really quite simple:

> **polliceor vobis hoc,**
> patres conscripti,
> **tantam in nobis consulibus fore diligentiam**
> tantam in vobis auctoritatem (fore)
> tantam in equitibus Romanis virtutem (fore)
> tantam in omnibus bonis consensionem (fore)
> **ut**
> **Catilinae profectione omnia patefacta (esse)**
> (Catilinae profectione omnia) illustrata (esse)
> (Catilinae profectione omnia) oppressa (esse)
> (Catilinae profectione omnia) vindicata esse
> **videatis.**

In both English and Latin, it is customary in balanced phrases to omit words to avoid repetition. English tends to omit from the final clause, Latin from the earlier clauses, e.g.

> **sed pleni omnes sunt libri, plenae sapientium voces, plena exemplorum vetustas.** (Cicero, *Pro Archia* 14)
>
> *But all books are full of examples, as are the sayings of philosophers and ancient lore.*

EXERCISE I

Here are some straightforward sentences to practise Overview:

1 hoc proelio trans Rhenum nuntiato, Suebi, qui ad ripas Rheni venerant, domum reverti coeperunt. (Caesar, *Bellum Gallicum* I.54).

2 equites nostri, cum funditoribus sagittariisque flumen transgressi, cum hostium equitatu proelium commiserunt. (Caesar, *B.G.* II.19)

3 his rebus cognitis, Caesar legiones equitatumque revocari atque in itinere resistere iubet. (Caesar, *B.G.* V.11)

4 postero die procul a castris hostes in collibus constiterunt, rarique se ostendere et lenius quam pridie nostros equites proelio lacessere coeperunt. (Caesar, *B.G.* V.17)

5 primo igitur concursu, cum vix pila coniecta essent, rettulit pedem media acies. (Livy XXIII.29)

6 itaque Segestani non solum perpetua societate atque amicitia, verum etiam cognatione se cum populo Romano coniunctos esse arbitrantur. (Cicero, *Verrines* II.iv.33)

7 Samnitibus optimum visum est committere rem fortunae et transigere cum Publilio certamen. (Livy IX.13)

8 inde inhabitantibus tristes diraeque noctes per metum vigilabantur; vigiliam morbus et, crescente formidine, mors sequebatur.
(Pliny, *Letters* VII.27)

9 sic Mithridates fugiens maximam vim auri atque argenti pulcherrimarumque rerum omnium, quas et a maioribus acceperat et ipse bello superiore ex tota Asia direptas in suum regnum congesserat, in Ponto omnem reliquit. (Cicero, *Pro Lege Manilia* 22)

10 Caesar, cum septimam legionem, quae iuxta constiterat, item urgeri ab hoste vidisset, tribunos militum monuit ut paulatim sese legiones coniungerent et conversa signa in hostes inferrent.
(Caesar, *B.G.* II.26)

Poetry

When you are translating poetry, Overview becomes even more important. Besides being forced into an unusual word order by the constraints of the metre, the poet often deliberately uses a specific word order to create certain sound patterns as well as a wide range of emotional effects. However, the metre does bring one bonus: in words which end in **-a**, scansion will usually indicate whether the **-a** is long or short, thus helping to identify the case of the word.

Example 3

> ecce autem gemini a Tenedo tranquilla per alta
> (horresco referens) immensis orbibus angues
> incumbunt pelago, pariterque ad litora tendunt.
> (Virgil, *Aeneid* II.203)

The thought-process might be as follows:

(*a*) **ecce autem:** *behold, however.*

(*b*) **gemini:** *twin.* Look out for a masculine or neuter noun in the genitive singular, or a masculine nominative plural noun.

(*c*) **a Tenedo:** *from Tenedos.*

(*d*) **tranquilla:** *peaceful.* Scansion shows that it is a short -a. Look for a feminine noun in the nominative singular or a neuter noun in the nominative/accusative plural.

(*e*) **per alta:** *over the deep (seas).* It is possible that **tranquilla** agrees with **alta**.

(*f*) **horresco referens:** *I shudder recalling.* Obviously this is a parenthesis which can be ignored at present.

(*g*) Go back and pick up **gemini**, which is the only word so far which appears unconnected.

(*h*) **immensis:** *huge* – dative or ablative plural?

(*i*) **orbibus:** *circles, coils.* Since this is also dative or ablative plural, **immensis** and **orbibus** probably go together.

(*j*) **angues:** *snakes* – nominative or accusative plural? Could **gemini** go with this word?

(*k*) **incumbunt:** *(they) lean on, press forward.* Is there a plural noun which could be the subject of this verb? Note that this verb is usually followed by a preposition or a dative case.

(*l*) **pelago:** *the sea* – dative or ablative? Could this be governed by **incumbunt**?

(*m*) **pariterque:** *and equally.* Which two words/phrases/clauses does **-que** join? Since there has not been another adverb so far to parallel **pariter**, **-que** must join the two clauses.

(*n*) **ad litora:** *to the shore* (Poetic Plural used instead of singular).

(*o*) **tendunt:** *(they) hurry.*

(*p*) The only possible subject for **incumbunt** and **tendunt** is **angues**. Since there is no genitive singular noun, **gemini** must agree with **angues:** *twin snakes.*

(*q*) Go back to (*k*) and (*l*). The only word with which **pelago** can be associated is **incumbunt:** *(they) lean upon the sea.*

(*r*) Now translate the whole sentence:

Behold, however, over the peaceful sea from Tenedos (recalling it makes me shudder!) two snakes breasting the sea with their enormous coils came speeding together towards the shore.

EXERCISE 2

Translate:

1 Romulus septem et triginta regnavit annos, Numa tres et quadraginta; cum valida tum temperata et belli et pacis artibus erat civitas. (Livy 1.21)

2 multas et locis altis positas turres Hispania habet, quibus et speculis et propugnaculis adversus latrones utuntur. (Livy XXII.19)

3 forte evenit ut agrestes Romani ex Albano agro, Albani ex Romano praedas in vicem agerent. (Livy I.22)

4 "obsides" inquit "in civitates remitte! id et privatim parentibus et publice populis gratum erit." (Livy XXII.22)

5 scribendi recte sapere est et principium et fons. (Horace, *Ars Poetica* 309)

6 nunc vero venio ad gravissimam querelam et atrocissimam suspicionem tuam, quae non tibi ipsi magis quam cum omnibus civibus tum maxime nobis, qui a te conservati sumus, providenda est. (Cicero, *Pro Marcello* 7)

7 Cornelius quidam sacerdos, et nobilis et sacerdotii religionibus venerandus et castitate vitae sanctus, repente mota mente conspicere se procul dixit pugnam acerrimam pugnari.
(Aulus Gellius XV.18)

8 erat e regione oppidi collis sub ipsis radicibus montis, egregie munitus atque ex omni parte circumcisus; quem si tenerent nostri, et aquae magna parte et pabulatione libera prohibituri hostes videbantur.
(Caesar, *Bellum Gallicum* VII.36)

EXERCISE 3

Translate:

1 *Death the Leveller*

    pallida mors aequo pulsat pede pauperum tabernas
      regumque turres.
(Horace, *Odes* I.4)

2 *A Cool Head*

    aequam memento rebus in arduis
    servare mentem.
(Horace, *Odes* II.3)

3 *Sacrifice*

> Laocoon, ductus Neptuno sorte sacerdos,
> sollemnes taurum ingentem mactabat ad aras.
> > (Virgil, *Aeneid* II.201)

4 *A Poet in Love*

> vivamus, mea Lesbia, atque amemus,
> rumoresque senum severiorum
> omnes unius aestimemus assis.
> > (Catullus 5)

5 *A Declaration of Love*

> nulla potest mulier tantum se dicere amatam
> vere, quantum a me, Lesbia, amata, mea, es.
> > (Catullus 87)

6 *Farewell at a Brother's Grave*

> multas per gentes et multa per aequora vectus
>   advenio has miseras, frater, ad inferias
> ut te postremo donarem munere mortis
>   et mutam nequiquam alloquerer cinerem.
> > (Catullus 101)

7 *A poet's claim to immortality*

> exegi monumentum aere perennius
> regalique situ pyramidum altius,
> quod non imber edax, non Aquilo impotens
> possit diruere aut innumerabilis
> annorum series et fuga temporum.
> > (Horace, *Odes* III.30)

8 *An invitation to dinner!*

> cenabis bene, mi Fabulle, apud me
> paucis, si tibi di favent, diebus,
> si tecum attuleris bonam atque magnam
> cenam, non sine candida puella
> et vino et sale et omnibus cachinnis.
> > (Catullus 13)

9 *The shipwrecked Aeneas decides to reconnoitre.*

> at pius Aeneas, per noctem plurima volvens,
> ut primum lux alma data est, exire locosque
> explorare novos, quas vento accesserit oras,
> qui teneant (nam inculta videt) hominesne feraene,
> quaerere constituit, sociisque exacta referre.
> > (Virgil, *Aeneid* I.305)

10 *The Trojan Horse*

　　　　　　fracti bello fatisque repulsi
ductores Danaum, tot iam labentibus annis,
instar montis equum divina Palladis arte
aedificant, sectaque intexunt abiete costas.
　　　　　　　　　　　(Virgil, *Aeneid* II.13)

EXERCISE 4

1 *The mysterious disappearance of King Romulus*

Romana pubes, sedato tandem pavore, postquam ex tam turbido die serena et tranquilla lux rediit, ubi vacuam sedem regiam vidit, etsi satis credebat patribus, qui proximi steterant, sublimem raptum procella, tamen velut orbitatis metu icta maestum aliquamdiu silentium obtinuit. (Livy I.16.2)

2 *Galba, one of Caesar's generals, having assumed that an attack was unlikely, now hears that the Gauls are in fact massing to attack.*

his nuntiis acceptis, Galba, cum neque opus hibernorum munitionesque plene essent perfectae, neque de frumento reliquoque commeatu satis esset provisum, quod, deditione facta obsidibusque acceptis, nihil de bello timendum existimaverat, consilio celeriter convocato, sententias exquirere coepit.
(Caesar, *Bellum Gallicum* III.3)

3 *Crassus prepares to fight in an area where Roman armies have previously been defeated.*

eodem fere tempore, P. Crassus, cum in Aquitaniam pervenisset, quae pars, ut ante dictum est, et regionum latitudine et multitudine hominum ex tertia parte Galliae est aestimanda, cum intellegeret in eis locis sibi bellum gerendum ubi paucis ante annis L. Valerius Praeconinus legatus exercitu pulso interfectus esset atque unde L. Manilius proconsul impedimentis amissis profugisset, non mediocrem sibi diligentiam adhibendam intellegebat. (Caesar, *Bellum Gallicum* III.20)

4 *The Germans attack, even though they have just asked for a truce.*

at hostes, ubi primum nostros equites conspexerunt, quorum erat quinque milium numerus, cum ipsi non amplius octingentos equites haberent, quod ei qui frumentandi causa ierant trans Mosam nondum redierant, nihil timentibus nostris, quod legati eorum paulo ante a Caesare discesserant atque is dies indutiis erat ab iis petitus, impetu facto, celeriter nostros perturbaverunt.
(Caesar, *Bellum Gallicum* IV.12)

5 *Aeneas prepares to obey divine instructions to leave Dido.*

at pius Aeneas, quamquam lenire dolentem
solando cupit et dictis avertere curas,
multa gemens, magnoque animum labefactus amore,
iussa tamen divum exsequitur classemque revisit.

(Virgil, *Aeneid* IV.393)

6 *Need for a fire-brigade*

cum diversam partem provinciae circumirem, Nicomediae
vastissimum incendium multas privatorum domos et duo publica
opera, quamquam via interiacente, Gerusian et Iseon
absumpsit.

(Pliny, *Letters* X.33)

7 *An appeal to the Bithynian king to hand over Hannibal*

patres conscripti, qui Hannibale vivo numquam se sine insidiis
futuros existimarent, legatos in Bithyniam miserunt, in his
Flamininum, qui ab rege peterent ne inimicissimum suum secum
haberet sibique dederet.

(Nepos XXIII.12)

8 *Horace bewails to Postumus the relentless passage of time.*

eheu! fugaces, Postume, Postume,
labuntur anni nec pietas moram
　rugis et instanti senectae
　　afferet indomitaeque morti.

(Horace, *Odes* II.14)

9 *After death*

iam iam non domus accipiet te laeta, nec uxor
optima nec dulces occurrent oscula nati
praeripere et tacita pectus dulcedine tangent.

(Lucretius III.894)

10 *Treachery*

cum Pyrrhus rex in terra Italia esset et unam atque alteram pugnas
prospere pugnasset et pleraque Italia ad regem descivisset, tum
Ambraciensis quispiam Timochares, regis Pyrrhi amicus, ad C.
Fabricium consulem furtim venit ac praemium petivit et, si de
praemio conveniret, promisit regem venenis necare, idque facile esse
factu dixit, quoniam filius suus pocula in convivio regi
ministraret.

(Aulus Gellius III.8)

11 *Ovid is sent into exile.*

cum subit illius tristissima noctis imago,
  qua mihi supremum tempus in urbe fuit,
cum repeto noctem, qua tot mihi cara reliqui,
  labitur ex oculis nunc quoque gutta meis.

(Ovid, *Tristia* I.iii)

12 *Juno takes pity on the dying Dido.*

tum Iuno omnipotens, longum miserata dolorem
difficilesque obitus, Irim demisit Olympo
quae luctantem animam nexosque resolveret artus.

(Virgil, *Aeneid* IV.693)

13 *An officer is sent with cavalry to reconnoitre.*

qui ubi adequitavit portis, subsistere extra munimenta ceteris
iussis, ipse cum duobus equitibus vallum intravit, speculatusque
omnia cum cura renuntiat insidias profecto esse. (Livy XXII.42)

14 *A storm looms over the Trojan fleet.*

postquam altum tenuere rates nec iam amplius ullae
apparent terrae, caelum undique et undique pontus,
tum mihi caeruleus supra caput astitit imber
noctem hiememque ferens, et inhorruit unda tenebris.

(Virgil, *Aeneid* III.192)

15 *Despite the atrocities he has committed, Mithridates still goes unpunished.*

is enim qui uno die tota in Asia, tot in civitatibus, uno nuntio
atque una significatione litterarum cives Romanos necandos
trucidandosque denotavit, non modo adhuc poenam nullam suo
dignam scelere suscepit, sed ab illo tempore annum iam tertium et
vicesimum regnat. (Cicero, *Pro Lege Manilia* III.7)

16 *Pompey has all the qualities a general needs to win this war.*

quare cum bellum sit ita necessarium ut neglegi non possit, ita
magnum ut accuratissime sit administrandum, et cum ei
imperatorem praeficere possitis, in quo sit eximia belli scientia,
singularis virtus, clarissima auctoritas, egregia fortuna, dubitatis,
Quirites, quin hoc tantum boni, quod vobis ab dis immortalibus
oblatum et datum est, in rem publicam conservandam atque
amplificandam conferatis?

(Cicero, *Pro Lege Manilia* XVI.49)

Part III: Medieval Latin

Introduction

Latin literature is considered to have reached the peak of achievement in the two centuries that roughly span the period 100 BC to AD 100. This era abounded in great writers of prose (e.g. Cicero, Caesar, Livy, Pliny and Tacitus) and of poetry (e.g. Virgil, Catullus, Horace, Ovid, Martial and Juvenal). The highly sophisticated and elegant language of that literature is known as Classical Latin, so-called because it was thought to have set a standard of excellence and correctness.

Yet even Cicero, whose speeches and philosophical writings have always been regarded as a model of classical Latinity, used the simpler Latin of everyday speech when writing letters. To one correspondent he is at pains to point out:

> **causas agimus subtilius, ornatius; epistolas vero cotidianis verbis texere solemus.**
>
> *In my speeches in the law-courts, I use a more formal, more ornate style; but in my letters I usually employ everyday words.*

These **cotidiana verba** point to the spoken Latin of everyday conversation, called by scholars Vulgar Latin (derived from the noun **vulgus, -i** (*n*), *common people*). The nature of this conversational Latin can be glimpsed in the plays of Plautus, in the Satyricon of Petronius and in the graffiti which have survived on the walls of Pompeii, as well as in the letters of Cicero and his correspondents.

It was this informal, loosely-structured form of the language which, after the collapse of the Empire in the 5th century AD, formed the foundation of the Latin-based languages of Europe (French, Italian, Portuguese, Romanian and Spanish) which are known collectively as the Romance languages.

It was also this form of Latin which, during the Dark Ages, was deliberately chosen by the Fathers of the Church for their Christian writings. For instance, St Jerome (AD 331–420) declared:

volo pro legentis facilitate abuti sermone vulgato.
To make things easy for the reader, I intend to make use of the common spoken idiom.

This was certainly the principle he adopted in his translation of the Bible from Hebrew and Greek into Latin (known as the Vulgate).

And so, when the great revival of literature written in Latin took place in the Middle Ages, that literature found its means of expression in the Latin of the only book with which everyone was familiar, the Vulgate.

Naturally, better-educated men who were versed in the literature of Classical Latin tended to keep to classical norms in their own writings. The result of this wide variety of practice is that Medieval Latin encompasses everything from "imitation-Cicero" to something verging on Italian or French. Nevertheless, it is misleading to think of Medieval Latin as some kind of survival of the classical tongue. It is a language in its own right, with well-defined characteristics and a distinctive flavour of its own.

Some Characteristic Features of Medieval Latin

1 *Changes in spelling:*

oe/ae may become **e**,	e.g.	coepit	→ cepit
		meae	→ mee
		quaedam	→ quedam
h may become **ch**,	e.g.	mihi	→ michi
		nihil	→ nichil
h may be inserted,	e.g.	abiit	→ habiit
		clam	→ chlam
		ostium	→ hostium
h may be omitted,	e.g.	haurire	→ aurire
		homines	→ omines
p may become **b**,	e.g.	nuper	→ nuber
		scripturus	→ scribturus
p may be inserted between **m** and **n**,	e.g.	columna	→ columpna
		damnari	→ dampnari
t (medial) becomes **c**,	e.g.	etiam	→ eciam
		petierat	→ pecierat
		tristitia	→ tristicia

t (final) becomes **d**,   e.g. inquit   → inquid
          reliquit   → reliquid

Confusion of single and double consonants:
    Insertion, e.g. satisfacio   → satisfaccio
          tulisset   → tullisset
    Omission, e.g. immo   → imo
          nullo   → nulo
          reddita   → redita

Omission of short vowels between consonants:
     e.g. aspera   → aspra
       oculus   → oclus
       dominus   → domnus

2 Meanings of forms:

(*a*) Gerund: **dicendo** = *by saying*   (Classical)
          while saying (Medieval)

   e.g. tu turrim circueas **considerando** si fumum egredi videris.
    Go round the tower **looking closely** (to see) *if you can see smoke emerging*.

    dominus meus **equitando** dicit horas suas.
    My master says his hours (prayers) **while he is riding along**.

(*b*) Present Participle:

   (1) **audiens:** (i) used in Classical Latin for an action going on at the same time as the main verb – *while hearing*;
        (ii) in Medieval Latin it can mean either *hearing* or *having heard*, as in English.

    e.g. vir sanctus haec **audiens** iussit.
    Having heard *this, the saint gave orders*.

   (2) With parts of the verb **esse** to form continuous tenses,

    e.g. iuxta quam terram **erat** quidam miles **manens**.
    A certain soldier **was living** *near this land*.

   (3) **accedens** = *approaching* (Classical)
        = *he/she approached* (Medieval)

    e.g. Leo papa per se ad eum **accedens**.
    Leo the Pope in person **approached** *him*.

(*c*) Past Participle:

   (1) When used with parts of the verb **esse**, it lost its past meaning, e.g.

    dictum est = *it has been said* or *it was said* (Classical)
         = *it is said* (Medieval) (= **dicitur** in Classical)

(2) When used with parts of the verb **habere**, it formed a past tense, e.g.

habeo factum = *I have done* (= **feci** in Classical)
episcopum **invitatum habes**, *you have invited* the bishop

(d) Impersonal Verbs:

(1) Greater frequency of use, e.g.

dum **nescitur** ubi venerabile corpus esset collocatum **effoditur** exquirendo.
while it was not known where the body of the saint lay, in the search for it digging operations were begun.

(2) Extension of use, e.g.

venitur = **venit** (as in the following lines from a poem by Bede)

O quam beata civitas   *O how blessed the city*
In qua redemptor **venitur**!   *To which the Redeemer has come!*

(e) Subjunctive:
The use of the subjunctive is unpredictable, e.g.

postquam **bibit** ac poculum **redderet** . . .
After he drank and handed back the cup.

(There is no grammatical reason for changing from the indicative **bibit** to the subjunctive **redderet**.)

3 *Vocabulary:*

(a) Classical words acquired new meanings, e.g.

comes = "count"
dux = "duke"
unus = "a"   (fecit unum parvum foramen, *he made a small hole.*)
aliqui = "people" (duo aliqui, *two people*)
contra = "to" (contra eum perrexit, *he spoke to him*)
super = "on" (misereor super turbam, *I take pity on the crowd*)

(b) Distinctions of meaning became blurred, especially in the use of pronouns and pronoun adjectives, e.g.

suus used for **eius** (*his*)
ei used for **sibi**
ipse used for **is** or **ille**.

(1) induit **se** vestimentis **suis**, dextrarium **eius** ascendit.
*He dressed **himself** in **his** (the king's) clothes and mounted **his** (the king's) charger.*

(2) peciit ab **eo** ut aliquid **ei** daret.
*He asked **him** to give **him** something.*

(3) vendam **ipsum**. *I will sell **it**.*

(c) Classical words were supplanted by their Vulgar Latin equivalents, e.g.

vesper was replaced by **serum**
urbs   was replaced by **civitas**
equus   was replaced by **caballus**.

(d) New words came into the language from many sources, especially from Greek, e.g.

ecclesia   *church*
presbyter   *priest*
mysterium   *sacred rite*

4 Sentence Construction:

(a) Blurring of case distinctions, e.g.

in eo loco venitur, *They came **to that place*** (ablative for accusative)
Idus Maias accepit, *He received (it) **on the Ides of May*** (accusative for ablative)
ripae relati sunt, *They were carried back **to the bank*** (dative for **ad** + accusative)

In place of the Ablative Absolute other cases are employed, e.g.

(1) Nominative:

interea, **nox atra cadens**, Aurora reportat alma diem.
*Meanwhile, **as black night departed**, gracious Dawn brought back the light of day.*

qui, machinis constructis **omnia**que **genera** tormentorum **adhibita**, invadunt civitatem.
***Having** constructed siege-engines and **brought into action all kinds of artillery**, they attacked the city.*

(2) Accusative:

itaque, **liberatam civitatem**, Attellanem fugant.
*Therefore, **when they had freed the city**, they put Attila to flight.*

(b) Reported Speech:

The Classical Accusative and Infinitive construction is still found, but **quod, quia, quoniam** and **ut** (with the indicative or subjunctive) appear frequently, e.g.

scio **quod** non **moriar**, *I know that I will not die.*

audivimus **quia** pugnare **vis**, *We have heard that you wish to fight.*

confido **quoniam** hoc fieri **permisit** Deus, *I believe that God allowed this to happen.*

clamor factus est communis **ut** filiam vestram in uxorem **habebit**.
It is common knowledge that he will marry your daughter.

(c) Word Order:
The long periodic Latin sentence tends to disappear and shorter sentences predominate. Instead of the complex word order of Classical Latin, we find an order of words much closer to that of English and other modern European languages, e.g.

interrogavit ergo eum: "quis es tu?" cui ille: "apocrisiarius sum regis Alexandri, missus nunciare tibi quia moram facit in campo exspectans te. unde, si tibi placet, constitue diem praeliandi.

So he asked him, "Who are you?" To which he replied, "I am the deputy of King Alexander, sent to announce to you that he is whiling away the time on the plain waiting for you. So, if you don't mind, fix a day for the battle."

EXERCISE A

Translate:

Abbot Samson

Abbas Samson mediocris erat stature, fere omnino calvus, vultum habens nec rotundum nec oblongum, naso eminente, labiis grossis, oculis cristallinis et penetrantis intuitus, auribus clarissimi auditus, superciliis in altum crescentibus et sepe tonsis; ex parvo frigore cito raucus; die elec-
5 cionis sue quadraginta et septem annos etatis habens, et in monachatu decem et septem annos; paucos canos habens in rufa barba, et paucissimos inter capillos nigros, et aliquantulum crispos; set infra xiiii annos post eleccionem suam totus albus efficitur sicut nix.

homo supersobrius, numquam desidiosus, multum valens, et volens
10 equitare vel pedes ire donec senectus prevaluit, que talem voluntatem temperavit; qui, audito rumore de capta cruce et perdicione Jerusalem, femoralibus cilicinis cepit uti et cilicio loco staminis, et carnibus et carneis abstinere; carnes tamen voluit sibi anteferri sedens ad mensam, ad augmentum scilicet elemosine. lac dulce et mel et consimilia dulcia libencius quam
15 ceteros cibos comedebat.

mendaces et ebriosos et verbosos odio habuit; quia virtus sese diligit et aspernatur contrarium. murmuratores cibi et potus, et precipue monachos murmuratores condempnans, tenorem antiquum conservans quem olim habuit dum claustralis fuit. hoc autem virtutis in se habuit
20 quod numquam ferculum coram eo positum voluit mutare. quod cum ego novicius vellem probare si hoc esset verum, forte servivi in refectorio; et cogitavi penes me ut ponerem coram eo ferculum quod omnibus aliis displiceret in disco nigerimo et fracto. quod cum ipse vidisset, tanquam non videns erat. facta autem mora, penituit me hoc fecisse; et statim,
25 arepto disco, ferculum et discum mutavi in melius et asportavi: ille vero emendacionem talem moleste tulit iratus et turbatus.

The Chronicle of Jocelin of Brakelond

cepit = coepit

EXERCISE B

Translate:

A Fortune-teller Meets the Unforeseen

audivi quod astrologus quidam, cum aliquando vera divinaret sicut eciam demones quedam prevident futura, rex, de cuius familia erat, cepit ei valde credere et in eius divinacionibus confidere.

quadam autem die stabat valde tristis coram rege. cum rex ab eo
5 quereret quare tristaretur et mestus esset, nolebat dicere ei. tandem ad multam instanciam lugens et dolens in secreto dixit regi: "domine, respexi

in astralabio et pro certo ex disposicione stellarum perpendi quod non potestis vivere nisi dimidio anno."

quo audito, rex credidit et cepit singulis diebus angustiari, macerari et valde tristis esse, ita quod milites multum mirabantur et dolebant. nam rex more solito nolebat eos hylariter videre vel loqui eis.

tandem ad multas preces et instanciam unius qui magis familiaris erat ei, confessus est quod clericus eius, qui optimus erat astronomus, de morte imminente predixerat ei.   tunc miles ille metuens ne rex nimia tristicia absorberetur et gravem incurrens infirmitatem moreretur (nam et multi metu moriuntur moriendi), vocato coram omnibus astronomo, dixit ei: "quomodo tu certus es de morte regis?"

qui respondit: "certus sum de morte eius quam ex arte mea, que infallibilis est, perpendi."

cui miles: "melius debes scire de te ipso quam de alio. scis quanto victurus es tempore?"

at ille: "scio quod (utique et certus sum) quod citra viginti annos non moriar."

cui miles: "mentitus es in caput tuum." et, extracto cultello, coram cunctis occidit eum. tunc rex attendens quod divinaciones astronomi mendaces essent, ressumptis viribus confortatus est et postea diu vixit.

The Exempla of Jacques de Vitry No. 20

Part IV: Tables

Section A: Summary of the Uses of Cases

Case	Use	Example	Translation
Nom.	Subject	servus laborat.	*The slave is working.*
Acc.	Direct Object	servum specto.	*I am watching the slave.*
	After certain prepositions (See pp. 22–23.)	per agros	*through the fields*
	Moving towards		
	(a) with preposition	ad **urbem**	*to the city*
	(b) without preposition	**Romam**	*to Rome*
		domum	*(to) home*
	Length of time (See p. 6.)	**duos dies** manebat.	*He stayed for two days.*
		puer **duos annos** natus	*a boy two years old*
	Distance (See p. 6.)	urbs decem **milia passuum** abest.	*The city is ten miles away.*
		via quindecim **pedes** lata	*a road fifteen feet wide*
	Exclamation	o **me miserum**!	*Oh dear me!*
	Subject in Accusative and Infinitive (See p. 34.)	vidi **puerum** adesse.	*I saw (that) the boy was present.*
Gen.	To link nouns	pater **pueri**	*the boy's father*
		viae **urbis**	*the city streets*
		aditus **speluncae**	*the approach to the cave*
		rami **arboris**	*the branches of the tree*
	Descriptive	vir **summae virtutis**	*a man of the biggest courage*
	Subjective	iniuriae **Gallorum**	*wrongs done by the Gauls*
	Objective	iniuriae **Gallorum**	*wrongs done to the Gauls*
	Partitive	nihil **pecuniae**	*no money*
		plus **aquae**	*more water*
		aliquid **novi**	*something new; some news*
	Value	**quanti** est hic liber?	*How much is this book?*

	With certain Impersonal Verbs (See p. 58.)	me taedet **laboris.**	*I am tired of work.*
		me pudet **stultitiae.**	*I am ashamed of my folly.*
	Characteristic	est **boni consulis** senatum consulere.	*It is the mark of a good consul to consult the senate.*
Dat.	To indicate a "transfer"	fabulam **puellae** narro.	*I tell the girl a story.*
		librum **puero** do.	*I give a book to the boy.*
	With certain verbs (See p. 10.)	**puellae** credo.	*I believe the girl.*
	With certain adjectives (See p. 12.)	locus **castris** idoneus	*a place suitable for camp*
	Predicative (See p. 13.)	puer **patri** auxilio est.	*The boy is a help to his father.*
	With Gerundive (See p. 62.)	**mihi** eundum est.	*I must go.*
	Possession	**mihi** est domus.	*I have a house; the house is mine.*
Abl.	After certain prepositions (See pp. 23–24.)	cum patre	*with father*
	Moving from (See p. 20.)		
	(a) with preposition	ex **urbe**	*out of the city*
	(b) without preposition	**Roma**	*from Rome*
		domo	*from home*
	Time "at", "on", "in" (See p. 18.)	tertia **hora**	*at the third hour*
		eo **die**	*on that day*
		paucis **diebus**	*in a few days*
	Causal	**vulneribus** mortuus est.	*He died from his wounds.*
	Instrumental	**virgis** caesi sunt.	*They were beaten with sticks.*
	Descriptive	vir **summa virtute**	*a man of the highest courage*
		taurus **brevibus cornibus**	*a short-horned bull*
	With comparative adjectives and adverbs	quis est me **ignavior?**	*Who is lazier than I?*
		celerius curro **fratre.**	*I run faster than my brother.*
	Adverbial (Manner)	magna **voce**	*in a loud voice; loudly*
		summa **vi**	*with the utmost force*
	With certain verbs (See p. 16.)	**gladio** usus est.	*He used a sword.*
	With certain adjectives (See p. 16.)	dignus **laude**	*worthy of praise*
	Measure	uno **pede** altior	*one foot taller*
	Price	magno **domum** emi.	*I paid a high price for the house.*
	Respect	nostri hostes **virtute** praestabant.	*Our men surpassed the enemy in courage.*
	Ablative Absolute (See p. 30.)	**hoc viso,** discessit.	*After seeing this, he left.*

Section B: Nouns

		Group 1	Group 2		Group 3		Group 4		Group 5
Sing.	Nom.	puella	servus	puer	baculum	vox	nomen	manus	cornu	dies
	Acc.	puellam	servum	puerum	baculum	vocem	nomen	manum	cornu	diem
	Gen.	puellae	servi	pueri	baculi	vocis	nominis	manus	cornus	diei
	Dat.	puellae	servo	puero	baculo	voci	nomini	manui	cornu	diei
	Abl.	puella	servo	puero	baculo	voce	nomine	manu	cornu	die
Plur.	Nom.	puellae	servi	pueri	bacula	voces	nomina	manus	cornua	dies
	Acc.	puellas	servos	pueros	bacula	voces	nomina	manus	cornua	dies
	Gen.	puellarum	servorum	puerorum	baculorum	vocum	nominum	manuum	cornuum	dierum
	Dat.	puellis	servis	pueris	baculis	vocibus	nominibus	manibus	cornibus	diebus
	Abl.	puellis	servis	pueris	baculis	vocibus	nominibus	manibus	cornibus	diebus

1 *Vocative Case.* This case is used when someone or something is addressed by name. It is only in the singular of Group 2 nouns ending in **-us** that it has a different ending from the nominative case, e.g. **Sexte, Marce, Corneli, Gai, amice.**

2 The *stem* of a noun is that part which remains when the genitive singular ending is removed, e.g. **puella**, genitive singular **puellae**, stem **puell-**; **vox, vocis,** stem **voc-**; **nomen, nominis,** stem **nomin-**.

3 In Group 3 nouns, there is no standard form for the nominative singular (e.g. **mater, vestis, urbs,** etc.); and there are two forms of the genitive plural (**-um** and **-ium**).
Other forms found in Group 3 are:
Acc. Sing.: **vim, Neapolim, Tiberim**
Abl. Sing.: **vi, navi, mari**
Acc. Plur.: **-is** for **-es,** e.g. **navis**

4 **domus** usually has the same endings as **manus.** Common exceptions are ablative singular (**domo**) and the special form **domi,** *at home.*

5 *Gender:*
(a) Group 1 nouns are all feminine except those which are men's names, jobs that men did, or the names of certain rivers, e.g. **Caligula, -ae** (*m*); **nauta, -ae** (*m*), sailor; **Matrona, -ae** (*m*), Marne.

(b) Group 2 nouns ending in **-us** or **-er** are nearly all masculine, but names of cities, islands and trees are feminine, e.g. **Corinthus, -i** (*f*), Corinth; **laurus, -i** (*f*), bay-tree. Group 2 nouns ending in **-um** are neuter.

(c) Most nouns in Group 3 are either masculine or feminine, but nearly all nouns of the following types are neuter:
ending in **-en, -inis**: e.g. **nomen, nominis** (*n*)
ending in **-us, -oris**: e.g. **corpus, corporis** (*n*)
ending in **-us, -eris**: e.g. **onus, oneris** (*n*)

(d) Group 4 nouns ending in **-us** are mostly masculine, but two common exceptions are **manus, -us** (*f*) and **domus, -us** (*f*).

(e) Group 5 nouns are all feminine except **dies, diei** (*m*) and **meridies, -ei** (*m*). When **dies** refers to a fixed day it is feminine, e.g. **die constituta,** *on the appointed day.*

6 *Locative:* See page 20.

Section C: Adjectives

		Groups 1/2			Group 3			
		Masc.	Fem.	Neut.	Masc./Fem.	Neut.	Masc./Fem.	Neut.
Sing.	Nom.	magn**us**	magn**a**	magn**um**	omn**is**	omn**e**	ingens	ingens
	Acc.	magn**um**	magn**am**	magn**um**	omn**em**	omn**e**	ingent**em**	ingens
	Gen.	magn**i**	magn**ae**	magn**i**	omn**is**	omn**is**	ingent**is**	ingent**is**
	Dat.	magn**o**	magn**ae**	magn**o**	omn**i**	omn**i**	ingent**i**	ingent**i**
	Abl.	magn**o**	magn**a**	magn**o**	omn**i**	omn**i**	ingent**i**	ingent**i**
Plur.	Nom.	magn**i**	magn**ae**	magn**a**	omn**es**	omn**ia**	ingent**es**	ingent**ia**
	Acc.	magn**os**	magn**as**	magn**a**	omn**es**	omn**ia**	ingent**es**	ingent**ia**
	Gen.	magn**orum**	magn**arum**	magn**orum**	omn**ium**	omn**ium**	ingent**ium**	ingent**ium**
	Dat.	magn**is**	magn**is**	magn**is**	omn**ibus**	omn**ibus**	ingent**ibus**	ingent**ibus**
	Abl.	magn**is**	magn**is**	magn**is**	omn**ibus**	omn**ibus**	ingent**ibus**	ingent**ibus**

1 In general, nouns and adjectives of the same group have the same case endings. Thus,
magnus has the same endings as **servus**
magna has the same endings as **puella**
magnum has the same endings as **baculum**.
However, in Group 3, whereas most nouns have their ablative singular ending in **-e**, most adjectives have their ablative singular ending in **-i**. Exceptions are **dives, -itis** (*rich*), **pauper, -eris** (*poor*), **vetus, -eris** (*old*) and comparative adjectives, all of which have their ablative singular ending in **-e**.

2 Some adjectives of Groups 1/2 end in **-er** in the nominative singular masculine, e.g.
noster, nostra, nostrum
miser, misera, miserum
The endings of the other cases are the same as for **magnus, -a, -um**.

3 There is no standard form for the nominative singular endings of Group 3 adjectives.

4 Some common adjectives of Groups 1/2 have the genitive singular ending in **-ius** and the dative singular ending in **-i**: **solus** (*alone*), **totus** (*all*), **ullus** (*any*), **nullus** (*none*), **uter** (*which*), **neuter** (*neither*), **alter** (*the other*).

5 Adjectives are sometimes used as nouns, e.g. **nostri** (*our men*), **boni** (*good people*), **bona** (*goods*), **multa** (*many things*).

Section D: Comparison of Adjectives

1 Adjectives have Positive, Comparative and Superlative forms. The Comparative can usually be recognised by the ending **-ior**. The Superlative can usually be recognised by the endings **-issimus, -errimus** or **-illimus**, e.g.

Positive	Comparative	Superlative
ignavus	**ignavior**	**ignavissimus**
felix	**felicior**	**felicissimus**
pulcher	**pulchrior**	**pulcherrimus**
facilis	**facilior**	**facillimus**

2 Comparative adjectives have the same endings as **melior** in the table opposite. The Comparative has several possible meanings, e.g. **ignavior** may mean *lazier, more lazy, rather lazy, too lazy*.

3 Superlative adjectives have the same endings as **magnus, -a, -um**. The Superlative also has several possible meanings, e.g. **ignavissimus** may mean *laziest, most lazy, very lazy, exceedingly lazy*.

4 Some adjectives have irregular Comparative and Superlative forms, e.g.

bonus, good **melior**, better **optimus**, best
malus, bad **peior**, worse **pessimus**, worst
magnus, big **maior**, bigger **maximus**, biggest
parvus, small **minor**, smaller **minimus**, smallest
multus, much **plus**, more **plurimus**, most
multi, many **plures**, more **plurimi**, most

5 The Comparative Adjective forms:

	Singular		Plural	
	M./F.	N.	M./F.	N.
Nom.	melior	melius	meliores	meliora
Acc.	meliorem	melius	meliores	meliora
Gen.	melioris		meliorum	
Dat.	meliori		melioribus	
Abl.	meliore		melioribus	

Section E: Adverbs

Adverbs are of various types. Two of the most common types are:

1 Adverbs derived from adjectives. There are three common endings:
  (a) **-e**, e.g. **longe** (from **longus**), **maxime** (from **maximus**)
  (b) **-o**, e.g. **subito** (from **subitus**), **tuto** (from **tutus**)
  (c) **-iter** or **-ter**, e.g. **fortiter** (from **fortis**), **audacter** (from **audax**)

2 Adverbs based on prepositions, e.g.:

postea (from **post ea**). Compare **antea, praeterea, propterea** and **interea** (based on the prepositions **ante, praeter, propter, inter**).

Section F: Comparison of Adverbs

Adverbs have Positive, Comparative and Superlative forms.

1 The Comparative can be recognised by the ending **-ius**. The Superlative can be recognised by the endings **-issime, -errime** or **-illime**, e.g.

Positive	Comparative	Superlative
ignave	ignavius	ignavissime
feliciter	felicius	felicissime
pulchre	pulchrius	pulcherrime
facile	facilius	facillime

2 Some adverbs have irregular Comparative and Superlative forms (compare the corresponding adjectives on page 144), e.g.

bene, well	**melius**, better	**optime**, best
male, badly	**peius**, worse	**pessime**, worst
magnopere, greatly	**magis**, more	**maxime**, most
paulum, a little	**minus**, less	**minime**, least
multum, much	**plus**, more	**plurimum**, most

3 The Comparative adverb, like the corresponding adjective, has several possible meanings, e.g. **ignavius** may mean *more lazily, rather lazily, too lazily.*

4 The Superlative adverb also has several possible meanings, e.g. **ignavissime** can mean *most lazily, very lazily, in an extremely lazy way.*

Section G: *quam* + Superlative

quam + a Superlative adjective or adverb has a special meaning, e.g.

quam plurimi, *as many as possible*
quam celerrime, *as quickly as possible*
quam primum, *as soon as possible*
milites quam plurimos duxit, *he brought as many soldiers as he could.*

Section H: Demonstrative Adjectives

		Masc.	Fem.	Neut.	Masc.	Fem.	Neut.	Masc.	Fem.	Neut.
Sing.	Nom.	hic	haec	hoc	ille	illa	illud	is	ea	id
	Acc.	hunc	hanc	hoc	illum	illam	illud	eum	eam	id
	Gen.	huius	huius	huius	illius	illius	illius	eius	eius	eius
	Dat.	huic	huic	huic	illi	illi	illi	ei	ei	ei
	Abl.	hoc	hac	hoc	illo	illa	illo	eo	ea	eo
Plur.	Nom.	hi	hae	haec	illi	illae	illa	ei	eae	ea
	Acc.	hos	has	haec	illos	illas	illa	eos	eas	ea
	Gen.	horum	harum	horum	illorum	illarum	illorum	eorum	earum	eorum
	Dat.	his	his	his	illis	illis	illis	eis	eis	eis
	Abl.	his	his	his	illis	illis	illis	eis	eis	eis

Notes:

1 **haec** mulier cum **eis** pueris ambulabat. *This woman was walking with those boys.*
  ille senator risit. *That senator laughed.*
  eam puellam vidimus. *We saw that girl.*

2 The above Demonstrative Adjectives are also used as 3rd person pronouns, e.g.

  haec cum **eis** ambulabat. *She was walking with them.*
  ille risit. *He laughed.*
  eam vidimus. *We saw her.*

3 The genitive forms may be used to indicate possession, e.g.

  patrem **eius** vidimus. *We saw his/her father.*
  amicos **illorum** servavi. *I saved their friends.*

  (See also Note 2 on page 150.)

4 The adjective **iste, ista, istud** (*that of yours*) has the same endings as **ille**. It can also be used as a pronoun, most often in court cases, speaking contemptuously of "the accused".

		Masc.	Fem.	Neut.	Masc.	Fem.	Neut.
Sing.	Nom.	idem	eadem	idem	ipse	ipsa	ipsum
	Acc.	eundem	eandem	idem	ipsum	ipsam	ipsum
	Gen.	eiusdem	eiusdem	eiusdem	ipsius	ipsius	ipsius
	Dat.	eidem	eidem	eidem	ipsi	ipsi	ipsi
	Abl.	eodem	eadem	eodem	ipso	ipsa	ipso
Plur.	Nom.	eidem	eaedem	eadem	ipsi	ipsae	ipsa
	Acc.	eosdem	easdem	eadem	ipsos	ipsas	ipsa
	Gen.	eorundem	earundem	eorundem	ipsorum	ipsarum	ipsorum
	Dat.	eisdem	eisdem	eisdem	ipsis	ipsis	ipsis
	Abl.	eisdem	eisdem	eisdem	ipsis	ipsis	ipsis

Notes:

1 **idem, eadem, idem**, *the same*, has the same forms as **is, ea, id** with the addition of **-dem**. Note that **-m-** is changed to **-n-** in the accusative singular (masc. and fem.) and in the genitive plural; and the nominative and accusative singular neuter is **idem**.

2 **ipse, ipsa, ipsum** is used to give emphasis to a noun or pronoun, e.g.

ego **ipse** veni.   *I **myself** came.*
ipse venit.   *He came **himself**.*
Caesarem **ipsum** vidimus.   *We saw Caesar **himself**.*
aedificia **ipsa** vidimus.   *We saw the buildings **themselves**.*
                   *the **very** buildings.*
                   *the **actual** buildings.*

Section I: Interrogative, Relative and Indefinite Pronouns

		Interrogative Pronoun (who? what?)			Relative Pronoun (who, which, that)			Indefinite Pronoun (a certain)		
		Masc.	Fem.	Neut.	Masc.	Fem.	Neut.	Masc.	Fem.	Neut.
Sing.	Nom.	quis?	quis?	quid?	qui	quae	quod	quidam	quaedam	quoddam
	Acc.	quem?	quem?	quid?	quem	quam	quod	quendam	quandam	quoddam
	Gen.	cuius?	cuius?	cuius?	cuius	cuius	cuius	cuiusdam	cuiusdam	cuiusdam
	Dat.	cui?	cui?	cui?	cui	cui	cui	cuidam	cuidam	cuidam
	Abl.	quo?	qua?	quo?	quo	qua	quo	quodam	quadam	quodam
Plur.	Nom.	qui?	quae?	quae?	qui	quae	quae	quidam	quaedam	quaedam
	Acc.	quos?	quas?	quae?	quos	quas	quae	quosdam	quasdam	quaedam
	Gen.	quorum?	quarum?	quorum?	quorum	quarum	quorum	quorundam	quarundam	quorundam
	Dat.	quibus?	quibus?	quibus?	quibus	quibus	quibus	quibusdam	quibusdam	quibusdam
	Abl.	quibus?	quibus?	quibus?	quibus	quibus	quibus	quibusdam	quibusdam	quibusdam

Notes:
1 The Interrogative and Relative Pronouns have the same forms, except in the nominative and accusative singular.

2 The Interrogative Adjective has the same forms as the Relative Pronoun, e.g. **quod** templum visitavisti? **Which** *temple did you visit?*

3 **quidam, quaedam, quoddam** (*a certain*) is a compound of the Relative Pronoun and the ending **-dam**. It has the same forms as the Relative Pronoun, except that **-m-** changes to **-n-** before **-d-**. (Cf. **idem**.) **quidam** is used both as a pronoun and as an adjective, e.g.

quidam advenit. *A* **certain** *man has arrived.*
homines **quosdam** vidimus. *We saw* **some** *men.*

4 **aliquis, aliquis, aliquid** is the usual word for *someone/something*, e.g.
   aliquem misit. *He sent someone.*
   aliquid vini bibimus. *We drank some wine.*

   aliquis has the same forms as **quis, quis, quid**.

5 Words for *anyone/anything* include
   (a) **quisquam, quidquam** (or **quicquam**), used after negatives or **vix** (*scarcely, hardly*), e.g.
       vix **quisquam** venit. *Scarcely anyone came.*
       nec **quidquam** apparuit. *And nothing appeared.*

       The forms are the same as for **quis, quis, quid** followed by the suffix **-quam**.

   (b) **quis, quis, quid**, used after **si, nisi, ne, num, quo, quanto**, e.g.
       si **quis** te viderit, . . . *If anyone sees you, ...*

6 **quisquis, quidquid** means *whoever/whatever*. It has the same forms as **quis, quis, quid** in both parts, e.g.
   quoquo modo, *in whatever way*

   In the neuter, both **quidquid** and **quicquid** are found in the nominative and accusative singular.

7 **quicunque, quaecunque, quodcunque** means *whoever/whatever*. It is a compound of the relative **qui, quae, quod** and the ending **-cunque**, e.g.
   quacunque de re, *for whatever reason*

   cf. **quivis, quaevis, quodvis** } *anyone (anything) you like,*
       quilibet, quaelibet, quodlibet } *any at all*

8 **-nam** is sometimes attached to question words for emphasis, usually to express surprise or incredulity, e.g.
   quisnam? *who (on earth)?* **ubinam?** *where (in the world)?*

149

Section J: Personal Pronouns and Possessive Adjectives

Personal Pronouns

		1st Person	2nd Person
Sing.	Nom.	ego	tu
	Acc.	me	te
	Gen.	mei	tui
	Dat.	mihi	tibi
	Abl.	me	te
Plur.	Nom.	nos	vos
	Acc.	nos	vos
	Gen.	nostrum / nostri	vestrum / vestri
	Dat.	nobis	vobis
	Abl.	nobis	vobis

Possessive Adjectives

1st Person	2nd Person
meus, -a, -um	tuus, -a, -um
noster, nostra, nostrum	vester, vestra, vestrum

Notes:

1 The personal pronouns are used as Reflexive Pronouns in the 1st and 2nd person, e.g. **me** servavi. *I saved* **myself**. **nos** liberavimus. *We set* **ourselves** *free*.

2 A special Reflexive pronoun is used for the 3rd person (singular and plural) meaning *himself, herself, itself, themselves*:

		Possessive Adjective
Acc.	se/sese	
Gen.	sui	suus, -a, -um
Dat.	sibi	
Abl.	se/sese	

3 The preposition **cum** is attached to Personal, Reflexive and Relative Pronouns, e.g. **mecum**, *with me*; **nobiscum**, *with us*; **secum**, *with himself*; **quibuscum**, *with whom*.

4 **nostrum** and **vestrum** are partitive genitives, e.g. **quis vestrum**. *which of you?*

Section K: Numerals

Cardinal numerals are the numbers used in counting: "one," "two," "three," etc.

Ordinal numerals give the order in a series: "first," "second," "third," etc.

		Cardinals	Ordinals
1	I	unus, -a, -um	primus
2	II	duo, duae, duo	secundus
3	III	tres, tres, tria	tertius
4	IV	quattuor	quartus
5	V	quinque	quintus
6	VI	sex	sextus
7	VII	septem	septimus
8	VIII	octo	octavus
9	IX	novem	nonus
10	X	decem	decimus
11	XI	undecim	undecimus
12	XII	duodecim	duodecimus
13	XIII	tredecim	tertius decimus
14	XIV	quattuordecim	quartus decimus
15	XV	quindecim	quintus decimus
16	XVI	sedecim	sextus decimus
17	XVII	septendecim	septimus decimus
18	XVIII	duodeviginti	duodevicesimus
19	XIX	undeviginti	undevicesimus
20	XX	viginti	vicesimus
21	XXI	viginti unus	vicesimus primus
22	XXII	viginti duo	vicesimus secundus
23	XXIII	viginti tres	vicesimus tertius
30	XXX	triginta	tricesimus
40	XL	quadraginta	quadragesimus
50	L	quinquaginta	quinquagesimus
60	LX	sexaginta	sexagesimus
70	LXX	septuaginta	septuagesimus
80	LXXX	octoginta	octogesimus
90	XC	nonaginta	nonagesimus
100	C	centum	centesimus
101	CI	centum (et) unus	centesimus primus
120	CXX	centum (et) viginti	centesimus vicesimus
200	CC	ducenti, -ae, -a	ducentesimus
300	CCC	trecenti, -ae, -a	trecentesimus
400	CCCC	quadringenti, -ae, -a	quadringentesimus
500	D	quingenti, -ae, -a	quingentesimus
600	DC	sescenti, -ae, -a	sescentesimus
700	DCC	septingenti, -ae, -a	septingentesimus
800	DCCC	octingenti, -ae, -a	octingentesimus
900	DCCCC	nongenti, -ae, -a	nongentesimus
1000	M	mille	millesimus
2000	MM	duo milia	bis millesimus

	M.	F.	N.	M.	F.	N.	M./F.	N.
Nom.	unus	una	unum	duo	duae	duo	tres	tria
Acc.	unum	unam	unum	duos	duas	duo	tres	tria
Gen.	unius	unius	unius	duorum	duarum	duorum	trium	trium
Dat.	uni	uni	uni	duobus	duabus	duobus	tribus	tribus
Abl.	uno	una	uno	duobus	duabus	duobus	tribus	tribus

N.B. The genitive and dative endings of **unus** are like **solus, totus**, etc. (See page 143.)

Notes:
(a) Of the cardinals, only the following decline (i.e. change their endings): **unus, duo, tres** (see table opposite); **ducenti** to **nongenti** and **milia** (the plural of **mille**).
(b) The "hundreds" (**ducenti** to **nongenti**) are declined like the plural of **magnus, -a, -um**.
(c) **milia** is a plural noun of Group 3 and is generally followed by the genitive case, e.g. **tria milia servorum**, *3000 slaves*.
(d) All the ordinals are declined like **magnus, -a, -um**.

Section L: Verbs

(a) *Principal Parts*

When we refer to Latin verbs, we normally give four principal parts, e.g.

	Present	Present Infinitive	Perfect Active	Supine	Meaning
Group 1	porto	portare (1)	portavi	portatum	to carry
Group 2	habeo	habere (2)	habui	habitum	to have
Group 3	mitto	mittere (3)	misi	missum	to send
Group 4	audio	audire (4)	audivi	auditum	to hear

Most verbs in Groups 1, 2 and 4 follow the above patterns. There is no standard form for the verbs in Group 3. This section will help you if you know which verb you are dealing with but are in some doubt about the form used.

All parts of the verb can be identified from the four principal parts. The following table of the verb **portare** illustrates this:

Principal Parts	**porto, portare**(1) Present stem: **porta-**		**portavi** Perfect stem: **portav-**		**portatum** Supine stem: **portat-**	
Indicative	*Active* Present porto Imperf. portabam Future portabo	*Passive* portor portabar portabor	Perfect Pluperf. Fut. Perf.	*Active* portavi portaveram portavero	Perfect Pluperf. Fut. Perf.	*Active* — — —	*Passive* portatus sum portatus eram portatus ero
Subjunctive	Present portem Imperf. portarem	porter portarer	Perfect Pluperf.	portaverim portavissem	Perfect Pluperf.	— —	portatus sim portatus essem
Infinitive	Present portare	portari	Perfect	portavisse	Perfect Future	— portaturus esse	portatus esse portatum iri
Participle	Present portans	—	—	—	Perfect Future	— portaturus	portatus —
Imperative	Present porta portate	portare portamini	—	—	—	—	—

(b) *Person Endings*

		Active		Passive	
		All tenses except Perfect	Perfect	Present Imperfect Future	Perfect Pluperfect Future Perf.
Sing.	1	**-o, -m**	**-i**	**-r**	See Note (c)
	2	**-s**	**-isti**	**-ris**	
	3	**-t**	**-it**	**-tur**	
Plur.	1	**-mus**	**-imus**	**-mur**	
	2	**-tis**	**-istis**	**-mini**	
	3	**-nt**	**-erunt**	**-ntur**	

(c) *Agreement of Subject and Verb*

In the Perfect, Pluperfect and Future Perfect tenses Passive, the perfect participle passive (**-us, -a, -um**) agrees with the subject of the verb in gender, number and case, e.g.

puer laudat**us** est.	*The boy has been (was) praised.*
matres laudat**ae** sunt.	*The mothers have been (were) praised.*
aedificium laudat**um** est.	*The building has been (was) praised.*

(d) *Meanings of Tenses*

Tense	Active	Passive
Present	**portat**, *he carries, is carrying*	**portatur**, *he is carried, is being carried*
Imperfect	**portabat**, *he carried he kept carrying he was carrying he used to carry he began to carry he tried to carry*	**portabatur**, *he was carried he was being carried he used to be carried he kept being carried*
Future	**portabit**, *he will carry*	**portabitur**, *he will be carried*
Perfect	**portavit**, *he carried he has carried*	**portatus est**, *he was carried he has been carried*
Pluperfect	**portaverat**, *he had carried*	**portatus erat**, *he had been carried*
Future Perfect	**portaverit**, *he will have carried*	**portatus erit**, *he will have been carried*

ACTIVE

Indicative

Group	Present	Imperfect	Future	Perfect	Pluperfect	Future Perfect
1	porto portas portat portamus portatis portant	portabam portabas portabat portabamus portabatis portabant	portabo portabis portabit portabimus portabitis portabunt	portavi portavisti portavit portavimus portavistis portaverunt	portaveram portaveras portaverat portaveramus portaveratis portaverant	portavero portaveris portaverit portaverimus portaveritis portaverint
2	habeo habes habet habemus habetis habent	habebam habebas habebat habebamus habebatis habebant	habebo habebis habebit habebimus habebitis habebunt	habui habuisti habuit habuimus habuistis habuerunt	habueram habueras habuerat habueramus habueratis habuerant	habuero habueris habuerit habuerimus habueritis habuerint
3	mitto mittis mittit mittimus mittitis mittunt	mittebam mittebas mittebat mittebamus mittebatis mittebant	mittam mittes mittet mittemus mittetis mittent	misi misisti misit misimus misistis miserunt	miseram miseras miserat miseramus miseratis miserant	misero miseris miserit miserimus miseritis miserint
	capio capis capit capimus capitis capiunt	capiebam capiebas capiebat capiebamus capiebatis capiebant	capiam capies capiet capiemus capietis capient	cepi cepisti cepit cepimus cepistis ceperunt	ceperam ceperas ceperat ceperamus ceperatis ceperant	cepero ceperis ceperit ceperimus ceperitis ceperint
4	audio audis audit audimus auditis audiunt	audiebam audiebas audiebat audiebamus audiebatis audiebant	audiam audies audiet audiemus audietis audient	audivi audivisti audivit audivimus audivistis audiverunt	audiveram audiveras audiverat audiveramus audiveratis audiverant	audivero audiveris audiverit audiverimus audiveritis audiverint

Notes:
1 The 3rd person plural of the Perfect Tense often ends in **-ere** instead of **-erunt**, e.g. **portavere** = **portaverunt**.
2 Contracted forms are found in the Perfect and Pluperfect, e.g. **portasti** = **portavisti**; **amassem** = **amavissem**; **servasse** = **servavisse**; **amarat** = **amaverat**.

ACTIVE

Subjunctive

Group	Present	Imperfect	Perfect	Pluperfect
1	portem portes portet portemus portetis portent	portarem portares portaret portaremus portaretis portarent	portaverim portaveris portaverit portaverimus portaveritis portaverint	portavissem portavisses portavisset portavissemus portavissetis portavissent
2	habeam habeas habeat habeamus habeatis habeant	haberem haberes haberet haberemus haberetis haberent	habuerim habueris habuerit habuerimus habueritis habuerint	habuissem habuisses habuisset habuissemus habuissetis habuissent
3	mittam mittas mittat mittamus mittatis mittant	mitterem mitteres mitteret mitteremus mitteretis mitterent	miserim miseris miserit miserimus miseritis miserint	misissem misisses misisset misissemus misissetis misissent
	capiam capias capiat capiamus capiatis capiant	caperem caperes caperet caperemus caperetis caperent	ceperim ceperis ceperit ceperimus ceperitis ceperint	cepissem cepisses cepisset cepissemus cepissetis cepissent
4	audiam audias audiat audiamus audiatis audiant	audirem audires audiret audiremus audiretis audirent	audiverim audiveris audiverit audiverimus audiveritis audiverint	audivissem audivisses audivisset audivissemus audivissetis audivissent

PASSIVE

Indicative

Group	Present	Imperfect	Future
1	portor portaris portatur portamur portamini portantur	portabar portabaris portabatur portabamur portabamini portabantur	portabor portaberis portabitur portabimur portabimini portabuntur
2	habeor haberis habetur habemur habemini habentur	habebar habebaris habebatur habebamur habebamini habebantur	habebor habeberis habebitur habebimur habebimini habebuntur
3	mittor mitteris mittitur mittimur mittimini mittuntur	mittebar mittebaris mittebatur mittebamur mittebamini mittebantur	mittar mitteris mittetur mittemur mittemini mittentur
	capior caperis capitur capimur capimini capiuntur	capiebar capiebaris capiebatur capiebamur capiebamini capiebantur	capiar capieris capietur capiemur capiemini capientur
4	audior audiris auditur audimur audimini audiuntur	audiebar audiebaris audiebatur audiebamur audiebamini audiebantur	audiar audieris audietur audiemur audiemini audientur

Perfect	Pluperfect	Future Perfect
portatus sum portatus es portatus est portati sumus portati estis portati sunt	portatus eram portatus eras portatus erat portati eramus portati eratis portati erant	portatus ero portatus eris portatus erit portati erimus portati eritis portati erunt
habitus sum habitus es habitus est habiti sumus habiti estis habiti sunt	habitus eram habitus eras habitus erat habiti eramus habiti eratis habiti erant	habitus ero habitus eris habitus erit habiti erimus habiti eritis habiti erunt
missus sum missus es missus est missi sumus missi estis missi sunt	missus eram missus eras missus erat missi eramus missi eratis missi erant	missus ero missus eris missus erit missi erimus missi eritis missi erunt
captus sum captus es captus est capti sumus capti estis capti sunt	captus eram captus eras captus erat capti eramus capti eratis capti erant	captus ero captus eris captus erit capti erimus capti eritis capti erunt
auditus sum auditus es auditus est auditi sumus auditi estis auditi sunt	auditus eram auditus eras auditus erat auditi eramus auditi eratis auditi erant	auditus ero auditus eris auditus erit auditi erimus auditi eritis auditi erunt

Note: In the 2nd person singular, the ending **-re** is sometimes used instead of **-ris**, e.g. **mittere = mitteris**.

PASSIVE

Subjunctive

Group	Present	Imperfect	Perfect	Pluperfect
1	porter porteris portetur portemur portemini portentur	portarer portareris portaretur portaremur portaremini portarentur	portatus sim portatus sis portatus sit portati simus portati sitis portati sint	portatus essem portatus esses portatus esset portati essemus portati essetis portati essent
2	habear habearis habeatur habeamur habeamini habeantur	haberer habereris haberetur haberemur haberemini haberentur	habitus sim habitus sis habitus sit habiti simus habiti sitis habiti sint	habitus essem habitus esses habitus esset habiti essemus habiti essetis habiti essent
3	mittar mittaris mittatur mittamur mittamini mittantur	mitterer mittereris mitteretur mitteremur mitteremini mitterentur	missus sim missus sis missus sit missi simus missi sitis missi sint	missus essem missus esses missus esset missi essemus missi essetis missi essent
	capiar capiaris capiatur capiamur capiamini capiantur	caperer capereris caperetur caperemur caperemini caperentur	captus sim captus sis captus sit capti simus capti sitis capti sint	captus essem captus esses captus esset capti essemus capti essetis capti essent
4	audiar audiaris audiatur audiamur audiamini audiantur	audirer audireris audiretur audiremur audiremini audirentur	auditus sim auditus sis auditus sit auditi simus auditi sitis auditi sint	auditus essem auditus esses auditus esset auditi essemus auditi essetis auditi essent

ACTIVE

	Participle	Infinitive	Imperative
Present	port**ans**	port**are**	port**a** port**ate**
Future	portat**urus**	portat**urus esse**	—
Perfect	—	porta**visse**	—
Present	hab**ens**	hab**ere**	hab**e** hab**ete**
Future	habit**urus**	habit**urus esse**	—
Perfect	—	habu**isse**	—
Present	mitt**ens**	mitt**ere**	mitt**e** mitt**ite**
Future	miss**urus**	miss**urus esse**	—
Perfect	—	mis**isse**	—
Present	capi**ens**	cap**ere**	cap**e** cap**ite**
Future	capt**urus**	capt**urus esse**	—
Perfect	—	cep**isse**	—
Present	audi**ens**	aud**ire**	aud**i** aud**ite**
Future	audit**urus**	audit**urus esse**	—
Perfect	—	audi**visse**	—

Note the following irregular imperatives:
- **duc, ducite,** *lead!*
- **scito, scitote,** *know!*
- **dic, dicite,** *say!*
- **fac, facite,** *do!*

158

PASSIVE

	Participle	Infinitive	Imperative
Present	—	port**ari**	port**are**
			port**amini**
Future	—	portat**um iri**	—
Perfect	portat**us**	portat**us esse**	—
Present	—	hab**eri**	hab**ere**
			hab**emini**
Future	—	habit**um iri**	—
Perfect	habit**us**	habit**us esse**	—
Present	—	mitt**i**	mitt**ere**
			mitt**imini**
Future	—	miss**um iri**	—
Perfect	miss**us**	miss**us esse**	—
Present	—	cap**i**	cap**ere**
			cap**imini**
Future	—	capt**um iri**	—
Perfect	capt**us**	capt**us esse**	—
Present	—	aud**iri**	aud**ire**
			aud**imini**
Future	—	audit**um iri**	—
Perfect	audit**us**	audit**us esse**	—

Gerund   **Gerundive**

Acc. porta**nd**um   porta**nd**us, -a, -um
Gen. porta**nd**i   habe**nd**us, -a, -um
Dat. porta**nd**o   mitte**nd**us, -a, -um
Abl. porta**nd**o   capie**nd**us, -a, -um
                         audie**nd**us, -a, -um

Compare:
habe**nd**um
mitte**nd**um
capie**nd**um
audie**nd**um

IRREGULAR VERBS

Indicative

	Present	Imperfect	Future	Perfect	Pluperfect	Future Perfect
esse	sum es est sumus estis sunt	eram eras erat eramus eratis erant	ero eris erit erimus eritis erunt	fui fuisti fuit fuimus fuistis fuerunt	fueram fueras fuerat fueramus fueratis fuerant	fuero fueris fuerit fuerimus fueritis fuerint
posse	possum potes potest possumus potestis possunt	poteram poteras poterat poteramus poteratis poterant	potero poteris poterit poterimus poteritis poterunt	potui potuisti potuit potuimus potuistis potuerunt	potueram potueras potuerat potueramus potueratis potuerant	potuero potueris potuerit potuerimus potueritis potuerint
velle	volo vis vult volumus vultis volunt	volebam volebas volebat volebamus volebatis volebant	volam voles volet volemus voletis volent	volui voluisti voluit voluimus voluistis voluerunt	volueram volueras voluerat volueramus volueratis voluerant	voluero volueris voluerit voluerimus volueritis voluerint
nolle	nolo nonvis nonvult nolumus nonvultis nolunt	nolebam nolebas nolebat nolebamus nolebatis nolebant	nolam noles nolet nolemus noletis nolent	nolui noluisti noluit noluimus noluistis noluerunt	nolueram nolueras noluerat nolueramus nolueratis noluerant	noluero nolueris noluerit noluerimus nolueritis noluerint
malle	malo mavis mavult malumus mavultis malunt	malebam malebas malebat malebamus malebatis malebant	malam males malet malemus maletis malent	malui maluisti maluit maluimus maluistis maluerunt	malueram malueras maluerat malueramus malueratis maluerant	maluero malueris maluerit maluerimus malueritis maluerint

Although these are called Irregular Verbs, they have many features in common with regular verbs:
(a) the person endings;
(b) the Perfect, Pluperfect and Future Perfect are regular;

Subjunctive

	Present	Imperfect	Perfect	Pluperfect
esse	sim sis sit simus sitis sint	essem esses esset essemus essetis essent	fuerim fueris fuerit fuerimus fueritis fuerint	fuissem fuisses fuisset fuissemus fuissetis fuissent

	Participle	Infinitive	Imperative
Pres.	—	esse	es este
Fut.	futurus	futurus esse*	—
Perf.	—	fuisse	—

	Present	Imperfect	Perfect	Pluperfect
posse	possim possis possit possimus possitis possint	possem posses posset possemus possetis possent	potuerim potueris potuerit potuerimus potueritis potuerint	potuissem potuisses potuisset potuissemus potuissetis potuissent

	Participle	Infinitive	Imperative
Pres.	—	posse	—
Fut.	—	—	—
Perf.	—	potuisse	—

*__fore__ is an alternative form of __futurus esse__ in all of its forms.

	Present	Imperfect	Perfect	Pluperfect
velle	velim velis velit velimus velitis velint	vellem velles vellet vellemus velletis vellent	voluerim volueris voluerit voluerimus volueritis voluerint	voluissem voluisses voluisset voluissemus voluissetis voluissent

	Participle	Infinitive	Imperative
Pres.	volens	velle	—
Fut.	—	—	—
Perf.	—	voluisse	—

	Present	Imperfect	Perfect	Pluperfect
nolle	nolim nolis nolit nolimus nolitis nolint	nollem nolles nollet nollemus nolletis nollent	noluerim nolueris noluerit noluerimus nolueritis noluerint	noluissem noluisses noluisset noluissemus noluissetis noluissent

	Participle	Infinitive	Imperative
Pres.	nolens	nolle	noli nolite
Fut.	—	—	—
Perf.	—	noluisse	—

	Present	Imperfect	Perfect	Pluperfect
malle	malim malis malit malimus malitis malint	mallem malles mallet mallemus malletis mallent	maluerim malueris maluerit maluerimus malueritis maluerint	maluissem maluisses maluisset maluissemus maluissetis maluissent

	Participle	Infinitive	Imperative
Pres.	—	malle	—
Fut.	—	—	—
Perf.	—	maluisse	—

(c) the Imperfect Subjunctive is formed from the Present Infinitive and the person endings;
(d) the Imperfect Indicative **-bam, -bas, -bat**, etc. is regular; (**-ram, -ras, -rat**, etc. in the verb **esse** is not unlike this);
(e) **-ro, -ris, -rit**, etc. in the verb **esse** is not unlike **-bo, -bis, -bit**, etc.
(f) **noli, nolite** + infinitive = *don't*.........., e.g. **noli abire.** *Don't go away.*

Indicative

	Present	Imperfect	Future
ire	eo is it **imus** itis eu**nt**	ibam ibas ibat ibamus ibatis ibant	ibo ibis ibit ibimus ibitis ibu**nt**

Perfect	Pluperfect	Future Perfect
iv**i** iv**isti** iv**it** iv**imus** iv**istis** iv**erunt**	iveram iveras iverat iveramus iveratis iverant	iver**o** iver**is** iver**it** iverimus iver**itis** iver**int**

	Present	Imperfect	Future
fieri	fio fis fit (fi**mus**) (fi**tis**) fiu**nt**	fie**bam** fie**bas** fie**bat** fie**bamus** fie**batis** fie**bant**	fiam fies fiet fiemus fietis fient

Perfect	Pluperfect	Future Perfect
factus sum factus es factus est facti sumus facti estis facti sunt	factus eram factus eras factus erat facti eramus facti eratis facti erant	factus ero factus eris factus erit facti erimus facti eritis facti erunt

Subjunctive

	Present	Imperfect
ire	eam eas eat eamus eatis eant	**ir**em **ir**es **ir**et **ir**emus **ir**etis **ir**ent

Perfect	Pluperfect
iverim iveris iverit iverimus iveritis iverint	ivissem ivisses ivisset ivissemus ivissetis ivissent

	Participle	Infinitive	Imperative
Pres.	iens, euntis	ire	i ite
Fut.	it**urus**	it**urus esse**	—
Perf.	—	iv**isse**	—

	Present	Imperfect
fieri	fiam fias fiat fiamus fiatis fiant	fierem fieres fieret fieremus fieretis fierent

Perfect	Pluperfect
factus sim factus sis factus sit facti simus facti sitis facti sint	factus essem factus esses factus esset facti essemus facti essetis facti essent

	Participle	Infinitive	Imperative
Pres.	—	fieri	—
Fut.	—	fact**um iri**	—
Perf.	fact**us**	fact**us esse**	—

ACTIVE
Indicative

	Present	Imperfect	Future
ferre	fero fers fert	ferebam ferebas ferebat	feram feres feret
	ferimus fertis ferunt	ferebamus ferebatis ferebant	feremus feretis ferent

Perfect	Pluperfect	Future Perfect
tuli tulisti tulit	tuleram tuleras tulerat	tulero tuleris tulerit
tulimus tulistis tulerunt	tuleramus tuleratis tulerant	tulerimus tuleritis tulerint

Subjunctive

Present	Imperfect	Perfect	Pluperfect
feram feras ferat	ferrem ferres ferret	tulerim tuleris tulerit	tulissem tulisses tulisset
feramus feratis ferant	ferremus ferretis ferrent	tulerimus tuleritis tulerint	tulissemus tulissetis tulissent

	Participle	Infinitive	Imperative
Pres.	ferens	ferre	fer ferte
Fut.	laturus	laturus esse	—
Perf.	—	tulisse	—

PASSIVE
Indicative

Present	Imperfect	Future
feror ferris fertur	ferebar ferebaris ferebatur	ferar fereris feretur
ferimur ferimini feruntur	ferebamur ferebamini ferebantur	feremur feremini ferentur

Perfect	Pluperfect	Future Perfect
latus sum latus es latus est	latus eram latus eras latus erat	latus ero latus eris latus erit
lati sumus lati estis lati sunt	lati eramus lati eratis lati erant	lati erimus lati eritis lati erunt

Subjunctive

Present	Imperfect
ferar feraris feratur	ferrer ferreris ferretur
feramur feramini ferantur	ferremur ferremini ferrentur

Perfect	Pluperfect
latus sim latus sis latus sit	latus essem latus esses latus esset
lati simus lati sitis lati sint	lati essemus lati essetis lati essent

	Participle	Infinitive	Imperative
Pres.	—	ferri	ferre ferimini
Fut.	—	latum iri	—
Perf.	latus	latus esse	—

DEPONENT VERBS

These verbs have mainly *passive* forms but *active* meanings.
There are only *three* principal parts, e.g.

Present	Infinitive	Perfect	Meaning
mor**or**	mor**ari**	mor**atus sum**	to delay
sequ**or**	sequ**i**	sec**utus sum**	to follow

Indicative

| Present
Imperfect
Future | sequ**or**
sequ**ebar**
sequ**ar** | I follow
I was following
I shall follow | Perfect
Pluperfect
Fut. Perf. | sec**utus sum**
sec**utus eram**
sec**utus ero** | I have followed
I had followed
I shall have followed |

Subjunctive

Present Imperfect	sequ**ar** sequ**erer**

Perfect Pluperfect	sec**utus sim** sec**utus essem**

Participle

| Present
Future
Perfect | sequ**ens**
sec**uturus**
sec**utus** | following
about to follow
having followed |

Infinitive

| Present
Future
Perfect | sequ**i**
sec**uturus esse**
sec**utus esse** | to follow
to be about to follow
to have followed |

Imperative

sequ**ere** sequ**imini** } follow!

SEMI-DEPONENT VERBS

A few verbs are deponent only in the perfect, pluperfect and future perfect tenses. These are called semi-deponent verbs.

audeo	audere (2)	ausus sum	*to dare*
gaudeo	gaudere (2)	gavisus sum	*to be glad*
soleo	solere (2)	solitus sum	*to be accustomed*
fido	fidere (3)	fisus sum	*to trust*
confido	confidere (3)	confisus sum	*to trust*
diffido	diffidere (3)	diffisus sum	*to distrust*

DEFECTIVE VERBS

Defective verbs have no present, imperfect or future forms. These tenses are supplied by the perfect, pluperfect and future perfect.

Indicative

memini	I remember	odi	I hate	novi	I know
memineram	I remembered	oderam	I hated	noveram	I knew
meminero	I shall remember	odero	I shall hate	novero	I shall know

Subjunctive

meminerim	oderim	noverim
meminissem	odissem	novissem

Participle

—	osurus about to hate	—

Infinitive

meminisse to remember	odisse to hate	novisse to know

Imperative

memento } remember! mementote

A Simplified Guide to Pronunciation

Consonants

Most consonants are pronounced as in English, but the following should be noted:

b before **s** or **t** is pronounced as English *p*: **urbs**.
c is always hard and pronounced as English *k*: **cibus**.
g is hard, as in English "get": **gemit**.
gn in the middle of a word is pronounced as the *ngn* in English "hangnail": **magnus**.
i before a vowel is a consonant and pronounced as English *y*: **ianua**.
r should be rolled: **ramus**.
s is pronounced as in English "sing", never as in "roses": **civis**.
t is always hard as in "take", never soft as in "nation": **taceo**.
v is pronounced as English *w*: **villa**.

Vowels and Diphthongs

The following approximations are offered for the pronunciation of short and long vowels. In addition, long vowels should be held for a longer time than short ones.

SHORT
a = English "aha!" (first "a") (**pater**)
e = English "pet" (**ego**)
i = English "skit" (**iterum**)
o = English "for" (**omnēs**)
u = English "put" (**ubi**)

LONG
ā = English "aha!" (second "a") (**māter**)
ē = English "they" (**dēscendō**)
ī = English "ski" (**īra**)
ō = English "holy" (**in hortō**)
ū = English "true" (**ūnus**)

The diphthong **ae** is pronounced as the *y* in English "sky" (**amicae**).
The diphthong **au** is pronounced as the *ow* in English "how" (**audit**).
The diphthong **ei** is pronounced as the *ay* in English "say" (**deinde**).

Stress Accent

When Latin was spoken, certain syllables were stressed. The following is the general rule for deciding where the stress should fall:

(a) In a word of two syllables, the accent is on the first syllable, e.g. **ámo** and **únus**.
(b) In a word of more than two syllables,
  (i) the stress falls on the second last syllable if that syllable contains a long vowel or a short vowel followed by two consonants, e.g. **amátis** and **deféssus**;
  (ii) otherwise the stress falls on the third last syllable, e.g. **celériter** and **sollícitus**.

Medieval Latin

It is not easy to reconstruct the pronunciation of Medieval Latin with any certainty. Indeed, it probably varied from area to area and it is likely that in each particular area it was pronounced very much like the emergent Romance language there. It must be remembered that it is only in fairly recent times that any internationally accepted pronunciation of Classical Latin has become current among scholars. In the Middle Ages, only the Church exercised any standardising influence; and, since the Church was Rome-centred, that standard tended to be Italian-based. Ecclesiastical Latin pronunciation is fairly similar to that of Classical Latin, apart from the following features:

1 c (before **a**, **o** or **u**) is pronounced 'k' as in English 'came' (i.e. the same as Classical Latin).
c (before **e** or **i**) is pronounced 'ch' as in English 'church', e.g. **in excelsis** sounds like *een ex-chel-sees*; **celum** (= **caelum**) **is pronounced** *chay-loom*.
c (replacing a **t** in Classical Latin) is pronounced 'ts' as in the Italian/English word pizza, e.g. **gratia** becomes **gracia**, pronounced *grah-tsee-ah*.

2 g (before **a**, **o** or **u**) is pronounced 'g' as in English 'good', (i.e. the same as Classical Latin).
g (before **e** or **i**) is pronounced 'j' as in English 'jury', e.g. **spargens** sounds like *spar-jens*.

3 sc (before **a**, **o** or **u**) is pronounced 'sk' as in English 'skill', (i.e. the same as Classical Latin).
sc (before **e** or **i**) is pronounced 'sh' as in English 'sheep', e.g. **suscipe** sounds like *soo-shee-pay*; **nescio** is pronounced *nay-shee-oh*.

4 ae and oe become e and are pronounced 'ay' as in English 'bay' or 'prey', e.g. **suae** becomes **sue** and sounds like *soo-ay*, and **coepit** becomes **cepit** and sounds like *chay-pit*.

5 gn is pronounced 'ny' as in French 'magnifique' or like the sond in the middle of the English word 'canyon', e.g. **Agnus Dei** sounds like *An-yoos Day-ee*.

6 i is pronounced 'ee' as in English 'keep', e.g. **civis** sounds like *chee-vees*.

Vocabulary

A

a, ab (+ *abl.*), by, from, away from
  a fronte, at the front, in front
  a tergo, in the rear, from behind
abbas, -atis (*m*), abbot
abeo, -ire, -ii, -itum, to go away, leave
abhinc (+ *acc.*), ago
abicio (3), **-ieci, -iectum**, to throw away
abies, -ietis (*f*), fir-tree
abripio (3), **-ripui, -reptum**, to carry off
absorbeo (2), to devour
abstineo (2), **-tinui, -tentum**, to refrain from
abstuli, see **aufero**
absum, abesse, afui, to be distant from, absent
absumo (3), **-sumpsi, -sumptum**, to take away, destroy
ac, and, as
accedo (3), **-cessi, -cessum**, to approach
accidit (3), **accidit**, it happens
accipio (3), **-cepi, -ceptum**, to receive, take, suffer, welcome
accurate, carefully
accuso (1), to accuse
acer, acris, acre, fierce, keen
acies, -ei (*f*), line of battle, battle
acriter, fiercely, eagerly
ad (+ *acc.*), to, up to, until, at, towards, for, with a view to
adeo, to such a degree, so much, so
adequito (1), to gallop up to
adgredior, see **aggredior**
adhibeo (2), to employ, apply
adhuc, still, as yet, hitherto
adimo (3), **-emi, -emptum** (+ *dat.*), to take away (from)
adiuvo (1), **-iuvi, -iutum**, to help
administro (1), to carry out, perform, administer
admirationi esse (+ *dat.*), to be a cause of wonder/amazement (to)
admiror (1), to admire, wonder at
admitto (3), **-misi, -missum**, to commit
adstantes, -ium (*m.pl*), bystanders
adsum, adesse, adfui, to be present, be near
adulescens, -entis (*m*), young man
advenio (4), **-veni, -ventum**, to come to, reach, arrive
adventus, -us (*m*), arrival
adversus (+ *acc.*), against
adversus, -a, -um, facing, opposite, from the front
  adverso flumine, upstream
advesperascit (3), **-avit**, it grows dark
aedificium, -i (*n*), building
aedifico (1), to build
aedilis, -is (*m*), aedile (Roman magistrate)
aeger, aegra, aegrum, ill, sick
aegroto (1), to be ill
Aeneas, -ae (*m*) (*acc.* **Aenean**), Aeneas, leader of the exiled Trojans
Aeolia, -ae (*f*), Aeolia (island home of king of the winds)
Aeolus, -i (*m*), Aeolus (king of the winds)
aeque, equally
aequor, -oris (*n*), an even surface, the sea
aequus, -a, -um, equal, fair, equitable, level, calm
aes, aeris (*n*), bronze

aestas, -atis (*f*), summer
aestimo (1), to estimate, value, judge
aestuarium, -i (*n*), estuary
aetas, -atis (*f*), age
affero, -ferre, attuli, allatum, to bring
afficio (3), **-feci, -fectum**, to affect, treat, inflict
affirmo (1), to declare
affligo (3), **-flixi, -flictum**, to throw down, cast down
Africa, -ae (*f*), Africa (Roman province roughly equivalent to modern Tunisia and Libya)
ager, agri (*m*), field, territory, land
aggredior (3), **-gressus sum**, to attack
agmen, -inis (*n*), line of march, column (of people)
ago (3), **egi, actum**, to do, carry, drive, carry off, spend (time), discuss
  gratias agere (+ *dat.*), to thank
agrestis, -is, -e, wild, rustic
agricola, -ae (*m*), farmer
Albanus, -a, -um, belonging to the town of Alba
albus, -a, -um, white
Alexandria, -ae (*f*), Alexandria (capital of Roman province of Egypt)
aliquamdiu, for a while, for some time
aliquando, at some time or other, at long last, at times
aliquantulum, a little
aliquis, -quis, -quid, someone, something
alligo (1), to tie to, bind to
alloquor (3), **-locutus sum**, to speak to, address
almus, -a, -um, kindly
Alpes, -ium (*f.pl*), the Alps
alter, -era, -erum, the one, the other, the second
altum, -i (*n*), deep water, the deep
altus, -a, -um, high, deep
amans, -antis, loving
Ambiorix, -igis (*m*), Ambiorix (Gallic leader)
Ambraciensis, -is, -e, from Ambracia (a town in Epirus)
ambulo (1), to walk
amicitia, -ae (*f*), friendship
amicus, -i (*m*), friend
amitto (3), **-misi, -missum**, to lose
amo (1), to love, like

amor, -oris (*m*), love
amplifico (1), to enlarge, extend
amplius, more, more than
Amulius, -i (*m*), Amulius (king of Alba Longa)
an, whether, if, or, (or just indicating a question)
ancilla, -ae (*f*), female slave, maidservant
ancora, -ae (*f*), anchor
  in ancoris, at anchor
anguis, -is (*m*), snake
angustio (1), to distress
angustus, -a, -um, narrow
anima, -ae (*f*), breath, soul
animadverto (3), **-verti, -versum**, to notice
animus, -i (*m*), mind, spirit, will
  in animo habere, to intend
annon, or not
annus, -i (*m*), year
ante (+ *acc.*), before, in front of
ante (*adverb*), before, previously
antea, before, previously
antefero, -ferre, -tuli, -latum, to put before
antequam, before
antiquus, -a, -um, ancient
antrum, -i (*n*), cave
aperio (4), **-ui, apertum**, to open
appareo (2), to appear
appropinquo (1) (+ *dat.*), to approach, draw near (to)
Aprilis, -is, -e, April, of April
apud (+ *acc.*), among, at the house of
aqua, -ae (*f*), water
aquila, -ae (*f*), eagle, standard
Aquilo, -onis (*m*), North Wind
Aquitania, -ae (*f*), Aquitania (region in south-west Gaul)
ara, -ae (*f*), altar
arbitror (1), to think, consider
arbor, -oris (*f*), tree
arcesso (3), **-ivi, -itum**, to send for, summon
arduus, -a, -um, steep, difficult
arena, -ae (*f*), sand, arena
argentum, -i (*n*), silver
Ariovistus, -i (*m*), Ariovistus (German chief)
arma, -orum (*n.pl*), arms, weapons
arripio (3), **-ui, -reptum**, to seize
ars, artis (*f*), art, skill
artus, -us (*m*), limb
as, assis (*m*), an **as** (least valuable of the Roman coins)

ascendo (3), **-scendi, -scensum,** to climb
Asia, -ae (*f*), Asia (Roman province, roughly western half of Turkey)
aspernor (1), to despise
asporto (1), to take away
asto (1), to stand
astralabium, -i (*n*), astrolabe
astrologus, -i (*m*), astrologer
astronomus, -i (*m*), astronomer, astrologer
at, but
Atalanta, -ae (*f*), Atalanta (king's daughter who was a very fast runner)
Athenae, -arum (*f.pl*), Athens
atque, and
atrium, -i (*n*), hall
atrox, -ocis, fierce, severe, dreadful
attendo (3), **-di, -tum,** to realise
attingo (3), **-tigi, -tactum,** to touch, reach, border on
auctor, -oris (*m*), author, instigator
auctoritas, -atis (*f*), authority, influence
audacia, -ae (*f*), daring, courage
audeo (2), **ausus sum,** to dare
audio (4), to hear, listen, listen to
auditus, -us (*m*), hearing
aufero, -ferre, abstuli, ablatum, to take away
aufugio (3), **-fugi,** to run away
augmentum, -i (*n*), growth, increase
Augustus, -i (*m*), Augustus (first emperor of Rome, earlier called Octavian)
auris, -is (*f*), ear
aurum, -i (*n*), gold
aut, or
  aut ... aut ..., either ... or ...
autem, however, but, now
auxilia, -orum (*n.pl*), reinforcements
auxilium, -i (*n*), help, assistance
  auxilio esse (+ *dat.*), to be of assistance (to), help
averto (3), **-verti, -versum,** to turn away
avis, -is (*f*), bird
avunculus, -i (*m*), uncle
avus, -i (*m*), grandfather
Axona, -ae (*f*), the River Aisne (in north-east France)

——————— B ———————

baculum, -i (*n*), stick
Baiae, -arum (*f.pl*), Baiae (town near Naples)
balneum, -i (*n*), bath
barba, -ae (*f*), beard
barbarus, -i (*m*), barbarian; (*pl*) the natives
beatus, -a, -um, happy
Belgae, -arum (*m.pl*), the Belgae (Gallic tribe)
bellum, -i (*n*), war
  bellum gerere, to wage war
bene, well
  rem bene gerere, to be successful
beneficium, -i (*n*), act of kindness, favour
bestia, -ae (*f*), wild beast
bibo (3), **bibi,** to drink
biduum, -i (*n*), (period of) two days
Bithynia, -ae (*f*), Bithynia (Roman province in north of Turkey)
bona, -orum (*n.pl*), goods, possessions
boni, -orum (*m.pl*), the good (citizens), patriots
bonus, -a, -um, good
  bono esse (+ *dat.*), to be of advantage (to), benefit
brevis, -is, -e, short
  brevi (tempore), in a short time
Britanni, -orum (*m.pl*), the Britons
Britannia, -ae (*f*), Britain
Britannicus, -a, -um, British
Brundisium, -i (*n*), Brindisi (port in heel of Italy)

——————— C ———————

cachinnus, -i (*m*), loud laugh, guffaw
cado (3), **cecidi, casum,** to fall
caecus, -a, -um, blind
caedo (3), **cecidi, caesum,** to kill
caelum, -i (*n*), heaven, sky
caeruleus, -a, -um, dark-blue, dark
Caesar, -aris (*m*), Julius Caesar (general, politician and, latterly, dictator)
calidus, -a, -um, hot, warm
calor, -oris (*m*), heat
calvus, -a, -um, bald
Campania, -ae (*f*), Campania (area near Naples)
campus, -i (*m*), plain

candidus, -a, -um, white, fair
canis, -is (*m*), dog
Cannae, -arum (*f.pl*), Cannae (village in Apulia)
Cantium, -i (*n*), Kent
canto (1), to sing
cantus, -us (*m*), singing
canus, -a, -um, white, grey
capillus, -i (*m*), hair
capio (3), **cepi, captum,** to take, capture, seize
  consilium capere, to adopt a plan
Capitolium, -i (*n*), the Capitol (on the Capitoline Hill)
Capreae, -arum (*f.pl*), Capri (island off Bay of Naples)
captivus, -i (*m*), prisoner
Capua, -ae (*f*), Capua (chief city of Campania)
caput, -itis (*n*), head
  capitis damnare, to condemn to death
carcer, -eris (*m*), prison
carmen, -inis (*n*), song, hymn, poem
carneus, -a, -um, of flesh, of meat
caro, carnis (*f*), meat
Carthaginienses, -ium (*m.pl*), the Carthaginians
Carthago, -inis (*f*), Carthage
carus, -a, -um, dear, precious, esteemed
castitas, -atis (*f*), purity, chastity
Castor, -oris (*m*), Castor (twin brother of Pollux)
castra, -orum (*n.pl*), camp
  castra ponere, to pitch camp
Catilina, -ae (*m*), Catiline (a Roman who plotted revolution)
Cato, -onis (*m*), Cato (a stern judge of morals)
caupo, -onis (*m*), innkeeper
caupona, -ae (*f*), inn
causa, -ae (*f*), cause, reason
causa (+ *gen.*), for the sake of
cautus, -a, -um, careful, cautious
cecidi, see **cado** and **caedo**
cedo (3), **cessi, cessum,** to yield, give way, withdraw, move back
celer, celeris, celere, swift
celeritas, -atis (*f*), speed
celeriter, quickly
celsus, -a, -um, high
cena, -ae (*f*), dinner
ceno (1), to dine
centum, hundred

centurio, -onis (*m*), centurion (a "sergeant-major" in the army)
certamen, -inis (*n*), contest
certe, certainly, surely, at least
certus, -a, -um, certain, definite
  pro certo habere, to be sure
  certiorem facere, to inform
ceteri, -ae, -a, the rest, the others
Christianus, -a, -um, Christian
cibus, -i (*m*), food
Cicero, -onis (*m*), Cicero (Roman orator and writer)
cilicinus, -a, -um, made of hair-cloth
cilicium, -i (*n*), shirt made of Cilician goat's hair
cinis, cineris (*m*), ash, ashes
circiter, about
circum (+ *acc.*), round, around
circumcido (3), **-cidi, -cisum,** to cut (all) round
circumdo (1), **-dedi, -datum,** to surround
circumeo, -ire, -ii, -itum, to go round, surround
circumsto (1), **-steti,** to stand round, surround
circumvenio (4), **-veni, -ventum,** to surround, catch, trap
Circus, -i (*m*), Circus Maximus (stadium for chariot-racing)
cista, -ae (*f*), chest
cito, quickly
citra (+ *acc.*), on this side of
civis, -is (*m*), citizen
civitas, -atis (*f*), state, city
clades, -is (*f*), defeat, disaster
clam, secretly, without being seen
clamo (1), to shout, call
clamor, -oris (*m*), shout, shouting, noise
clarus, -a, -um, clear, famous, distinguished
classis, -is (*f*), fleet
claudo (3), **-si, -sum,** to close, shut
claudus, -a, -um, lame
claustralis, -is, -e, confined to the monastery
clericus, -i (*m*), priest
Clodius, -i (*m*), Clodius (a political agitator and gang-leader in Rome)
coegi, see **cogo**
coepi, I began
cogito (1), to think
cognatio, -onis (*f*), kinship, relationship

cognosco (3), **-novi, -nitum,** to learn, find out
cogo (3), **coegi, coactum,** to force, compel, collect
cohors, -ortis (*f*), cohort (tenth part of a legion)
collega, -ae (*m*), colleague
colligo (3), **-legi, -lectum,** to collect, gather
collis, -is (*m*), hill
colloco (1), to place, station
colloquium, -i (*n*), meeting, discussion
colloquor (3), **-locutus sum,** to converse with, talk
colo (3), **colui, cultum,** to cultivate, dwell, worship
comedo (3), **-edi, -esum,** to eat
comes, -itis (*m*), companion, comrade
comiter, affably, amiably, courteously
commeatus, -us (*m*), supplies, provisions
committo (3), **-misi, -missum,** to entrust
proelium committere, to join battle
commoveo (2), **-movi, -motum,** to move
communis, -is, -e, common
comparo (1), to get ready, obtain, acquire
compello (3), **-puli, -pulsum,** to drive
complures, -es, -a, several
comprehendo (3), **-hendi, -hensum,** to seize, arrest
concido (3), **-cidi,** to fall
concido (3), **-cidi, -cisum,** to kill, destroy
concurro (3), **-curri, -cursum,** to run together, rush up
concursus, -us (*m*), a rushing together, clash
condemno (1), to condemn
condicio, -onis (*f*), condition, terms
confero, -ferre, -tuli, collatum, to confer, bestow
conficio (3), **-feci, -fectum,** to finish
confido (3), **-fisus sum** (+ *dat.*), to trust
confirmo (1), to establish
confiteor (2), **-fessus sum,** to confess, admit
confligo (3), **-xi, -ctum,** to fight
conforto (1), to strengthen greatly
confugio (3), **-fugi,** to flee for refuge, take refuge
congero (3), **-gessi, -gestum,** to gather

conicio (3), **-ieci, -iectum,** to hurl, throw
in vincula conicere, to throw into chains, imprison
coniungo (3), **-iunxi, -iunctum,** to join
coniuratus, -i (*m*), conspirator
coniuro (1), to conspire
conor (1), to try
conscendo (3), **-scendi, -scensum,** to board, go on board
conscisco (3), **-ivi, -itum,** to decree, decide on
mortem sibi consciscere, to commit suicide
conscribo (3), **-scripsi, -scriptum,** to enrol
patres conscripti, senators
consensio, -onis (*f*), agreement, unanimity
consensus, -us (*m*), agreement
conservo (1), to preserve, protect
consido (3), **-sedi, -sessum,** to sit down, encamp
consilium, -i (*n*), plan, advice, council
consilium capere, to adopt a plan
consimilis, -is, -e, like, similar
consisto (3), **-stiti,** to stand, halt, take up a position
conspectus, -us (*m*), sight
conspicio (3), **-spexi, -spectum,** to catch sight of
constat, it is agreed
constituo (3), **-ui, -utum,** to decide, fix
consuesco (3), **-suevi, -suetum,** to accustom oneself, become accustomed
consul, -ulis (*m*), consul
consulatus, -us (*m*), consulship
consulo (3), **-ui, -ultum** (+ *acc.*), to consult; (+ *dat.*) to look after
consulto (1), to consult
contemno (3), **-tempsi, -temptum,** to despise
contendo (3), **-tendi, -tentum,** to strive, hasten, fight
continens, -entis, continuous, mainland
contineo (2), **-ui, -tentum,** to confine, hold
contra (+ *acc.*), against
contrarius, -a, -um, opposite, opposing
convenio (4), **-veni, -ventum,** to come together, meet, assemble, be agreed

converto (3), **-ti, -versum,** to turn
conviva, -ae (*m*), guest
convivium, -i (*n*), banquet
convoco (1), to call together
coorior (4), **coortus sum,** to arise, break out
copiae, -arum (*f.pl*), forces, troops
coquus, -i (*m*), cook
coram (+ *abl.*), in the presence of, before the eyes of
Corinthus, -i (*f*), Corinth (city in Greece)
costa, -ae (*f*), side
cotidianus, -a, -um, daily
cotidie, every day, daily
cras, tomorrow
creber, -bra, -brum, frequent, thick
credo (3), **credidi, creditum** (+ *dat.*), to believe
creo (1), to create, appoint, elect
cresco (3), **crevi, cretum,** to grow, increase
crispus, -a, -um, curly
cruciatus, -us (*m*), torture
crucio (1), to torture
crudelis, -is, -e, cruel
crux, crucis (*f*), cross
crystallinus, -a, -um, sparkling, twinkling, bright
cubiculum, -i, (*n*), bedroom
cubo (1), **-ui, -itum,** to lie down, sleep
  cubitum ire, to go to bed
culina, -ae (*f*), kitchen
culpo (1), to blame
cultellus, -i (*m*), small knife
cum (+ *abl.*), with
cum (+ *indic.*), when, whenever
  cum primum, as soon as
cum (+ *subj.*), when, since, although
cum ... tum ..., both ... and ...
cuncti, -ae, -a, all (together)
cupidus, -a, -um (+ *gen.*), desirous (of), eager (to)
cupio (3), **-ivi, -itum,** to want, wish, be anxious to
cur, why
cura, -ae (*f*), care, anxiety
  curae esse (+ *dat.*), to be a cause of anxiety (to)
Curia, -ae (*f*), Senate-house
curo (1), to attend to, look after
curro (3), **cucurri, cursum,** to run
custodio (4), to guard
custos, -odis (*m*), guard

--------- **D** ---------

daemon, -onis (*m*), spirit
damno (1), to condemn
  capitis damnare, to condemn to death
Danai, -orum (*m.pl*), Greeks
de (+ *abl.*), about, concerning, down from
dea, -ae (*f*), goddess
debeo (2), I ought, owe
decem, ten
decerno (3), **-crevi, -cretum,** to decree, pass a resolution
decet, it is right
decimus, -a, -um, tenth
decurro (3), **-(cu)curri, -cursum,** to run down
dedecus, -oris (*n*), disgrace
  dedecori esse (+ *dat.*), to bring shame (upon)
dedi, see **do**
deditio, -onis (*f*), surrender
dedo (3), **dedidi, deditum,** to hand over, give up
  se dedere, to surrender
deduco (3), **-duxi, -ductum,** to bring, escort
defendo (3), **-di, -sum,** to defend
defessus, -a, -um, tired, weary
deinde, then
delecto (1), to please, delight
deleo (2), **-evi, -etum,** to destroy
delibero (1), to debate, consider well
dementia, -ae (*f*), madness
demitto (3), **-misi, -missum,** to send down
denique, in short, in fact, finally
denoto (1), to mark, mark down
depello (3), **-puli, -pulsum,** to drive down
descendo (3), **-di, -sum,** to descend, climb down, go down
descisco (3), **-ivi, -itum,** to revolt from
describo (3), **-scripsi, -scriptum,** to write down, transcribe
desertus, -a, -um, deserted
desidiosus, -a, -um, lazy, indolent
desilio (4), **-ui, -sultum,** to jump down
desino (3), **-sii, -situm** (+ *infin.*), to cease, stop
desisto (3), **-stiti** (+ *infin.*), to cease, stop
despero (1), to give up hope, despair

deterreo (2), to deter
detineo (2), -ui, -tentum, to hold back, detain
detrimentum, -i (*n*), loss, damage
deus, -i (*m*) (*nom.pl* di), god
dexter, -tra, -trum, right
dico (3), dixi, dictum, to say, tell
dictum, -i (*n*), word
dies, -ei (*m*), day
difficilis, -is, -e, difficult
dignus, -a, -um (+ *abl.*), worthy (of), deserving
diligenter, carefully, hard
diligentia, -ae (*f*), attention to duty, diligence, alertness
diligo (3), -lexi, -lectum, to love
dimidius, -a, -um, half
diripio (3), -ui, -reptum, to plunder
diruo (3), -ui, -utum, to destroy
dirus, -a, -um, dreadful
discedo (3), -cessi, -cessum, to go away, leave
discipulus, -i (*m*), pupil
disco (3), didici, to learn
discrimen, -inis (*n*), danger, risk, crisis
discus, -i (*m*), dish
displiceo (2) (+ *dat.*), to displease
dispositio, -onis (*f*), arrangement
dissentio (4), -sensi, -sensum, to differ from, disagree
dissimilis, -is, -e, unlike
dissimulo (1), to keep secret
diu, for a long time
diversus, -a, -um, facing opposite directions, distant, isolated
dives, -itis, rich
divido (3), -visi, -visum, to divide, separate
divinatio, -onis (*f*), prophecy
divino (1), to foresee, foretell
divinus, -a, -um, divine
divitiae, -arum (*f.pl*), riches, wealth
divus, -a, -um, divine
  divi, divorum (or divum) (*m.pl*), gods
do (1), dedi, datum, to give
  dono dare, to give as a gift
doceo (2), -ui, doctum, to teach, tell, inform
doleo (2), to mourn, grieve, be sorry
dolor, -oris (*m*), grief, pain
dolus, -i (*m*), trick
dominus, -i (*m*), master, lord
domus, -us (*f*), house, home
  domi, at home

domo, from home
domum, homewards
donec, until, as long as
dono (1), to give, present
dormio (4), to sleep
dubito (1), to doubt, hesitate
dubius, -a, -um, doubtful, uncertain
ducenti, -ae, -a, two hundred
duco (3), duxi, ductum, to lead, take, marry, draw, choose
ductor, -oris (*m*), leader
dulcedo, -inis (*f*), sweetness
dulcis, -is, -e, sweet, melodious
dum, while, until, as long as, provided that
dummodo, provided that
Dumnorix, -igis (*m*), Dumnorix (Gallic leader)
duo, duae, duo, two
duodecim, twelve
durus, -a, -um, hard, harsh
dux, ducis (*m*), leader, general

E

e, ex (+ *abl.*), out of, from
ebrius, -a, -um, given to drinking
ecce! look! behold!
edax, -acis, eating, corroding
edo, esse (3), edi, esum, to eat
educo (3), -xi, -ctum, to lead out, bring up, rear
efficio (3), -feci, -fectum, to accomplish
effugio (3), -fugi, to escape
ego, I
egredior (3), -gressus sum, to go out, disembark
egregie, remarkably well, excellently
egregius, -a, -um, outstanding, excellent, exceptional
eheu! alas!
electio, -onis (*f*), election, appointment
eleemosyna, -ae (*f*), alms
emendatio, -onis (*f*), correction, change
eminens, -entis, prominent
emitto (3), -misi, -missum, to send out, let stop
emo (3), emi, emptum, to buy
enim, for
eo, to that place, there
eo, ire, ivi, itum, to go

obviam ire (+ *dat.*), to go to meet
eo magis, all the more
epistola, -ae (*f*), letter
equitatus, -us (*m*), cavalry
equites, -um (*m.pl*), horsemen, cavalry, the **equites** (Knights)
equito (1), to ride
equus, -i (*m*), horse
eripio (3), **-ui**, **-reptum**, to snatch from, rescue
erro (1), to wander
eruditus, -a, -um, learned, scholarly
erumpo (3), **-rupi**, **-ruptum**, to burst out, break out
essedarius, -i (*m*), chariot-warrior
et, and, also
et . . . et . . ., both . . . and . . .
etenim, for
etiam, also, even
etiamsi, even if
Etruria, -ae (*f*), Etruria (area to the north of Rome)
etsi, although, even if
evenio (4), **-veni**, **-ventum**, to turn out, happen
eventus, -us (*m*), outcome
ex (+ *abl.*), out of, from
exaudio (4), to hear distinctly
excedo (3), **-cessi**, **-cessum**, to go out, leave
excito (1), to rouse, waken
exemplum, -i (*n*), example
exeo, -ire, -ii, -itum, to go out, leave
exerceo (2), to exercise
exercitatio, -onis (*f*), practice
exercitus, -us (*m*), army
exigo (3), **-egi**, **-actum**, to spend, complete, inquire into
exiguus, -a, -um, small
eximius, -a, -um, extraordinary, remarkable
existimo (1), to think, consider
exitium, -i (*n*), destruction
exitio esse (+ *dat.*), to be a cause of destruction (to), destroy
expeditio, -onis (*f*), expedition
expello (3), **-puli**, **-pulsum**, to drive out, expel
explico (1), to explain
explorator, -oris (*m*), scout
exploro (1), to reconnoitre
expono (3), **-posui**, **-positum**, to lay open, expose, land (troops)
exquiro (3), **-quisivi**, **-quisitum**, to seek, ask

exsequor (3), **-secutus sum**, to follow
exspecto (1), to wait, wait for
extra (+ *acc.*), outside
extraho (3), **-xi**, **-ctum**, to pull out, draw
extremus, -a, -um, last, furthest
exuo (3), **-ui**, **-utum**, to take off

─────────── F ───────────

fabula, -ae (*f*), story
facetus, -a, -um, witty, clever
facile, easily
facile factu, easy to do
facilis, -is, -e, easy
facio (3), **feci**, **factum**, to make, do
iter facere, to journey, travel, march
Faesulae, -arum (*f.pl*), Faesulae (town in Etruria)
fallo (3), **fefelli**, **falsum**, to deceive
falsus, -a, -um, false
falsa dicere, to tell lies
falx, falcis (*f*), sickle, pruning-hook
fames, -is (*f*), hunger
familia, -ae (*f*), household
familiaris, -is, -e, intimate
fata, -orum (*n.pl*), the fates, destiny
faveo (2), **favi**, **fautum** (+ *dat.*), to favour, support
fax, facis (*f*), torch, firebrand
felix, -icis, lucky, happy
femorale, -is (*n*), covering for thighs, drawers, underpants
fera, -ae (*f*), wild beast
ferculum, -i (*n*), dish, course
fere, almost, roughly
feriatus, -a, -um, on holiday
fero, ferre, tuli, latum, to carry, bring, endure
ferocitas, -atis (*f*), fierceness, ferocity
ferociter, fiercely
ferox, -ocis, fierce
festino (1), to hurry
fides, -ei (*f*), faith, loyalty, pledge
fidem laedere, to break a promise
fido (3), **fisus sum** (+ *dat.*), to trust
filia, -ae (*f*), daughter
filius, -i (*m*), son
finis, -is (*m*), end
fines, -ium (*m.pl*), territory
finitimus, -a, -um, neighbouring
fio, fieri, factus sum, to be done, happen, become
firmus, -a, -um, strong

Flamininus, -i (*m*), Flamininus (Roman general who conquered Philip of Macedon)
flamma, -ae (*f*), flame
flecto (3), **-xi, -xum**, to bend
fleo (2), **-evi, -etum**, to weep
fletus, -us (*m*), weeping
flos, floris (*m*), flower
fluctus, -us (*m*), wave
flumen, -inis (*n*), river
fons, fontis (*m*), fount, origin
foras, out of doors
fore, future infinitive of **esse**
forma, -ae (*f*), shape, figure, beauty
formido, -inis (*f*), fear
fortasse, perhaps
forte, by chance
fortis, -is, -e, brave, strong
fortiter, bravely
fortuna, -ae (*f*), fortune, good fortune, luck
forum, -i (*n*), market-place, forum
fossa, -ae (*f*), ditch
fragor, -oris (*m*), noise, crash
frango (3), **fregi, fractum**, to break
frater, -tris (*m*), brother
freno (1), to curb, restrain
fretus, -a, -um (+ *abl.*), relying (on)
frigidus, -a, -um, cold
frigus, -oris (*n*), cold
frons, frontis (*f*), front, forehead
  a fronte, at the front, in front
frumentor (1), to forage, fetch corn
frumentum, -i (*n*), corn
  res frumentaria, corn-supply
fuga, -ae (*f*), flight
  in fugam dare, to put to flight
fugax, -acis, fleeting, transitory
fugio (3), **fugi**, to flee, run away
fumus, -i (*m*), smoke
funditor, -oris (*m*), slinger
fundo (3), **fudi, fusum**, to pour, drive away, rout
fundus, -i (*m*), farm, farm-house
fur, furis (*m*), thief
furtim, stealthily, secretly
furtum, -i (*n*), theft
fustis, -is (*m*), club, stick
futurus, -a, -um, future, about to be

——————— G ———————

Gala, -ae (*m*), Gala (king of the Numidians)

Galli, -orum (*m.pl*), Gauls
Gallia, -ae (*f*), Gaul
Gallicus, -a, -um, Gallic
gaudeo (2), **gavisus sum**, to be glad, rejoice
gemini, -ae, -a, twin
gemo (3), **-ui, -itum**, to groan
gens, gentis (*f*), race, clan, tribe
gero (3), **gessi, gestum**, to wear, carry on, (passive) happen
  bellum gerere, to wage war
  rem bene gerere, to be successful
  res gestae, achievements
  se gerere, to behave
Gerusia, -ae (*acc.* **-an**) (*f*), senate-house (in a Greek city)
gladiator, -oris (*m*), gladiator
gladius, -i (*m*), sword
  gladium stringere, to draw a sword
Graecia, -ae (*f*), Greece
Graecus, -a, -um, Greek
grandis, -is, -e, large
gratiae, -arum (*f.pl*), thanks
  gratias agere (+ *dat.*), to thank
gratus, -a, -um, pleasing, agreeable
gravis, -is, -e, heavy, serious
grossus, -a, -um, thick
gutta, -ae (*f*), drop, tear

——————— H ———————

habeo (2), to have, hold, consider
  orationem habere, to deliver a speech
habito (1), to live, dwell
Hannibal, -alis (*m*), Hannibal (Carthaginian general)
haud, not, by no means
Hector, -oris (*m*), Hector (son of Priam, King of Troy)
Helvetii, -orum (*m.pl*), Helvetii (Swiss)
Herculaneum, -i (*n*), Herculaneum (town near Pompeii)
heri, yesterday
hesternus, -a, -um, of yesterday
hiberna, -orum (*n.pl*), winter-quarters
hic, haec, hoc, this
hic, here
hiemo (1), to winter, spend the winter
hiems, hiemis (*f*), winter, storm
hilariter, cheerfully
hinc, from here
Hippomenes, -is (*m*), Hippomenes

(youth who won Atalanta as his bride by beating her in a race)
Hispania, -ae (*f*), Spain
hodie, today
homo, hominis (*m*), man, fellow, person
homines, -um (*m.pl*), people
honestas, -atis (*f*), honour, good reputation
hora, -ae (*f*), hour
Horatius Flaccus, Horace (Roman poet)
horreo (2), to shudder
horresco (3), **horrui**, to shudder
horribilis, -is, -e, frightening, terrible, dreadful
hortor (1), to encourage, urge
hortus, -i (*m*), garden
hostis, -is (*m*), enemy
huc, here, hither, to this place

——————— I ———————

iaceo (2), to lie
iacio (3), **ieci, iactum**, to throw
iam, now, already, by this time
ianitor, -oris (*m*), door-keeper
ianua, -ae (*f*), door
ibi, there
ictus, -a, -um, struck, stricken
idem, eadem, idem, the same
identidem, time and again
idoneus, -a, -um, suitable
Idus, Iduum (*f.pl*), Ides (13th or 15th day in Roman month)
igitur, therefore
ignavus, -a, -um, cowardly, lazy
ignominia, -ae (*f*), disgrace
ignosco (3), **-novi, -notum** (+ *dat.*), to forgive, pardon
ille, illa, illud, that; he, she, it
illustro (1), to illuminate, make clear
imago, -inis (*f*), likeness, image, vision, ghost
imber, imbris (*m*), rain, storm-cloud
immemor, -oris, forgetting, unmindful
immensus, -a, -um, endless, huge
imminens, -entis, imminent
immo, in fact, on the contrary
immortalis, -is, -e, immortal
impedimenta, -orum (*n.pl*), baggage
impedio (4), to hinder
impeditus, -a, -um, hindered, hampered

imperator, -oris (*m*), general, emperor
imperium, -i (*n*), command, power
impero (1) (+ *dat.*), to order, command; (+ *acc.*) to demand
impetro (1), to have a request granted
impetus, -us (*m*), attack, advance
impotens, -entis, uncontrolled, furious
improbus, -a, -um, wicked, depraved
improvisus, -a, -um, unexpected
impune, without punishment
in (+ *abl.*), in, on
in (+ *acc.*), into, towards, against
inambulo (1), to walk about
incendium, -i (*n*), fire
incendo (3), **-di, -sum**, to burn, set on fire
incola, -ae (*m*), inhabitant
incultus, -a, -um, unkempt, uncultivated
incumbo (3), **-cubui, -cubitum** (+ *dat.*), to lean upon, breast
incurso (1), to run into
inde, from there, after that, then
indignus, -a, -um (+ *abl.*), unworthy (of)
indomitus, -a, -um, ungovernable
indutiae, -arum (*f.pl*), truce
ineo, -ire, -ii, -itum, to go into
infallibilis, -is, -e, infallible
inferiae, -arum (*f.pl*), sacrifice in honour of the dead
infero, -ferre, -tuli, illatum, to carry in, import
infirmitas, -atis (*f*), weakness
inflammo (1), to set on fire, inflame
infra (+ *acc.*), inside, within, below
ingenium, -i (*n*), ability, intelligence, character
ingens, -entis, huge, great
ingredior (3), **-gressus sum**, to go into, enter
inhabito (1), to live in, dwell in
inhorreo (2), to shudder, tremble
inimicus, -a, -um, hostile, enemy
inimicus, -i (*m*), personal enemy
iniquus, -a, -um, uneven, unjust
iniussu (+ *gen.*), without the orders (of)
innocens, -entis, innocent, guiltless
innoxius, -a, -um, harmless
innumerabilis, -is, -e, countless
inopinans, -antis, unsuspecting
inquit, he/she says, said
insequor (3), **-secutus sum**, to pursue closely

insidiae, -arum (*f.pl*), ambush, plot
insignia, -ium (*n.pl*), decorations, badges
instantia, -ae (*f*), insistence
instar (*indeclinable*), a likeness; (+ *gen.*) like
instituo (3), **-ui, -utum**, to set up, begin
institutum, -i (*n*), practice, custom
insto (1), **-stiti**, to press on
instruo (3), **-struxi, -structum**, to set in order
  aciem instruere, to draw up a line of battle
insuetus, -a, -um, unaccustomed
insula, -ae (*f*), island
integro (1), to make whole
intellego (3), **-lexi, -lectum**, to understand, realise
inter (+ *acc.*), between, among
  inter se, one another
interdiu, by day, during the day
interea, meanwhile
interest, it is important
interficio (3), **-feci, -fectum**, to kill
interiaceo (2), to lie between
intermitto (3), **-misi, -missum**, to interrupt, let pass
interrumpo (3), **-rupi, -ruptum**, to break through, break down
intimus, -a, -um, innermost
  intima, -orum (*n.pl*), the inmost parts, heart
intro (1), to enter
introduco (3), **-duxi, -ductum**, to bring in
intexo (3), **-ui, -textum**, to weave, join together
intuitus, -us (*m*), look
inutilis, -is, -e, useless
invado (3), **-vasi, -vasum**, to attack
invideo (2), **-vidi, -visum** (+ *dat.*), to envy
invito (1), to invite, summon
invitus, -a, -um, unwilling(ly)
ipse, ipsa, ipsum, -self
ira, -ae (*f*), anger
irascor (3), **iratus sum** (+ *dat.*), to be angry (with)
iratus, -a, -um, angry
Iris, -is (*f*) (*acc.* **Irim**), Iris (goddess of the rainbow)
is, ea, id, this, that; he, she, it
Iseum, -i, (*n*), temple of Isis (Egyptian goddess of fertility)

iste, ista, istud, that, that over there
ita, in this way, so
Italia, -ae (*f*), Italy
itaque, and so, therefore
item, likewise, also, in the same way
iter, itineris (*n*), journey, march, way
  iter facere, to journey, march
iterum, again, a second time
Ithaca, -ae (*f*), Ithaca (Greek island ruled by Ulysses)
iubeo (2), **iussi, iussum**, to order
iudices, -um (*m.pl*), members of the jury
Iuno, -onis (*f*), Juno (queen of the gods)
Iuppiter Stator, Jupiter the Protector
iussi, see **iubeo**
iussum, -i (*n*), order
iuvenis, -is (*m*), young man
iuxta, nearby

─────────── K ───────────

Kalendae, -arum (*f.pl*), Kalends (first day of a Roman month)

─────────── L ───────────

labefacio (3), **-feci, -factum**, to shake
Labienus, -i (*m*), Labienus (one of Caesar's generals)
labor (3), **lapsus sum**, to slip
labor, -oris (*m*), work, toil
laboro (1), to work, be hard pressed, be in difficulties
labrum, -i (*n*), lip
lac, lactis (*n*), milk
Lacedaemonius, -a, -um, Spartan, Lacedaemonian
lacesso (3), **-ivi, -itum**, to harass, provoke
lacrima, -ae (*f*), tear
lacrimo (1), to weep
laedo (3), **laesi, laesum**, to harm, hurt
laete, joyfully, gladly
laetus, -a, -um, happy, glad
langueo (2), to be weary
Laocoon, -ontis (*m*), Laocoon (priest of Apollo at Troy)
lapis, -idis (*m*), stone
Lares, -um (*m.pl*), household gods
lateo (2), to be hidden, hide
Latinus, -a, -um, Latin, belonging to Latium

latitudo, -inis (*f*), breadth, width
latro, -onis (*m*), robber, brigand
laudo (1), to praise
laus, laudis (*f*), praise
   laudi esse (+ *dat.*), to be a credit (to)
lectus, -i (*m*), bed, couch
legatus, -i (*m*), ambassador, envoy, staff-officer, general
legio, -onis (*f*), legion
lego (3), **legi, lectum**, to read
lenio (4), to soothe, calm
lenis, -is, -e, gentle
leo, -onis (*m*), lion
levis, -is, -e, light, irresponsible, fickle
levitas, -atis (*f*), lightness
lex, legis (*f*), law
libenter, gladly, willingly
liber, libri (*m*), book
liber, -era, -erum, free
liberi, -orum (*m.pl*), children
libero (1), to set free
libertas, -atis (*f*), freedom, liberty
licet (2), **-uit**, it is allowed
   mihi licet, I am allowed
lictor, -oris (*m*), lictor, magistrate's attendant
ligneus, -a, -um, wooden
lingua, -ae (*f*), tongue, language
liquidus, -a, -um, liquid, flowing
littera, -ae (*f*), letter (of alphabet)
   litterae, -arum (*f.pl*), letter, dispatch(es), literature
litus, -oris (*n*), shore, beach
loco (1), to place
locus, -i (*m*), place, ground
Londinium, -i (*n*), London
longus, -a, -um, long
loquor (3), **locutus sum**, to speak, talk, say
luceo (2), **luxi**, to shine
luctor (1), to strain, struggle
luctus, -us (*m*), grief, distress
ludibrium, -i (*n*), mockery
   ludibrio esse (+ *dat.*), to be a laughing-stock
ludo (3), **lusi, lusum**, to play
ludus, -i (*m*), game, school
lugeo (2), to bewail
luna, -ae (*f*), moon
lupus, -i (*m*), wolf
lux, lucis (*f*), light, daylight
   prima luce, at dawn

M

Macedonia, -ae (*f*), Macedonia (country to the north of Greece)
macero (1), to waste away
macto (1), to reward, punish, sacrifice
macula, -ae (*f*), spot
maestitia, -ae (*f*), sadness
maestus, -a, -um, sad
magis, more
   eo magis, all the more
magister, -tri (*m*), schoolmaster
magistratus, -us (*m*), magistrate
magnopere, greatly
magnus, -a, -um, big, great, loud
maior, -oris, greater
   maiores, -um (*m.pl*), ancestors
male, badly
malo, malle, malui, to prefer
malus, -i (*m*), mast (of ship)
mandatum, -i (*n*), order
mane, in the morning
maneo (2), **mansi, mansum**, to remain
manus, -us (*f*), hand
mare, -is (*n*), sea
Masinissa, -ae (*m*), Masinissa (king of Numidia in north Africa)
Massilia, -ae (*f*), Marseilles
Massiva, -ae (*m*), Massiva (Numidian warrior captured by Scipio)
mater, -tris (*f*), mother
matrimonium, -i (*n*), marriage
   in matrimonium ducere, to marry
matrona, -ae (*f*), married woman
maturo (1), to hasten
maturus, -a, -um, early, earlier
maxime, very much, especially
maximus, -a, -um, biggest, greatest, very large
medicus, -i (*m*), doctor
mediocris, -is, -e, moderate, ordinary, middling
Mediolanum, -i (*n*), Milan (town in north of Italy)
medius, -a, -um, mid-, middle of
mel, mellis (*n*), honey
melior, -oris, better
Melita, -ae (*f*), Malta
memento! remember!
memor, -oris (+ *gen.*), mindful, remembering
Menapii, -orum (*m.pl*), Menapii (a Belgian tribe)
mendax, -acis, lying, deceitful

mendicus, -i (*m*), beggar
mens, mentis (*f*), mind, intellect, purpose
mensa, -ae (*f*), table
mensis, -is (*m*), month
mentior (4), **mentitus sum,** to lie, tell lies
mercator, -oris (*m*), merchant
meridies, -ei (*m*), mid-day
meto (3), **messui, messum,** to reap
metuo (3), **-ui, -utum,** to fear
metus, -us (*m*), fear
meus, -a, -um, my
miles, -itis (*m*), soldier, courtier
Miletus, -i (*f*), Miletus (town in western part of Turkey)
mille, a thousand
  milia passuum, miles
Milo, -onis (*m*), Milo (supporter of Cicero and rival of Clodius)
minae, -arum (*f.pl*), threats
ministro (1), to serve
minor (1) (+ *dat*.), to threaten
minor, -oris, smaller
minus, less
  si minus, if not
miror (1), to wonder, marvel at
mirus, -a, -um, wonderful, strange
miser, -a, -um, unhappy, wretched
miseror (1), to pity
Mithridates, -is (*m*), Mithridates (king of Pontus in north of Turkey)
mitto (3), **misi, missum,** to send
modo, only
modus, -i (*m*), way, manner
moenia, -ium (*n.pl*), (city) walls
moleste fero, I am annoyed
molestus, -a, -um, troublesome
monachatus, -us (*m*), monastic order
monachus, -i (*m*), monk
moneo (2), to warn, advise
mons, montis (*m*), mountain
monumentum, -i (*n*), monument
mora, -ae (*f*), delay
morbus, -i (*m*), disease, illness
morior (3), **mortuus sum,** to die
moror (1), to delay, stay
mors, mortis (*f*), death
  mortem sibi consciscere, to commit suicide
mortalis, -is, -e, mortal
mos, moris (*m*), custom, tradition
Mosa, -ae (*m*), River Meuse (in region of the Belgae)
motus, -us (*m*), movement, sudden rising

moveo (2), **movi, motum,** to move
mox, soon
mulier, -eris (*f*), woman
multitudo, -inis (*f*), large number, crowd
multo (+ *comparative*), much
multum, much
multus, -a, -um, much; (*pl*) many
munimentum, -i (*n*), defence, protection, fortification
munio (4), to defend, fortify
munitio, -onis (*f*), defence, fortification
munus, -eris (*n*), gift
murmurator, -oris (*m*), grumbler
murus, -i (*m*), wall
muto (1), to change
mutus, -a, -um, silent

——————— N ———————

nam, for
nanciscor (3), **nactus sum,** to obtain
narro (1), to tell
nascor (3), **natus sum,** to be born
Nasica, -ae (*m*), Nasica (branch of the Scipio family)
nasus, -i (*m*), nose
natio, -onis (*f*), nation, race, tribe
nato (1), to swim
natu, by birth
  natu minor, younger
natura, -ae (*f*), nature
natus, -a, -um, born, old
natus, -i (*m*), son, child
nauta, -ae (*m*), sailor
navalis, -is, -e, naval
navigo (1), to sail
navis, -is (*f*), ship
  navem conscendere, to go on board ship, embark
  navem solvere, to set sail
ne (+ *subjunctive*), lest, in case, that . . . not, that, to avoid, not to, not
-ne, (indicates a question)
  -ne . . . -ne . . ., whether . . . or . . .
ne . . . quidem, not even
Neapolis, -is (*f*) (*acc*. **Neapolim**), Naples
nec, and . . . not, nor
  nec . . . nec . . ., neither . . . nor . . .
necessarius, -a, -um, necessary
necesse est, it is necessary
necne, or not
neco (1), to kill

nefarius, -a, -um, abominable, wicked
neglego (3), -lexi, -lectum, to neglect, ignore
nego (1), to say that . . . not, deny
nemo, nullius, no one
Neptunus, -i (*m*), Neptune (god of the sea)
neque, and not, nor
    neque . . . neque . . ., neither . . . nor . . .
nequiquam, in vain
nescio (4) (+ *infin.*), not to know (how to)
neu, and not, nor
neve, and not, nor
nexus, -a, -um, twined, bound
Nicomedia, -ae (*f*), Nicomedia (capital of Bithynia)
niger, -gra, -grum, black
nihil, nothing
nimius, -a, -um, excessive
nisi, if . . . not, unless, except
nitor (3), nisus sum (nixus sum), to strive
nix, nivis (*f*), snow
nobilis, -is, -e, noble, famous
nobilitas, -atis (*f*), nobility, the nobles
nocens, -entis, guilty
noceo (2) (+ *dat.*), to harm
Nola, -ae (*f*), Nola (town in Campania)
nolo, nolle, nolui, to be unwilling, refuse
    noli(te) (+ *infin.*), refuse! don't!
nomen, -inis (*n*), name
non, not
Nonae, -arum (*f.pl*), Nones (5th or 7th day in Roman month)
nondum, not yet
nonne? surely?
nonnulli, -ae, -a, some
nonus, -a, -um, ninth
nos, we, us
noster, -tra, -trum, our
    nostri, -orum (*m.pl*), our men
notus, -a, -um, known
novicius, -i (*m*), novice
novus, -a, -um, new
nox, noctis (*f*), night
nubes, -is (*f*), cloud
nubo (3), nupsi, nuptum (+ *dat.*), to marry
nullus, -a, -um, no, none
num, surely . . . not? whether, if
Numa, -ae (*m*), Numa Pompilius (second king of Rome)
numerus, -i (*m*), number
Numida, -ae (*m*), Numidian
numquam, never
nunc, now
nuntio (1), to announce, report
nuntius, -i (*m*), messenger, message

———————— O ————————

ob (+ *acc.*), on account of, because of
obeo, -ire, -ii, -itum (+ *dat.*), to meet, die
obitus, -us (*m*), destruction, death
oblatus, see **offero**
obliviscor (3), oblitus sum (+ *gen.*), to forget
oblongus, -a, -um, longish, squarish
obsecro (1), to beseech, beg, implore
obses, -idis (*m*), hostage
obsideo (2), -sedi, -sessum, to besiege, blockade
obstinate, obstinately, stubbornly
obtineo (2), -ui, -tentum, to hold, keep, rule
obviam, in the way of
    obviam ire (+ *dat.*), to go to meet
occasio, -onis (*f*), opportunity, chance
occasus, -us (*m*), (sun-)set
occido (3), -cidi, -cisum, to kill
occurro (3), -curri, -cursum (+ *dat.*), to run to meet, meet, attack
octo, eight
oculus, -i (*m*), eye
odi, -isse, to hate
odium, -i (*n*), hatred
    odio esse (+ *dat.*), to be an object of hatred (to), be hated (by)
offero, -ferre, obtuli, oblatum, to offer
olim, once upon a time, one day
Olympus, -i (*m*), Mount Olympus (home of the gods in Greece)
omitto (3), -misi, -missum, to say nothing of, let go, neglect
omnino, altogether
omnipotens, -entis, all-powerful
omnis, -is, -e, every, all
onerarius, -a, -um, transporting freight
    navis oneraria, merchant-ship
onero (1), to burden, load
onus, oneris (*n*), burden, load
oportet te (+ *infin.*), you must, you ought
oppidum, -i (*n*), town

opprimo (3), **-pressi, -pressum,** to crush, overwhelm
oppugno (1), to attack
(ops), opem, opis (*f*), help
optimus, -a, -um, best, excellent, very good
opus, operis (*n*), work, task
opus est (+ *abl.*), there is need (of)
ora, -ae (*f*), shore, coast
oratio, -onis (*f*), speech
   orationem habere, to deliver a speech
orator, -oris (*m*), orator, speaker
orbis, -is (*m*), circle, coil
orbitas, -atis (*f*), bereavement
orbus, -a, -um (+ *abl.*), deprived (of), orphaned
Orgetorix, -igis (*m*), Orgetorix (chief of the Helvetii)
orior (4), **ortus sum,** to rise, begin
oro (1), to beg
ortus, -us (*m*), rising
osculum, -i (*n*), kiss
ostendo (3), **-tendi, -tentum,** to show
Ostia, -ae (*f*), Ostia (port of Rome)
ostium, -i (*n*), entrance, river-mouth
otium, -i (*n*), ease, leisure

──────── **P** ────────

pabulatio, -onis (*f*), foraging
pabulor (1), to forage, collect food
paco (1), to pacify, subdue
paedagogus, -i (*m*), tutor, slave in charge of children
paenitet me, I repent, am sorry
Pallas, -adis (*f*), Pallas Athena (the Greek goddess of wisdom)
pallidus, -a, -um, pale, pallid
panis, -is (*m*), bread
paratus, -a, -um, prepared, ready
parco (3), **peperci, parsum** (+ *dat.*), to spare
parens, -entis (*m*), parent
pareo (2) (+ *dat.*), to obey
pariter, equally, abreast, side by side
paro (1), to prepare
pars, partis (*f*), part, direction
partim, partly
passus, -us (*m*), step
   mille passus, a mile
   duo milia passuum, two miles
patefacio (3), **-feci, -factum,** to lay open, expose

patens, -entis, open
pateo (2), to lie open
pater, -tris (*m*), father
   patres, -um (*m.pl*), senators, elders
   patres conscripti (*m.pl*), senators
patior (3), **passus sum,** to allow, suffer, endure
patria, -ae (*f*), native land
patruus, -i (*m*), uncle
pauci, -ae, -a, few
paulatim, gradually
paulisper, for a short time
paulo (+ *comparative*), a little
paulum, little, a little
pauper, -eris, poor
pavor, -oris (*m*), fear, fright, panic
pax, pacis (*f*), peace
pectus, -oris (*n*), chest, breast, heart
pecunia, -ae (*f*), money
pedites, -um (*m.pl*), infantry
pelagus, -i (*n*), the sea
pello (3), **pepuli, pulsum,** to drive, push back, beat
penes (+ *acc.*), in the presence of
penetro (1), to pierce
per (+ *acc.*), through, over, across
perditio, -onis (*f*), destruction
perditus, -a, -um, corrupt, degenerate
perennis, -is, -e, lasting, everlasting
pereo, -ire, -ii, -itum, to pass away, perish
perficio (3), **-feci, -fectum,** to finish, complete
periculum, -i (*n*), danger, trial
   periculo esse (+ *dat.*), to be a source of danger (to), endanger
peritus, -a, -um (+ *gen.*), skilful, skilled (in)
permitto (3), **-misi, -missum,** to allow
permulti, -ae, -a, very many
permutatio, -onis (*f*), exchange
pernocto (1), to spend the night
perpauci, -ae, -a, very few
perpendo (3), **-di, -sum,** to weigh carefully, examine
perpetuus, -a, -um, continuous, unbroken
persuadeo (2), **-suasi, -suasum** (+ *dat.*), to persuade
perterritus, -a, -um, terrified
perturbo (1), to confuse, throw into confusion
pervenio (4), **-veni, -ventum** (**ad** + *acc.*), to reach, arrive at

pervigilo (1), to spend the night awake
pes, pedis (*m*), foot
  pedem referre, to retreat, withdraw
peto (3), **-ivi, -itum**, to seek, ask for, look for, stand for
Philippi, -orum (*m.pl*), Philippi (town in Macedonia)
philosophus, -i (*m*), philosopher
pietas, -atis (*f*), goodness, dutifulness, sense of duty
pila, -ae (*f*), ball
pilum, -i (*n*), javelin
pirata, -ae (*m*), pirate
piscor (1), to fish
pius, -a, -um, good, devout, dutiful
placeo (2) (+ *dat.*), to please
  mihi placet, I have decided
plaustrum, -i (*n*), wagon, cart
plene, completely, wholly
plenus, -a, -um, full
plerusque, -raque, -rumque, most
pluit, it is raining
plurimum posse, to be most powerful
plurimus, -a, -um, very much; (*pl*) very many
plus, pluris, more
poculum, -i (*n*), cup, goblet
poena, -ae (*f*), penalty, punishment
  poenas pendere, to pay the penalty
Poenus, -a, -um, Carthaginian
poeta, -ae (*m*), poet
polliceor (2), **pollicitus sum**, to promise
Pompeius, -i (*m*), Pompey (great Roman general and rival of Caesar)
pono (3), **posui, positum**, to place, put, site
  castra ponere, to pitch camp
pons, pontis (*m*), bridge
pontus, -i (*m*), sea
Pontus, -i (*m*), Pontus (country in the north of Turkey)
popularis, -is, -e, of the people, fellow-countryman
populus, -i (*m*), people
porta, -ae (*f*), gate
porto (1), to carry
portus, -us (*m*), harbour
possum, posse, potui, to be able
  plurimum posse, to be most powerful
post (+ *acc.*), after
post, behind, after
postea, afterwards

posteaquam, after
posterus, -a, -um, following, next
postquam, after, when
postremo, at last, finally
postremus, -a, -um, last
postridie, on the next day
postulo (1), to ask, demand, request
potens, -entis, powerful
potior (4) (+ *abl.*), to gain possession of
potus, -us (*m*), drink
prae (+ *abl.*), because of
praebeo (2), to give, provide, supply, show
praecipio (3), **-cepi, -ceptum** (+ *dat.*), to instruct, order
praecipue, especially
praeda, -ae (*f*), plunder, booty, loot
praedico (3), **-dixi, -dictum**, to predict
praedo, -onis (*m*), robber
praeficio (3), **-feci, -fectum** (+ *dat.*), to put in charge (of)
praemitto (3), **-misi, -missum**, to send on ahead
praemium, -i (*n*), reward
praepono (3), **-posui, -positum**, to prefer, deem more important
praeripio (3), **-ripui, -reptum**, to snatch
praesidium, -i (*n*), garrison
  praesidio esse (+ *dat.*), to be a means of protection (to), protect
praesto (1), **-stiti, -statum**, (+ *dat.*), to be superior (to); (+ *acc.*) to display
praeter (+ *acc.*), except, past, along
praetermitto (3), **-misi, -missum**, to let pass, overlook
praetor, -oris (*m*), praetor (senior magistrate)
praevaleo (2), to be superior, prevail
praevideo (2), **-vidi, -visum**, to foresee
preces, -um (*f.pl*), prayers, pleas
precor (1), to pray, beg
premo (3), **pressi, pressum**, to press, trouble, put under pressure, control
pretium, -i (*n*), price, bribe
pridie, on the previous day
primo, at first, first
primum, first
  ubi primum, as soon as
  ut primum, as soon as
primus, -a, -um, first
princeps, -cipis (*m*), emperor, leading citizen, leader

principium, -i (*n*), beginning
prius, previously
priusquam, before
privatim, privately
privatus, -a, -um, private
pro (+ *abl.*), for, in front of, instead of, in proportion to, on behalf of
probitas, -atis (*f*), goodness, integrity, honesty
probo (1), to prove
probus, -a, -um, honest, honourable
procedo (3), **-cessi, -cessum,** to go forward
procella, -ae (*f*), storm
proconsul, -is (*m*), proconsul
proconsularis, -is, -e, of a proconsul, proconsular
procul, far, far off, from afar, from a distance
proditor, -oris (*m*), traitor
prodo (3), **-didi, -ditum,** to betray
proelium, -i (*n*), battle
  proelium committere, to join battle
profectio, -onis (*f*), departure
profecto, certainly, assuredly
proficiscor (3), **profectus sum,** to set out
profugio (3), **-fugi,** to flee
progredior (3), **-gressus sum,** to go forward, advance
prohibeo (2) (+ *infin.*), to prevent (from)
proicio (3), **-ieci, -iectum,** to throw
prolabor (3), **-lapsus sum,** to fall down
promitto (3), **-misi, -missum,** to promise
pronuntio (1), to announce
prope (+ *acc.*), near
prope, near, nearby, almost
propter (+ *acc.*), on account of
propugnaculum, -i (*n*), defence, fortress
prospere, favourably
provideo (2), **-vidi, -visum,** to foresee, provide for, act with foresight, guard against
provincia, -ae (*f*), province (territory ruled by a Roman governor)
proximus, -a, -um, nearest, last
prudens, -entis, wise, sensible
prudentia, -ae (*f*), wisdom, good-sense
pubes, -is (*f*), youth, young men
publice, publicly, officially
publicus, -a, -um, public
pudet (2), **-uit,** it shames
  me pudet, I am ashamed
puella, -ae (*f*), girl
puer, -i (*m*), boy; (*pl*) children
pugna, -ae (*f*), battle, fight
pugno (1), to fight
pulcher, -chra, -chrum, beautiful
pullus, -i (*m*), chicken
pulso (1), to knock (at)
pulvis, -eris (*m*), dust
Punicus, -a, -um, Carthaginian
punio (4), to punish
purgo (1), to make clean, purify, justify, excuse
puto (1), to think
pyramis, -idis (*f*), pyramid
Pyrrhus, -i (*m*), Pyrrhus (king of Epirus, north of Greece)

─────────── Q ───────────

quadraginta, forty
quae cum ita sint, since this is so, in the circumstances
quaero (3), **-sivi, -situm,** to seek, ask, find out
quaeso, I beseech you, please
qualis, -is, -e, of what kind, as
quam, than
quam! how!
  tam . . . quam . . ., as . . . as . . .
quam (+ *superlative*), as . . . as possible
  quam primum, as soon as possible
quamdiu, how long, as long as
  tamdiu . . . quamdiu . . ., as long as
quamquam, although
quando, when
quantus, -a, -um, how big, how much, as
  tanto . . . quanto . . ., the more . . . the more . . .
  tantum . . . quantum . . ., as much as
quare, therefore, why
quartus, -a, -um, fourth
quattuor, four
-que, and
querela, -ae (*f*), complaint
qui, quae, quod, who, which
quia, because
quidam, quaedam, quoddam, a certain; (*pl*) some

quidem, indeed
   ne . . . quidem, not even
quies, -etis (*f*), peace, quiet, rest
quiesco (3), **quievi, quietum,** to rest
quin, without (see page 105)
quindecim, fifteen
quinque, five
quintus, -a, -um, fifth
quippe qui, inasmuch as
Quirites, -ium (*m.pl*), citizens of Rome
quis, quid, who, what, anyone, anything
quispiam, quaepiam, quidpiam, anyone, anything
quisquam, quidquam, anyone, anything
quisque, quaeque, quodque, each
quo, where to
quo (+ *comparative*), in order that
quod, because, that, which
quomodo, how
quoniam, since
quoque, also
quot, how many
quotie(n)s, how often, how many times

R

radix, -icis (*f*), root, foot (of hill)
raeda, -ae (*f*), coach, carriage
rapio (3), **-ui, raptum,** to seize
rarus, -a, -um, rare, thinly scattered
ratio, -onis (*f*), plan, method
ratis, -is (*f*), raft, ship
ratus, thinking (see **reor**)
raucus, -a, -um, hoarse
receptus, -us (*m*), retreat
recipio (3), **-cepi, -ceptum,** to take back, receive
   se recipere, to retreat, withdraw
recte, rightly (in moral sense)
recupero (1), to recover
reddo (3), **-didi, -ditum,** to give back, return
redeo, -ire, -ii, -itum, to go back, return
redimo (3), **-emi, -emptum,** to buy back, ransom
refectorium, -i (*n*), refectory, dining-hall
refero, -ferre, rettuli, relatum, to bring back, recall
   pedem referre, to retreat, withdraw

regalis, -is, -e, kingly, royal
regia, -ae (*f*), palace
regina, -ae (*f*), queen
regio, -onis (*f*), region, district
regius, -a, -um, royal
regno (1), to rule, reign
regnum, -i (*n*), kingdom
regredior (3), **-gressus sum,** to go back, return
religio, -onis (*f*), religious belief, scruple(s), respect for the gods
relinquo (3), **-liqui, -lictum,** to leave
reliquus, -a, -um, remaining, rest of
remaneo (2), **-mansi, -mansum,** to stay behind, remain
Remi, -orum (*m.pl*), Remi (Gallic tribe near Rheims, in France)
remitto (3), **-misi, -missum,** to send back
renuntio (1), to report
reor (2), **ratus sum,** to think
repello (3), **reppuli, repulsum,** to drive back, beat back
repente, suddenly
repeto (3), **-ivi, -itum,** seek again, revive
reporto (1), to bring back
reprehendo (3), **-di, -sum,** to scold, blame
res, rei (*f*), thing, matter, situation
   rem bene gerere, to be successful
   res frumentaria, corn-supply
   res gestae, achievements
   res novae, revolution
resisto (3), **-stiti** (+ *dat.*), to resist
resolvo (3), **-solvi, -solutum,** to unfasten, release
respicio (3), **-spexi, -spectum,** to look back, look
respondeo (2), **-di, -sum** (+ *dat.*), to reply
respublica, reipublicae (*f*), the state, the republic, country
resumo (3), **-sumpsi, -sumptum,** to take back
rete, -is (*n*), net
retineo (2), to hold back
revenio (4), **-veni, -ventum,** to come back, return
revera, really, in actual fact
reverto (3), **-verti, -versum,** to return (perfect participle **reversus**)
revertor (3), **reversus sum,** to return
reviso (3), to go back to
revoco (1), to call back, recall

rex, regis (*m*), king
Rhenus, -i (*m*), River Rhine
Rhodanus, -i (*m*), River Rhône
rideo (2), **risi, risum,** to laugh, smile
ripa, -ae (*f*), bank (of river)
risus, -us (*m*), laugh, smile
rogo (1), to ask
Roma, -ae (*f*), Rome
Romanus, -a, -um, Roman
Romulus, -i (*m*), Romulus (founder and first king of Rome)
rostrum, -i (*n*), speakers' platform
 Usually plural **rostra, -orum** (*n.pl*)
rotundus, -a, -um, round
Rubico, -onis (*m*), River Rubicon (in north of Italy)
rufus, -a, -um, red
ruga, -ae (*f*), wrinkle
ruina, -ae (*f*), ruin, downfall
rumor, -oris (*m*), rumour, gossip, talk
rumpo (3), **rupi, ruptum,** to burst, break
rursus, again
rus, ruris (*n*), country(side)
 ruri, in the country

───────── S ─────────

sacerdotium, -i (*n*), priesthood
sacerdos, -otis (*m*), priest
saepe, often
sagitta, -ae (*f*), arrow
sagittarius, -i (*m*), archer, bowman
Saguntum, -i (*n*), Saguntum (town on east coast of Spain)
sal, salis (*m*), salt, witty saying
salio (4), **-ui, saltum,** to leap
salus, -utis (*f*), safety
 saluti esse (+ *dat.*), to be the salvation (of), save
saluto (1), to greet, welcome, pay respects
sanctus, -a, -um, sacred, holy
Samnites, -ium (*m.pl*), Samnites (inhabitants of Samnium)
sapiens, -entis, wise
sapio (3), **-ii,** to be wise, know, understand
satis, enough, sufficiently
saxum, -i (*n*), rock
scelestus, -a, -um, wicked
scelus, -eris (*n*), crime
scientia, -ae (*f*), knowledge, skill
scilicet, doubtless

Scipio, -onis (*m*), Scipio (Roman general)
scio (4), to know; (+ *infin.*) to know how to
scribo (3), **scripsi, scriptum,** to write, describe
se, himself, herself, itself, themselves
 se recipere, to withdraw, retreat
seco (1), **-ui, sectum,** to cut
secretus, -a, -um, secret
secundus, -a, -um, second, favourable
sed, but
sedes, -is (*f*), seat; (*pl*) foundations
sedo (1), to calm
Segestani, -orum (*m.pl*), people of Segesta (in Sicily)
semper, always
senator, -oris (*m*), senator
senatus, -us (*m*), senate
senecta, -ae (*f*), old age
senectus, -utis (*f*), old age
senex, senis (*m*), old man
sententia, -ae (*f*), opinion
sentio (4), **sensi, sensum,** to feel, notice, realise
septem, seven
Septentriones, -um (*m.pl*), the North
septimus, -a, -um, seventh
sequor (3), **secutus sum,** to follow
serenus, -a, -um, bright, clear
series, -ei (*f*), series, succession
sero, late
sero (3), **sevi, satum,** to sow
servio (4), to serve
Servius, -i (*m*), Servius Tullius (sixth king of Rome)
servo (1), to save, keep, protect
servus, -i (*m*), slave
sese = **se**
seu . . . seu . . ., whether . . . or . . .
severus, -a, -um, stern, serious
sevoco (1), to call aside
sex, six
si, if
 si minus, if not
 si quis, if anyone
sic, thus, in this way
sica, -ae (*f*), dagger
sicut, just as
Sicilia, -ae (*f*), Sicily
signifer, -i (*m*), standard-bearer (of cohort)
significatio, -onis (*f*), sign
signum, -i (*n*), sign, standard (of cohort)

silentium, -i (*n*), silence
sileo (2), to be silent
silva, -ae (*f*), wood
similis, -is, -e, like, similar
simul, at the same time
simulac, as soon as
simulatque, as soon as
simulo (1), to pretend
sine (+ *abl.*), without
singularis, -is, -e, single, remarkable, exceptional
singuli, -ae, -a, singly, one at a time
sino (3), **sivi, situm**, to allow
situs, -us (*m*), position, site
sive ... sive ..., whether ... or ...
societas, -atis (*f*), alliance
socius, -i (*m*), ally, companion, accomplice
sol, solis (*m*), sun
soleo (2), **solitus sum**, to be accustomed
solitus, -a, -um, accustomed
sollemnis, -is, -e, solemn, religious
sollicito (1), to rouse, stir up
solor (1), to comfort
solum, only
    non solum ... verum etiam ..., not only ... but also ...
solus, -a, -um, alone
solvo (3), **solvi, solutum**, to loosen, set sail
    navem solvere, to set sail
somnus, -i (*m*), sleep
sonitus, -us (*m*), sound
sonorus, -a, -um, noisy, loud-sounding
soror, -oris (*f*), sister
sors, sortis (*f*), drawing of lots, lot
spatium, -i (*n*), space
spectaculum, -i (*n*), spectacle, show
spectator, -oris (*m*), spectator
specto (1), to look at
specula, -ae (*f*), watch-tower
speculator, -oris (*m*), scout
speculor (1), to watch, reconnoitre
spelunca, -ae (*f*), cave
spero (1), to hope
spes, -ei (*f*), hope
spolio (1), to plunder, loot, strip
spondeo (2), **spopondi, sponsum**, to pledge, promise
stamen, -inis (*n*), cloth shirt
statim, immediately
statio, -onis (*f*), outpost, guard-post

statua, -ae (*f*), statue
statura, -ae (*f*), height
stella, -ae (*f*), star
sto (1), **steti, statum**, to stand
strepitus, -us (*m*), noise, din
studeo (2), to study
studiosus, -a, -um, studious; (+ *gen.*) devoted (to)
studium, -i (*n*), zeal, eagerness
stultus, -a, -um, foolish
stupeo (2), to be aghast, amazed
suadeo (2), **suasi, suasum** (+ *dat.*), to advise, urge
sub (+ *abl.*), under
subeo, -ire, -ii, -itum, approach, occur
subito, suddenly
subitus, -a, -um, sudden, unexpected
sublimis, -is, -e, borne aloft
subsidium, -i (*n*), help; (*pl*) supplies
    subsidio esse (+ *dat.*), to be a help (to), help, support
subsisto (3), **-stiti**, to stay, remain
subvenio (4), **-veni, -ventum** (+ *dat.*), to come to the help (of)
succedo (3), **-cessi, -cessum**, to go under, follow, succeed
succido (3), **-cidi, -cisum**, to kill, cut down
Suebi, -orum (*m.pl*), Suebi (tribe in north of Germany)
sum, esse, fui, to be
sumministro (1), to supply
summus, -a, -um, greatest, supreme, most important, the top of
sumo (3), **sumpsi, sumptum**, to take, pick up
superbus, -a, -um, proud, arrogant
supercilium, -i (*n*), eyebrow
superior, -oris, superior, higher, previous
supero (1), to defeat, overcome
supersobrius, -a, -um, very sober
supplicium, -i (*n*), punishment
supra (+ *acc.*), above
supremus, -a, -um, last
surgo (3), **surrexi, surrectum**, to rise, get up
suscipio (3), **-cepi, -ceptum**, to undertake
suspicio, -onis (*f*), suspicion
suspicor (1), to suspect
sustineo (2), **-ui, -tentum**, to sustain, maintain
suus, -a, -um, his, her, their
    sui, -orum (*m.pl*), his own men
Syracusae, -arum (*f.pl*), Syracuse

T

taberna, -ae (*f*), hut, hovel, inn
tabula, -ae (*f*), writing-tablet
taceo (2), to be silent
tacitus, -a, -um, silent
taedet (2), **-uit**, it wearies
    me taedet (+ *gen.*), I am tired (of)
talis, -is, -e, such, of such a kind
tam, so
    tam ... quam ..., as ... as ...
tamdiu, so long
tamen, however, nevertheless
tamquam, as if
tandem, at length, at last
tango (3), **tetigi, tactum**, to touch
tanquam, as if
tantum, only
tantus, -a, -um, so great, such
    tantus ... quantus ..., as great ... as ...
Tarquinius, -i (*m*), (1) Tarquinius Priscus (fifth king of Rome); (2) Tarquinius Superbus (seventh and last king of Rome)
taurus, -i (*m*), bull
Taus, -i (*m*), River Tay (in Scotland)
telum, -i (*n*), weapon
temere, rashly, unthinkingly, without good reason
temperatus, -a, -um, steady, calm
tempero (1), to moderate, govern
tempestas, -atis (*f*), storm, weather
templum, -i (*n*), temple
tempto (1), to test, try
tempus, -oris (*n*), time
    brevi tempore, in a short time
tendo (3), **tetendi, tensum**, to stretch, aim, make for, hasten
tenebrae, -arum (*f.pl*), darkness
Tenedos, -i (*f*), Tenedos (island near Troy)
teneo (2), **-ui, tentum**, to hold, keep, occupy
tenor, -oris (*m*), tradition, rule
tepidus, -a, -um, warm
tergum, -i (*n*), back
    a tergo, in the rear, from behind
tero (3), **trivi, tritum**, to rub away, waste (time)
terra, -ae (*f*), land, earth, ground
terreo (2), to frighten, terrify
territo (1), to frighten, terrify
tertius, -a, -um, third
testis, -is (*m*), witness

theatrum, -i (*n*), theatre
Tiberis, -is (*m*), River Tiber
timeo (2), to be afraid, fear
Timochares, -is (*m*), Timochares (courtier of King Pyrrhus)
timor, -oris (*m*), fear
tonsus, -a, -um, shaven
torqueo (2), **torsi, tortum**, to twist, turn
tot, so many
totiens, so often
totus, -a, -um, all, the whole of
trado (3), **-didi, -ditum**, to hand over
traduco (3), **-duxi, -ductum**, to take across
trano (1), to swim across
tranquillus, -a, -um, peaceful, calm
trans (+ *acc.*), across
transeo, -ire, -ii, -itum, to cross
transfuga, -ae (*m*), deserter
transgredior (3), **-gressus sum**, to cross
transigo (3), **-egi, -actum**, to put an end to
trecenti, -ae, -a, three hundred
tremo (3), **-ui**, to tremble, shake
trepidus, -a, -um, fearful
tres, tres, tria, three
Treveri, -orum (*m.pl*), Treveri (a Belgian tribe)
tribunus militum, military tribune (officer in legion)
triclinium, -i (*n*), dining-room
triginta, thirty
tristis, -is, -e, sad, sorrowful
tristitia, -ae (*f*), sadness
tristor (1), to be sad
triumphus, -i (*m*), triumph
Troia, -ae (*f*), Troy
trucido (1), to slay, butcher
tu, you
tum, then, at that time
    cum ... tum ..., both ... and ...
    tum ... cum ..., at the time when
tumultus, -us (*m*), confusion, commotion
tunc, then
turbatus, -a, -um, agitated
turbidus, -a, -um, confused, disturbed
turbulentus, -a, -um, stormy
turpis, -is, -e, shameful
turris, -is (*f*), tower, castle, palace
tutus, -a, -um, safe
tuus, -a, -um, your
tyrannus, -i (*m*), tyrant

U

ubi, where, when
  ubi primum, as soon as
Ubii, -orum (*m.pl*), Ubii (Germanic tribe)
ubique, everywhere
Ulixes, -is (*m*), Ulysses (Greek hero)
ullus, -a, -um, any
ululatus, -us (*m*), howling, wailing, cry (of mourning)
umquam, ever
unda, -ae (*f*), wave
unde, whence, from where/which
undecim, eleven
undique, from all directions, everywhere
universus, -a, -um, entire, all together
unus, -a, -um, one
urbanus, -a, -um, of the city
urbs, urbis (*f*), city
urgeo (2), **ursi**, to press hard, put under pressure
usque ad (+ *acc.*), right up to, as far as
usus, -us (*m*), experience
  usui esse (+ *dat.*), to be of use (to)
ut (+ *indic.*), when, as, how
  ut primum, as soon as
ut (+ *subj.*), so that, that, to, how
uter, utra, utrum, which (of two)
utilis, -is, -e, useful
utique, assuredly
utor (3), **usus sum** (+ *abl.*), to use, employ, take advantage (of)
utrimque, on both sides
utrum, whether, if
uxor, -oris (*f*), wife

V

vacuus, -a, -um, empty
valde, very, very much, greatly
valedico (3), **-dixi, -dictum**, to say farewell
valeo (2), to be strong/vigorous
validus, -a, -um, strong
vallum, -i (*n*), rampart
vanus, -a, -um, empty
vasto (1), to lay waste
vastus, -a, -um, huge, violent
-ve, or
vehementer, violently, furiously, forcibly
veho (3), **vexi, vectum**, to carry; (*passive*) to sail
vel, or
velle, see **volo**
velut, as if, as though
vendo (3), **-didi, -ditum**, to sell
venenum, -i (*n*), poison
veneror (1), to revere, worship
venio (4), **veni, ventum**, to come
ventus, -i (*m*), wind
verber, -eris (*n*), whip, lash
verbero (1), to beat
verbosus, -a, -um, wordy, talkative
verbum, -i (*n*), word
vere, truly, rightly
vereor (2), to fear
Vergilius, -i (*m*), Virgil (Roman poet)
vergo (3), to be situated, lie
veritus, -a, -um, fearing
vero, truly, even
Verres, -is (*m*), Verres (corrupt governor of Sicily)
verum, but
verus, -a, -um, true
  vera dicere, to tell the truth
vester, -tra, -trum, your
vestimentum, -i (*n*), garment; (*pl*) clothes
vestis, -is (*f*), clothing
vestri, (1) from **vester** (above); (2) genitive of **vos**
veto (1), **-ui, vetitum**, to forbid, tell not to
vetus, -eris, old
vetustas, -atis (*f*), old age, antiquity
vexo (1), to annoy, harass
via, -ae (*f*), road, street
viator, -oris (*m*), traveller
vice alterna, alternately
  in vicem, in turn
vicesimus, -a, -um, twentieth
vicinus, -a, -um, neighbouring
victor, -oris (*m*), victor, conqueror
victoria, -ae (*f*), victory
vicus, -i (*m*), village
video (2), **vidi, visum**, to see, see to
videor (2), **visus sum**, to seem
vigilia, -ae (*f*), watch, keeping watch, wakefulness
vigilo (1), to keep watch, lie awake
vilicus, -i (*m*), farm-manager, overseer
villa, -ae (*f*), country-house, farm
vinclum, contracted form of **vinculum**
vinco (3), **vici, victum**, to conquer, overcome

vinculum, -i (*n*), chain, bond
   in vincula conicere, to throw into chains, imprison
vindico (1), to punish
vinum, -i (*n*), wine
violo (1), to violate, break (law)
vir, viri (*m*), man
vires, -ium (*f.pl*), strength
virga, -ae (*f*), rod, stick
virgo, -inis (*f*), girl, young woman
virtus, -utis (*f*), virtue, courage, valour
vis, vim (*acc.*), **vi** (*abl.*) (*f*), force, amount
visito (1), to visit
vita, -ae (*f*), life
vivo (3), **vixi, victum,** to live
vivus, -a, -um, alive, living

vix, scarcely, with difficulty
voco (1), to call, summon
volo, velle, volui, to wish, want, be willing
volo (1), to fly
voluntas, -atis (*f*), will, enthusiasm
Volusenus, -i (*m*), Volusenus (tribune in Caesar's army)
volvo (3), **volvi, volutum,** to roll, ponder
vos, you
vox, vocis (*f*), voice, saying
vulgo, commonly
vulnero (1), to wound
vulnus, -eris (*n*), wound
vultus, -us (*m*), face, countenance, expression

Index

References are to page numbers; numbers in brackets refer to sections within a note.

Ablative Absolute   30
Ablative Case   15; 18 (Time); 20 (Place); 23, 24 (Prepositions); 30 (Ablative Absolute); 58(*b*); 60 (3); 61(3); 67 (Dates); 71–72; 76; 141; 142–3
Accusative Case   5; 18 (Time); 20 (Place); 22–23 (Prepositions); 58(*d*); 60(1); 61(1); 67(1); 71–73; 140;142–3
Accusative and Infinitive   6; 34
ad   22; 45(4); 60(1); 61(1)
adeo   47
Adjective Agreement   74; 118; 143
an   37(4,6); 40
antequam   51(2); 52(4)

Case Recognition   71–73; 118; 142–3
causa   8; 45(4); 60(2); 61(2)
Comparatives   16(6); 45(3); 64(3); 144–5
Conditional sentences   54; 107–8
Correlatives   63
cum (preposition)   24
cum (conjunction)   51; 64(4), 88

Dative Case   10; 13 (Predicative Dative); 42(5); 57(1*b*); 58(*c*); 62; 71–73; 76; 141; 142–3
debere   55(3)
Deliberative Questions   38(8); 107(1); 108(2)
Deponents   29; 164
Direct Commands   107; 108
Direct Questions   36; 100(2)
donec   51
Doubting   105
dum   51; 91

Exclamations   6; 100(1)
Exhortations   107

Fearing   49; 94; 96(2)

Generic Subjunctive   103(5)
Genitive Case   7; 60(2); 61(2); 71–73; 140; 142–3
Gerund/Gerundive   11(4); 45(4); 60–62; 134; 159

Historic Infinitive   32

immo   39(4)
Impersonal Verbs   57; 135
Indirect Command   41; 93(2); 94(IIIc); 96(1)
Indirect Question   39
Indirect Statement   6(*g*); 34; 137
Infinitives   32; 49(6); 158–9
interest   58
ita   38(B); 47; 94(III)

licet   58(*c*); 109(2)
Locative Case   9; 20

ne   41; 44; 49; 96; 107; 108(3)
-ne   37(2); 40(2)
neque   42(3)
neu (neve)   42(3); 44(1)
nisi   54
Nominative Case   5; 71–73; 140; 142–3
nonne   37(3)
num   37(3); 39

oportere   55(3); 58(2*c*)
Oratio Obliqua   110
Overview   121

Participles   28; 45(6); 49(4); 134; 158–9
perinde ac si.   110(5)
Place   15(3); 20

posse 55(3); 160–1
Possession 7; 11(6); 140–1
postquam 51; 52(5)
Potential Subjunctive 108
Predicative Dative 13
Prefixes 78
Prepositions 22–24; 118
Price 8
priusquam 51(2); 52(4)
Purpose 44; 51(2); 94(II–III); 96(3); 103(1)

qualis 36; 63; 64
quam 64; 100; 145
quamdiu 51
quantus 36; 63
quin 104(4); 105
quis 36; 39; 148
quo 36; 45(3); 63(1); 64(3,4)
quoad 51
quod 26; 98; 148
quominus 109(4)
quot 37; 40(4); 63
quotiens 37; 51; 64(4)

refert 58
Relative Pronoun 26; 44(2); 98(2); 100(3); 101(4); 103; 148
Reported Speech 110
Result 47; 93(2); 103(3)

se and suus 35(4); 40(3); 42(4); 45(7); 49(5); 114; 135(3); 150
seu 55(4)
si 54; 107; 108
sic 38(B)
simulac 51
sive 55(4)
Space 6(*e*)
Subjunctive 107; 109; 152–65 (Tables)
Suffixes 79
Supine 45(5); 152

talis 47; 63
tamquam 110
tantum abest ut 48
tantus 47; 63
Time 6; 15; 18; 51; 66–68
tot 47; 63

ubi 51; 64(4)
ut 41–42; 44; 47; 49(3); 51; 57(2); 64(4); 93
utinam 107–8
utrum 37(5); 40(2)

Value 8(*c*)
velut si 110(5)
Vocative Case 5; 142

Wishes 107–8